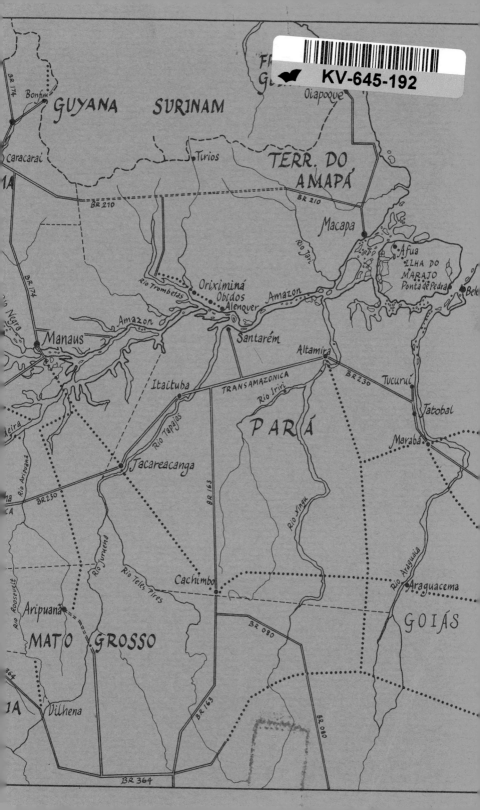

ASSAULT ON THE AMAZON

ASSAULT ON THE AMAZON

by

RICHARD BOURNE

LONDON
VICTOR GOLLANCZ LTD
1978

ISBN o 575 02358 9

Printed in Great Britain by
The Camelot Press Ltd, Southampton

For Juliet

CONTENTS

LIST OF ILLUSTRATIONS

following page 128

Outside and interior of traditional home (*photo: Alberto Tamer*)
Engine of the defunct Madeira–Mamoré railway
(*photo: Alberto Tamer*)
President Medici (*photo: Associated Press*)
TransAmazonica in the early construction phase (*photo: Abril*)
Camargo Corrêa workers (*photo: Abril*)
Camp followers (*photo: Abril*)
An Incra colonist near Itaituba (*photo: Abril*)
An Incra colonist near Altamira (*photo: Abril*)
Typical Incra *agrovila* (*photo: Claudia Andujar*)
Ariosto da Riva
Brickworks at the Indeco base
A squatter's family
A disappointed migrant (*photo: Abril*)
The high street of Amaporã, Parana (*photo: Abril*)
DNER housing
Iron shaft at the Serra dos Carajas
Daniel Ludwig (*photo: Abril*)
Zebu cattle (*photo: Paul Harrison*)
A DNER ferry
Typical dirt highway
Poolside of prestige hotel at Ruropolis President Medici
Traditional river transport (*photo: Paul Harrison*)
Housing at Aripuanã-Humboldt

Bandstand at Bragança
Dead jaguar (*photo: Abril*)
Skinned crocodile (*photo: Abril*)
Assimilated Indians
Non-assimilated Indians (*photo: Abril*)
Yanomama girl (*photo: Claudia Andujar*)

ACKNOWLEDGMENTS

The idea for this book first occurred to me in 1971, when I was researching a biography of Getulio Vargas in Brazil. For a long time it seemed impossible to find the resources of time and money which could make it practical. That it has become a reality, thanks to an extensive field trip in Amazonia in May–June 1976, is due to the kindness and support of the following people and institutions. They are in no way responsible for my opinions or conclusions, but I gratefully thank them all for their various kinds of help.

In Britain: Paul Barker, Editor of *New Society*, who gave me twelve weeks' leave of absence from my duties as assistant editor; Peter Flynn, Director of the Institute of Latin-American Studies, Glasgow University, who supported this project and whose university awarded me a research fellowship; the Astor Foundation and the Anglo-Brazilian Society, which made grants; Dora Basilio, a Brazilian artist living in London; Leslie Bethell, John Hemming, Peter Hall and David Donnison —who gave encouragement; Sergio Corrêa da Costa and Roberto Campos, successive Brazilian Ambassadors in London, whose attitude to the matters discussed in this book diverged considerably, but who wished me to see for myself; John Brooks of Lloyds Bank International; Liz Calder of Gollancz; Tony Garrett who drew the maps; and Jonathan, Toby and Camilla, who had to do without me for the first part of a hot British summer, and at weekends thereafter.

In Brazil: Francisco Basilio, of the Brazilian Portland Cement Association, São Paulo, and his son Jorge, of Rio de Janeiro; the Ministry of Transport, DNER (the federal roads agency, Departmento Nacional de Estradas de Rodagem) and IPR (DNER's research institute, Instituto de Pesquisas Rodoviarias) which gave crucial help with transport in Amazonia and statistical information; I should like to single out particularly Engineer Galileo Antenor de Araujo of IPR and, among many helpful and good-humoured DNER personnel from drivers to administrators, Engineers Antonio Lage of Cuiabá, Crisipo de Miranda of Manaus, Cesar Tuma of Altamira and Elmir Saady of Belem; the firms of Mendes Junior, Amazonia Mineração (known as AMZA), and Andrade Gutierrez, and particularly Mario Coutinho of Andrade Gutierrez in Manaus; Ariosto da Riva; Simon and Nancy Reed of São Paulo; Jane Braga, Zevi Ghivelder and Susan Branford, journalists; the Acre highways department (DER-Acre); and countless others.

Brazil uses metric units and, as most other countries now do the same, it seems wiser to retain this terminology here. Of the measures I refer to frequently it may be helpful to remember that one metre equals 1·09 yards; one kilometre equals 0·62 miles; one hectare equals 2·47 acres; one square kilometre equals 0·38 square miles; and one kilogramme equals 2·21 pounds. Official Brazilian policy of regular small devaluations also means that the cruzeiro, like the £ sterling, does not have a constant value over the period covered by the book. I have therefore sought to give more meaning to sums quoted in cruzeiros by translating them into average US dollar values for the year in question at the following rates to the dollar: 1968—3·4 cruzeiros; 1969—4·1 cruzeiros; 1970—4·6 cruzeiros; 1971—5·3 cruzeiros; 1972—5·9 cruzeiros; 1973—6·1 cruzeiros; 1974—6·8 cruzeiros; 1975—8·1 cruzeiros; 1976—10·5 cruzeiros.

ASSAULT ON THE AMAZON

PROLOGUE

IT IS AROUND 8 p.m. at Telles Pires, a construction camp by the river of the same name in northern Mato Grosso. The camp includes an airstrip and a ferry and more stinging insects than anyone can tolerate. It is the base for a private colonization scheme mounted by Indeco SA, a company which plans to build five new towns and a diversified agriculture in two million hectares of tropical forest. This has been another long hard day in the dry season, with work starting at 6 a.m. for some. A simple brick-making machine has been turning out the raw material for the new towns. A man who pauses—and there are few women to be seen—may hear a toucan call in the surrounding woods.

Then, suddenly, there is a hooting and a flashing from the 148-kilometre dirt road which leads to the new strategic road from Cuiabá to Santarem. People come out of their cabins to see, with all the expectation of the port when a fleet puts in. But the noisy exciting arrival here is a bus, loaded with 60 workers, many standing, which has just made the fourteen-hour journey from Cuiabá, the capital of Mato Grosso. As the men step down—rough, ill-shaven but cheerful—you notice that most are in their 20s, not in their 40s or 50s as you first thought. Quietly now they disperse to their dormitory hut, where they are provided with hammocks. But the atmosphere of their arrival lingers—a tingling mixture of loneliness, pioneering, hard labour and the myth of Eldorado.

Senhora Andrelina Freires, by contrast, has had four years in which to come to terms with her Eldorado. She is middle-aged, with five children, and that is the length of time she has been living in what some say is the best of the *agrovilas* (planned villages) near Altamira on the TransAmazonica highway. "We were only squatters in Ceará (a poor state in the Brazilian north-east) and we were told that we could have land after two years here. We were flown here by plane, and in the beginning our children nearly died of measles: four out of the six children next door did die," she says.

Her husband lives twelve kilometres away on the 100-hectare plot, which is the standard area given out by Incra (the government body called the Instituto Nacional de Colonização e Reforma Agraria), and he comes home every weekend to see his family. However, there is some complaining on this *agrovila*, Vale Piauiense, that Incra has let the colonists down. Its original plan had been to build the settlement closer to this group of plots, but there was no stone there, so many families are split for most of the time. Andrelina too is having to eat bought rice, because the access roads to the plots are so appalling that the lorries are charging nearly a third of the farmers' ultimate price just to bring out the crop. "But," says Andrelina, "we now have got our land."

Ever since 1971, when I realized that an unprecedented attempt was being made by the Brazilian government to occupy its Amazon region, I have been fascinated by the process, and anxious to know more about it. As I wrote in an article in *The Guardian* in February 1972—the first description of the roads and colonization programme to appear in Britain—"there is something poignant about trying to people this green moon at the present point in time". President Garrastazu Medici had launched the Programme of National Integration on 16 June 1970. This aimed to build a series of highways through the tropical forest; to bring 100,000 families from the north-east to live beside them; to tie 59·4 per cent of Brazil's land area more firmly to the more populous and developed parts of the country; and, in a region where almost all settlements had been alongside the waterways, to "fix the man to the land" in areas not at risk of flooding and to establish stable forms of agriculture on what had hitherto been empty spaces on a map.

Such a scheme, with the impetus it also gave to ranching and minerals extraction by major Brazilian and international companies, seemed anachronistic in the 1970s. Colonial values —of pioneering, and opening up new lands—had been in retreat for four decades in the international arena as the old colonial powers had been expelled from Africa and Asia, often removing their settlers as they went. And, by the 1970s, a new attitude towards the conservation of the world's resources was spreading, as much among the newly independent and developing countries as among the industrial states which had enjoyed them so disproportionately. Ecologists emphasized the relationships between all living species and their inanimate surroundings, and the distinction between resources that could or could not be renewed. From now on, man would try to treat his environment with more respect.

But there were also particular national reasons why the drive on Amazonia in the early 1970s seemed surprising, for Brazil's birth rate has been dropping and it has just become a predominantly urban country. Whereas the population had been growing at an annual rate of 3 per cent a year in the 1950s, this had fallen to an annual average of only 2·9 per cent in the 1960s. Furthermore, while the urban centres had multiplied in size and the 1970 census had shown that nearly a third of the population had migrated from its birthplace, it was becoming clearer that urbanization itself was a brake on demographic growth. And whereas 55 per cent of Brazilians lived in rural areas in 1960, 56 per cent were living in towns and cities in 1970. The basic demographic pressures to incorporate new lands for agriculture were and are weakening and the broad pyramid of the nation's age structure, which has made Brazil seem a land of teenagers and children, is now elongating towards the pattern of a more developed country.

In this book I seek to describe, analyse and synthesize an historic drive on the world's largest tropical forest region. Why is this human assault occurring now? What changes of policy, social content and geographical direction have occurred? Is it possible to estimate the costs and benefits, and has there been— as various sociologists, ecologists and anthropologists have feared there could be—any serious disaster? What does this say about the values of "development" to which most of the world's poorer countries subscribe, and which have bitten particularly deep in Brazil, both among the élite and the general public? How far is the Amazon venture a product of the needs of the conservative but "modernizing" military régime which has ruled Brazil since 1964?

Brazil was recently described by Henry Kissinger as "an

emerging power". Arthur Cesar Ferreira Reis, governor of the
state of Amazonas in the 1960s and one of the region's leading
historians and advocates, has described the occupation of
Amazonia as a test of his country's maturity. I believe this to be
true in two ways. First, that after Amazonia Brazilians will
have no more fresh land of their own to occupy, nor any new
natural resources to discover. This means that they are now, for
the first time since their daring forebears moved west in defiance
of the Spanish–Portuguese Treaty of Tordesillas, 1494—which
gave Portugal only the mouth of the Amazon and part of the
littoral of modern Brazil—in sight of their own limits. In
social and human terms, it is now possible to recognize that
the escape valve of an expanding frontier of settlement will
close within a few decades. In ecological terms, it means that it
will no longer be possible to plunder the land and the forests
and move on, seeking to avoid the consequences of man's
devastation.

Second, and more pervasive, Brazil in Amazonia is coming to
grips with its own futurist nationalism, which Stefan Zweig
identified in a book published in 1942 called *Brazil, Land of the
Future*. From the construction of the Volta Redonda steelworks
by Getulio Vargas in the early 1940s, to the transfer of the
capital to Brasilia by Juscelino Kubitschek in 1960, Brazilian
leaders have nourished a predominantly poor population with
symbols of future national greatness. President Medici's Trans-
Amazonica programme was accompanied by a similar futurist
rhetoric. But if the escape valve of an expanding frontier post-
pones social change in settled regions, by offering their victims a
second chance as migrants, the rôle of a futurist philosophy of
national development may be rather similar. A conservative
society can avoid changes its leaders dislike by offering hopes
and symbols instead. Tomorrow's prospects may become a
substitute consumer good when the problems of raising general
living standards today seem intractable. And when will
tomorrow come?

The maturity of an emerging power is not only demonstrated
by its performance in international relations, but by the way in
which it resolves its awkward domestic dilemmas. Amazonia
raises several of these for Brazil. Official government policy, and
virtually every Brazilian I have spoken to, subscribe equally to
a careful exploitation of this forest region and to the economic

development of their country. But if, in the worst eventuality, our grandchildren ask what became of this magnificent but fragile rainforest, and why there are still large numbers of poor people in Brazil, I hope this book will help to explain what happened.

I

AMAZONIA IN HISTORY

"For health, good ayre, pleasure, and riches I am resolved it [Amazonia] cannot be equalled by any region either in the East or West. Moreover the countrey is so healthfull, as of an hundred persons and more . . . we lost not any one, nor had one ill disposed to my knowledge, nor found any Calentura,[1] or other of those pestilent diseases which dwell in all hot regions, and so neere to the Equinoctiall line." Sir Walter Raleigh, Elizabethan captain, explorer and promoter.

"You call Sir Walter Raleigh a national hero. For us he was one of the biggest robbers ever to sail the coast of South America." Vera Pacheco Jordão, contemporary journalist and Brazilian cultural attaché in London, 1967.[2]

WHAT IS AMAZONIA? It is an area of approximately six million square kilometres (2·3 million square miles), covering part of six modern states, which is drained by the River Amazon itself. At some point in prehistory this huge basin drained into the Pacific but the growth of the Andes tilted the flow eastwards. Even so, the basin as a whole is fairly flat, and the main river drops only 64 metres (213 feet) between Peru and the Atlantic ocean, in a distance of 2,993 kilometres (1,860 miles). This huge system deposits nearly a fifth of all the fresh water which reaches the oceans each year. Even during the dry season the main river maintains an average speed of 2·5 kilometres (1·55 miles) an hour. The flow of water is unequalled—five times that of the River Congo, twelve times that of the Mississippi, and every 24 hours it pushes as much sweet water into the Atlantic as the River Thames carries past London in a year.

Not surprisingly an area so vast astride the Equator, undisturbed for over 100 million years, has developed its own ecology and climate. Its main characteristic is the tropical

forest, nourished by an annual rainfall which is over 203 centimetres (80 inches) in most places and which rises to 304
centimetres (120 inches) near the Atlantic coast. This forest
is, after the coniferous pine woods of Siberia, the second largest
reserve of natural woodlands in the world. But it is quite unlike
the Siberian forest because areas of one type of tree alone are
rare: hundreds of different species may be represented in a single
square mile. They include wild rubber and cocoa trees, valuable
hardwoods such as mahogany or Brazil rosewood, and pretty
flowering trees like the yellow and purple varieties of Ipé.
Trailing lianas hang from some of them, just as in a child's
picturebook of the jungle. But, except in flooded areas or where
the mature trees have been cut and a thick secondary growth
has appeared, it is not hard to walk around in the Amazon
forests. The high canopy of leaves and branches prevents much
sunlight reaching the ground, restricting the growth of plants
there. Instead there is a rich vegetable life at different heights
of the trees themselves. For a stranger, travelling by boat
through flooded woods beside the rivers, one of the most
beautiful sights is of the different coloured orchids, growing as
parasites on the trunks and branches of trees.

This diversified forest is complemented by an enormous range
of mammals, insects, reptiles and fish. Although it has attracted
the attention of scientists since the end of the eighteenth century
the sheer scale of the region, and the localized distribution of so
much of both flora and fauna, means that new varieties are
still being discovered. It is estimated that there are some 1,800
species of bird, many of them brightly coloured like the parrots.
There are, for example, 319 varieties of hummingbird alone.
There are possibly 2,000 species of fish, again locally distributed
because of the different chemical composition of the Amazon
tributaries. The richest waters for fish are the white-water
rivers like the Rio Madeira, which rise in the geologically young
Andes. Less nourishing are the black-water rivers like the Rio
Negro which joins the Amazon at Manaus, acid and rising in
the leached and ancient highlands of Guyana and Venezuela.
Similarly the clear-water rivers, rising to the south of the main
river in the ancient uplands of central Brazil, are poorer in
nutrients. Turtles and crocodiles are among the river creatures
which have suffered severe depredation by man, long before
the sharp increase in human activity in Amazonia over the last

decade. On the other hand the boto, the dolphin with red flesh which is supposed to have magical and erotic qualities, has benefited from a taboo on killing or eating it.

The forests themselves contain no large mammals, but many types of monkey, jaguar, deer, sloth and snake. Apart from the bats there are probably not too many new mammal species to be discovered: the risk now, as it has been for some 30 years, is that some of those with valuable skins such as the jaguars may be illegally hunted to extinction. The Victorian naturalist, H. W. Bates, collected over 14,700 insect species between 1848 and 1859 and there are undoubtedly many more which, though they may be known to individual forest dwellers or have turned up once in a scientific collection, have yet to be properly classified. Whereas it is often difficult to see creatures like the monkeys, which run off in the tops of the trees when they spot a human, no modern visitor to Amazonia can be unaware of the insects. This is as true of those which sting, like the pium fly, as of the clouds of butterflies which wheel and turn by the streams and pools, or the varied spiders which embellish the bushes.

Amazonia's climate, like its ecology, is also not as uniform or regular as is popularly believed. Generally the humidity is high, at least 80 per cent, and there is little seasonal variation in the temperature which runs at around 27 degrees C (80 degrees F). Because the Amazon itself runs parallel to the Equator there are alternate dry and rainy seasons on each side of the main river. In general the height of the rainy season in the south is between October and April, while in the north it is between April and August. During these periods most outdoor work, such as tree-felling or road-building, is at a standstill. In theory this alternation of the wet and dry seasons means that, while individual tributaries may rise or fall, the Amazon itself has a normal variation of only 9·6 metres (32 feet). But in fact the rainy seasons on either side of the main river overlap about once every four years and, more seriously, about once in every 23 years. The inhabitants of the Amazon valley rely on the annual floods to enrich the soil of the *varzea* flood-plain, raising crops on it during the six months when the waters drop. But when, as in 1952 and 1953 or 1975 and 1976, the rivers exceed the annual flood level and take longer to fall, there are serious losses to agriculture and housing. Rainfall in the region is not constant, on a monthly basis, from year to year. About a fifth comes in the form of unpredictable cloudbursts. Even the "dry" seasons are far from dry.

Nearly four-fifths of this remarkable region fall within the modern boundaries of Brazil, with the rest shared between Bolivia, Ecuador, Peru, Colombia and Venezuela. The history of Portuguese and Brazilian occupation of the area, following Pedro Cabral's discovery of Brazil for the Portuguese in 1500, is crucial to understanding the contemporary pressures to develop it. The salient point is that, under the demarcation between Spain and Portugal's nascent colonial empires which the Pope authorized in the Treaty of Tordesillas, 1494, Portugal would have had almost none of the Amazon basin. A steady expansion westwards up the rivers, by explorers, traders and settlers, was responsible for filching the heart of the South American continent out of the hands of Spain. Much of this took place without direct encouragement or leadership from the Portuguese mother country. The process was only completed in recent times. By the Treaty of Petropolis, 1903, Brazil bought the territory of Acre—about 18 degrees west of the original Tordesillas line—from Bolivia. Although the case of Acre had involved conflict between Brazilian rubber tappers and the Bolivian army, which was supported by rubber speculators in New York, the principle by which Brazil claimed the land was exactly the same as it had been for the previous four centuries. Whatever the legal theory of ownership, Brazilian citizens were actually using and in possession of the soil concerned. This is the legal doctine of *uti possidetis*, paraphrased in the British common law saying that "possession is nine points of the law". It is worth emphasizing therefore that, throughout history since Cabral's landing, Portuguese and Brazilians have been illegally moving westward beyond the currently agreed boundaries; that whenever diplomacy has regularized their situation their only claim to a new frontier line has been based on their own effective occupation; and that the latest instance of this occurred in the twentieth century.

The early exploration and penetration by Europeans occurred with all the chances, delays and repetitions that were typical of an area that seemed to offer no immediate prospects of wealth. None of the Indian tribes in Amazonia had developed an advanced civilization comparable to the Incas or Aztecs, although both near the modern city of Santarem and on the island of Marajó at the mouth of the Amazon there were peoples capable of making attractive pottery. Many of the Indian groups were actively hostile. The first European who can be proved to have found the mouth of the Amazon, sailing 50 miles up it, was a Spaniard, Vicente Yañez Pinzon. He arrived in what he called the Freshwater Sea (Mar Dulce) in February 1500 and claimed it for Spain. In the early 1530s the first Portuguese, Diogo Leite, may have reached the Amazon after sailing round the north-east coast of Brazil. And in 1541, in a daring voyage downstream chronicled by his chaplain, Gaspar de Carvajal, Francisco de Orellana set out from Quito to explore the interior and navigated the Amazon from its headwaters in the Andes to its conclusion. Out of this expedition, which clashed with an Indian tribe for whom the women fought with the men, emerged the legend of the Amazons—and the name of one of the world's greatest rivers.

Orellana, like Pinzon, was Spanish and throughout the sixteenth century there were sporadic clashes between the Dutch, the English and the Portuguese around the mouth of the river. In spite of their early voyages the Spanish, who were fully committed to exploiting the riches of Peru and Mexico, did not follow up their advantage. The Dutch and the English began growing sugar in parts of what is now Brazil, but their main interest in the mouth of the Amazon was mercantile. They were exporting Brazil dyewood and interested in the various natural products that would later be called the "drugs of Amazonia" on the European market. But they had no strong base of settlement near at hand, unlike the Portuguese who were colonizing north-eastern Brazil. After 1570 a series of small Portuguese settlements, trading posts and Jesuit missions began to be established along the banks of the main river. The Portuguese intermarried with the Amerindians, but it soon became clear that they could not easily turn hunters and gatherers into useful slaves or agricultural workers. By the end of the sixteenth century, however, the Portuguese had largely succeeded in expelling their European rivals from the area around the mouth of the Amazon.

It was in the seventeenth century that Portugal consolidated her hold on the lower Amazon, and staked her claim to the upper tributaries also. Belem, capital of the modern state of

Pará, was founded as the military Forte do Presepio on 12 January 1616. Half a dozen different religious orders, of whom the Jesuits were the most active, were proselytizing the Indians and trying to prevent them from being enslaved. Between 1580 and 1640 the Portuguese and Spanish crowns were temporarily united: although this had the disadvantage of exposing north-eastern Brazil to a Dutch occupation, it permitted Portuguese adventurers to push into the upper Amazon without protests from Madrid. The most important move was a large-scale expedition led by Pedro Teixeira in 1637, and only concluded just as the dynastic union was broken. Teixeira, who is recognized as the conqueror of Amazonia in modern Brazil, went up the Amazon with 1,200 Indian slaves, 87 soldiers and 45 boats. He took two years to reach Quito and then returned to the junction of the Napo and Aguarico rivers, where he erected a boundary mark which claimed the entire Amazon valley for Portugal.

Although the Treaty of Madrid, 1750, did not recognize quite all the land claimed by Teixeira as being Portuguese, this settlement confirmed that Portugal had won the lion's share of the river valley. In the mid eighteenth century scientists first began to take an interest in Amazonia, and the enlightened but autocratic Portuguese ruler, the Marquis de Pombal, demonstrated an unprecedented concern in Lisbon. It was he who expelled the Jesuits from Brazil in 1757, and he who tried to promote towns and agriculture in the Amazon basin to make the Portuguese presence more effective. The Jesuits were the object of intrigues both in Portugal and the Brazilian colony, partly inspired by their resistance to the enslaving of Indians. However, even though the Jesuits were opposed to slavery the culture shocks imposed by the religious orders—exposing Indians to European diseases in villages, altering their life-style—seem to have added to the more direct cruelties of the Portuguese settlers and caused a sharp reduction in the aboriginal population. Between 1743 and 1749, for example, 40,000 Indians are believed to have died of smallpox in villages organized by the religious orders.[3] During the mid eighteenth century there was the first significant immigration of families, mostly from the Azores rather than peninsular Portugal; they founded Macapá, the capital of Amapá, and Bragança in the state of Pará. Pombal was keen to get away from the extraction of woods and berries and flowers on which the economy of the region was based. Coffee, sugar cane and cocoa were grown in plantations near Belem. At the same time the administrators, who were put in to replace the Jesuits in charge of their Indian settlements, tried to increase their labour force by scouring the rivers for more Indians. In theory such Indians were to be allowed a year of freedom, in which to accustom themselves to the life of a town. In practice no such thing happened. The process helped to establish a network of towns, but at a high cost in Indian lives.

Although Amazonia had some population, strung out along the rivers and formed by miscegenation between Portuguese and Indians, with some admixture from African slaves, it was still semi-detached from the rest of Brazil at the time of independence. It was a year after Pedro I had declared the country's independence in 1822 that the British admiral, J. P. Grenfell, was able to make the concept stick in Amazonia. Independence accelerated the scientific exploration of the region and, immediately, set off social discontent around Belem: as many as 40,000 people died there in the smouldering rebellion which lasted for fifteen years and was known as the Cabanagem.

The product which really introduced Amazonia to the world was of course natural rubber, *hevea Brasilensis*. It was named and classified by the French botanist, Fusée Aublet, in 1762, but it only acquired a value after Charles Goodyear had discovered the vulcanization process in 1839. From then on the search for wild rubber trees in the Amazon and the trade and social processes that surrounded the extraction of the precious latex were to spearhead the development of the region. The frenzied period of the rubber boom lasted only from about 1890 to 1912, when the output of the eastern plantations overtook that of Amazonia. But it had developed more gradually, helped by the fact that Pedro II, Brazil's second emperor, had opened the Amazon to international shipping in 1866. Already, by 1876, the value of rubber was sufficiently attractive for the British botanist, Sir Henry Wickham, to take seeds to Kew; these were the foundation of the British plantations in Ceylon and Malaya. But it was the invention of the pneumatic tyre (1888) and of the motor car which created the sudden, insistent multiplication of demand.

Rubber did more than just establish a glossy, bubbly façade

of wealth—symbolized by the Opera House and tramways of Manaus. For the first time it locked Amazonia into the world of international capitalism and international humanitarian concern. It shifted numbers of extra people into a region which was still, compared with the rest of Brazil, almost empty. It set back the prospects of agriculture or any other type of exploitation. It prompted a rush for ownership of land and it pushed forward Brazilian penetration of the Amazon headwaters where some of the best natural rubber trees, like those which produced "Acre fine" rubber, grew wild.

Julio Arana, the austere tyrant whose cruel exploitation up the River Putumayo was exposed by Sir Roger Casement and others, was unusual in that he registered his Peruvian Amazon Rubber Company in the City of London. But the economics of the trade stretched all the way from small tributaries of tributaries of the Amazon, via the great clearing-house of Manaus, to the financiers of London and New York: it was a system in which Europe and North America speculated in demand, advancing money to Manaus, while the wholesalers in Manaus advanced loans to the merchants and strongarm men up river, who in their turn kept the rubber tappers themselves, the *seringueiros*, in an almost permanent debt slavery. The debts of the *seringueiros* were incurred from the moment the cost of their transport up river was set against their future earnings. They were grossly inflated by the exorbitant profit margin on knives and other necessities whose supply was monopolized by the river merchants. And the debts were rolled over, year after year, because the collection of rubber itself was a seasonal business. For the six months of the rains the tapper could not collect latex. Inevitably therefore people like Arana were paying the *seringueiros* a maximum of $2\frac{1}{2}$p a pound— but more usually only $\frac{1}{2}$p a pound—when the world market price for good rubber was 20p.

This was a system that generated enormous sums of money for the period. In 1906, for instance, £14 million worth of wild rubber ferried down from Manaus paid off 40 per cent of Brazil's annual debt. The state of Amazonas, whose capital Manaus is, was earning up to £1·6 million a year from the 20 per cent export tax which it levied on rubber. Manaus itself built a £500,000 Palace of Justice, a £400,000 Opera House, a telephone network and a floating harbour, and was given its

trams by the United States Rubber Company. Equally important, Amazonia was joined to Brazil and the rest of the world
by the latest communications available. Candido Rondon
and the Brazilian army laid telegraph lines into the interior,
while steamers plied regularly between Manaus and the ports
of Europe and North America. From 1898, for instance, the
Booth Line had weekly sailings from Manaus to Liverpool: at
the height of the boom over a decade later each cargo was
worth £1 million.

But the realities up river which lay behind the gaudy and
extravagant life of Manaus could be extremely unpleasant.
Malaria and yellow fever decimated the *seringueiros* and the
smoking process by which they turned the latex into hard,
easily transportable, balls shortened their lives. In Acre, for
instance, the owners of the rubber groves were known to give a
tapper his money at the end of the year, when he asked to
return home, and then shoot him in the back and remove it.
Many of the rubber barons, like Arana, Nicolas Suarez and
Germino Garrido y Otero, kept private armies whose task was
to cow the *seringueiros* and Indians, to prevent them from
escaping, and to stop others from encroaching on their territories. Chance sent Walt Hardenburg, an idealistic railway
engineer from the United States, into the Putumayo empire of
Arana in early 1908. He was shocked by what he saw and
launched a campaign in London, then the world's undisputed
centre for humanitarian causes, to get the Peruvian Amazon
Rubber Company to reform its practices. Two years later Sir
Edward Grey, Foreign Secretary in the Liberal government,
sent Sir Roger Casement to investigate Hardenburg's allegations. His report was sensational. Casement chronicled a reign
of terror by Arana's Barbadian overseers involving rape,
murder, floggings, and warfare between Peruvians and
Colombians in an area disputed by the two countries; within
five years the Indian population along the Putumayo had
dropped from 50,000 to 8,000. The report was followed by a
select committee inquiry in the House of Commons and
Arana's company was put into liquidation. Yet though the
Arana empire was probably the worst it was not unique and it
was only the fact that it had a registered office in London, and
was using British subjects to enforce its despotism, that allowed
it to become an international scandal. It was the collapse of the

rubber boom in 1911–12, rather than any gestures of control by governments in the Amazon region, which put paid to one of the worst chapters in the region's history.

One lasting effect of the rubber era was to bring more people into Brazilian Amazonia and, in the areas where most of the wild rubber trees grew, to spread them around. An earlier campaign, assisted by British pressure, had gradually eliminated slavery in Brazil in the course of the nineteenth century and the Indian tribes could not be relied on to provide a tractable or efficient army of rubber collectors. Instead the labour came from the Brazilian north-east. Stories of rapid rubber wealth in Amazonia were underscored for poor, landless north-easterners by the periodic droughts of their homeland. Geography explained why there had long been some human migration between the north-east and Amazonia. Eduardo Francisco Nogueira, the leader of the Cabanagem round Belem who was known as Angelim, was a Cearense who had moved to Pará to escape the great drought of 1827. The first north-easterners may have begun tapping as early as 1855. But it was a major drought in 1877, when Emperor Pedro II offered free shipping to Belem and Manaus for north-easterners, which started large waves moving westwards up the Amazon. By the peak of the boom 5,000 a week were passing upwards. The force of *seringueiros* led by José Placido de Castro, a gaucho from Rio Grande do Sul, which made Acre into Brazilian territory in 1902–3, was almost entirely north-eastern.

Amazonia's brief period of glory faded in 1912, when the output of the eastern plantations exceeded the rubber produced in Brazil. Attempts to set up comparable plantations in Amazonia foundered on the lack of a docile and stable labour force; the extractive, "get-rich-quick" psychology of the land-owners and merchants who could have financed them was too impatient to wait for the trees to mature; and the South American leaf blight, *Dothidella ulei*, attacked those plantations which were attempted. Thereafter, although there were brief revivals in the wild rubber business during the first and second world wars, Amazonia fell into relative decline. In spite of efforts, particularly by President Vargas during the Second World War and in the early 1950s, the region remained an economic backwater for half a century with all the problems of poverty and poor comunications.

By the 1960s, however, there was an established dialectic between international and Brazilian interest in the river valley, and a well-defined range of Brazilian attitudes. It is worth discussing these in some detail, because they permeate the much more vigorous activity in Amazonia which has developed over the past decade. Throughout its history since the arrival of the Europeans there was a sense in which, although Brazil had extended its sovereignty over it, Amazonia belonged to the world. The international interest has long comprised three contradictory but mutually supporting elements: economic greed, which was often ruthless and short-sighted; scientific curiosity; and a humanitarian and conservationist concern, whether directed at Indian tribes or the rich and beautiful wildlife. Without the scientists, with their disregard for nationalism and disinterest in national boundaries, the world would not have known of the existence of valuable products like wild rubber, and there could have been no runaway economic exploitation. Without the internationally supported exploitation there would have been no threat to Indians or wildlife, but nor would there have been the communications or information that could make international campaigns like the Putumayo possible.

Amazonia could only belong to the world in any metaphysical sense because Brazil did not have the scientists to explore the region itself, nor the capital to exploit it independently. At the same time, in spite of the rubber boom and a government attempt to move north-easterners to Amazonia in the Second World War in order to revive the industry, there were still relatively few Brazilians living there. The population was 1,876,025 in 1940, 2,372,508 in 1950 and still only 3,569,066 by 1960.[4] Given the huge size of the area this was the portrait of a human desert.

The international interest set up its own Brazilian antidote, stressing Brazilian sovereignty over the region. Whereas the Putumayo exposure had encouraged Brazil, for instance, to set up its Indian Protection Service as the first official effort to conserve the Amerindian heritage, it was quite possible for Brazilian nationalists to concentrate only on the predatory aspects of international interest. This train of thought was summarized by Arthur Ferreira Reis in a book published in 1968, *Amazonia and International Greed*. International greed

B

had been persistent; was a consequence of Brazil's lack of development; and justified a much more vigorous attempt by Brazilians themselves to open up, occupy and develop the basin.

A classic example of how the dialectic between international and Brazilian interest could work out in practice was provided by an abortive scheme to establish an international scientific institute for Amazonia under the auspices of Unesco. The first hint of this was dropped by President Vargas, when he visited Manaus in 1940. "The waters of the Amazon are continental," he remarked, and he proposed an international conference of countries with a stake in Amazonia to discuss the rational development of the valley. The idea for a high-level conference died when Peru and Ecuador had a sharp dispute over their Amazon boundaries in July 1941. But the momentum for international collaboration in the study and development of the region persisted in Brazil and it was the Brazilian delegation, at the first general conference of Unesco after the war, which put up a scheme for an international institute. An interim commission was set up in Manaus in 1948 to work out the details. As part of its study it commissioned the United States anthropologist, Charles Wagley, to investigate the social structure of the riverside community of Gurupá in Pará. Dubbing it "Itá" he described this vividly in his book *Amazon Town*, published five years later.

But if the interim commission had given one foreign academic an opportunity, the scheme for an institute itself had hit a powerful backlash of Brazilian nationalism. This was spearheaded by a former president, Artur Bernardes, who attacked the project in the Chamber of Deputies and before the National Security Council. "Political imperialism is being substituted in practice by another imperialism, economic. . . . Ratification of the treaty [setting up the Unesco institute] will mean the internationalization of Amazonia." He argued that with 56 states belonging to Unesco decisions about the institute would be taken by majority vote, overwhelming Brazilian interests. With the big powers dominating United Nations' bodies in the immediate aftermath of the Second World War this might indirectly hand them a lever on the future of Amazonia. Hostility to the idea in Brazil, and to a lesser extent in the other Amazon states, killed the institute.

But there was an interesting sequel. Out of the debates over the Unesco institute there emerged the resolve to establish a national scientific institute for Amazonia instead. INPA (Instituto Nacional de Pesquisas da Amazonia), set up in 1951 by President Vargas's last government, was the outcome. Over the last two decades this has been responsible for a steady output of basic research on botanical and ecological matters, publishing its own journal, *Acta Amazonica*. And like scientific institutes in many parts of the world INPA, which is based in Manaus, is not monoplized by nationals of the host territory. Dr Warwick Kerr, its present head, stated that 20 out of its 132 Manaus researchers in 1976 were not Brazilians.[5] Such foreigners have made a considerable contribution. Faisal Rahman, a Pakistani at INPA, has recently developed a new type of soya plant, which has up to 722 pods compared with a world average of between 80 and 400; he has also produced a red, seedless grapefruit as the result of adapting a North American tree to Amazonia. At the same time the existence of INPA has provided a temporary base for visiting foreign academics. One of the most critical scientific books about the recent highway programmes in Amazonia—*Amazon Jungle: Green Hell to Red Desert?*, published in 1975 by Robert Goodland and Howard Irwin, two ecologists from the United States— might never have appeared if the two authors had not been invited by INPA to arrange a three months' course in tropical ecology at Manaus. In terms of the dialectic between national and international interest in the region therefore a project which would have symbolized international collaboration had been turned into something which was to assert a national concern, which in practice was to increase international knowledge of the region, making possible better-informed attacks on Brazilian government policy.

The same kind of dialectic has been extremely important in the economic history of the region over the last decade, as will be seen later in chapter 5. A desire by Brazilian governments to assert national sovereignty and to promote economic development, partly stimulated by fear of foreign predators, has actually involved trying to harness the capital and technology of international companies to promote schemes in Amazonia. Yet this has deepened the risk that any profits accruing may be unequally shared between the overseas companies, Brazil in

general, or the inhabitants of any one locality in the basin. This
has been the paradox of the least developed part of a developing state, but it too has antecedents in the economic history of
the region. A good example in the inter-war period was Henry
Ford's ill-fated attempt to establish natural rubber plantations
on the Rio Tapajos in the 1930s. Ford was encouraged by the
Brazilian government, which was hoping to restore on a
rational basis an industry which had been virtually destroyed
by overseas competition. But although the car manufacturer
sank large sums of money into one million hectares at Belterra
and Fordlandia, problems of blight and faulty grafting had
caused him to write them all off by 1939. Had he succeeded,
however, United States-managed rubber might have become
as dominant in the region as the Firestone plantations were to
be in Liberia.

A third area of conflict between national aspirations and
international interests, this time humanitarian ones, has created
a similar zig-zag friction over the protection of the Amerindian
tribes of Amazonia. The Indian situation is discussed more
fully in chapter 8. Here it is worth recalling that international
pressure in the Casement era had an influence on the setting
up of the SPI, and that the Brazilian government invited three
international missions to look at the condition of the Indians
between 1970 and 1972 when it was clear that increased
development was a threat to their way of life. International
concern, which had also been fed by scandals in the old SPI
which had been publicized in the late 1960s, was a factor in the
creation of a successor body, FUNAI (Fundação Nacional do
Indio) and in the declaration of a Statute of the Indian by the
Medici government in 1973. In the 1970s, therefore, FUNAI
also began to employ foreign anthropologists directly as part of
a fresh attempt to assess the Indian societies and to mediate the
increasing dangers of cultural conflict with modern Brazil.
Three of these were involved in special projects of community
development: P. David Price, a United States citizen, who was
working among the Nambiquara of western Mato Grosso whose
traditional areas in the Guaporé valley have been invaded by
cattle ranchers over the past two decades; Peter Silverwood
Cope, a Briton, who was working with the Maku on the
Colombian border; and Kenneth Taylor, also a British anthropologist, who began a project among the Yanomama near the

Venezuelan border who might be affected by the new Peri-metral Norte road. But in January 1976 FUNAI announced that foreign anthropologists would no longer be allowed to work in a band 150 kilometres wide along Brazilian frontiers as this was a zone of national security. Thirteen anthropologists altogether were affected by this ban and the Yanomama project in particular, which had hardly begun and where there were no Brazilian personnel ready to continue it, was effectively killed.

There may have been ephemeral reasons for this decision—in personal disagreements, Brazilian nervousness over Cuban influence in Guyana, and a recent ruling by DASP (the Brazilian civil service department) that no foreigner could hold a statutory post. But it also fitted in with a history of friction between Brazil and outsiders over the protection of the Indian minorities. As a result of the dialectic between Brazil and humanitarian bodies abroad foreigners were actually being employed by Brazil in sensitive Indian areas in a rôle in which they might have to clash with the authorities and other Brazilians in order to maintain tribal rights. Yet no more absolute reason could have been given by a nation state for terminating this anomaly than military security along the state's borders.

The dialectic over Amazonia, with its often unpredictable results, has been rooted on the Brazilian side in a series of attitudes which have grown up towards the region. The first is one of national pride in the possession of what looks like so much space on a map, tempered by anxiety that it is so thinly populated and seems of only marginal value to the rest of the country. In Cuiabá, the capital of Mato Grosso, there was a car sticker in 1976 which boasted *"Amazonia Brasileirissima"*—"Amazonia is the most Brazilian". Historically this claim is apt, for it was in this region that Portuguese and Brazilian occupation moved the furthest from the Treaty of Tordesillas line, and it was the action of ordinary citizens, who were least touched by the mixture of other European stock, that was primarily responsible. The difficulties of this expansion—the discomforts of stings and diseases, the clashes with Indians, the obstacles of forest and distance, the fear of the unknown—merely increased the pride in it, particularly from the safer perspective of the central and southern parts of the country. And it was not lost on Brazilians who felt the rivalry with Argentina for

pre-eminence in South America that, without Amazonia, their
territory would be no bigger.

Such pride was, however, particularly by the 1950s and
1960s, becoming overshadowed by a fear that real Brazilian
sovereignty could be undermined by the human emptiness of
the area. For most of the 1940s and 1950s there had been no
net migration into Amazonia and even by the 1970 census,
when some economic development had begun in southern Pará,
Mato Grosso and Rondonia, there were no more than 0·84
inhabitants per square mile. Such a statistic greatly overstated
the real degree of occupation, for nearly all the people were
living alongside the rivers, and 47 per cent of them in towns.
For a nation which had justified extending its boundaries by
the principle of *uti possidetis* this was a worrying situation,
especially when the world's population was booming at around
3 per cent a year. One of the few groups of foreign settlers in
Amazonia in the twentieth century had come from a notoriously
over-populated country, Japan, and, although Brazil's neighbours also had plenty of unoccupied space, the casual asides of
foreign statesmen could be disturbing. In 1949, for example,
when condemning the need for any wars of territorial conquest,
the then Prime Minister of France, Georges Bidault, said,
"Such wars are ridiculous. In Amazonia there is so much land
that no one even knows what to do with it. So why not occupy
that?" By the 1960s the emptiness of Amazonia was being seen
in Brazil on the one hand as a reason for rejecting international
advice to limit the growth of the population, and on the other
as a geopolitical challenge. The arguments of strategic and
economic interest which had justified the transfer of the capital
from Rio de Janeiro inland to Brasilia in 1960 could, with
seeming logic, apply also to a more vigorous occupation of
Amazonia: indeed there was not much point in building
Brasilia unless it was to be used as the base for a new impetus
into the north and west, a line acted on by President Kubitschek
who also built the Belem–Brasilia road (the BR 153) and set on
foot a road link between Porto Velho, the capital of the
western territory of Rondonia, and Cuiabá, the capital of Mato
Grosso (the BR 364). The strategic approach came most
naturally to military eyes, which could see that Brazil faced
seven of her ten neighbours round the rim of Amazonia, and
became more influential after the military took power in the

1964 revolution. General Golbery do Couto e Silva, a leading figure in the first military government after 1964 as head of intelligence services—he is now head of the civil staff for President Geisel—published *Geopolitica do Brasil* in the mid 1960s. He underlined that the spread of population was still dangerously unbalanced towards the coast and the south.

But if the immense space of Amazonia had set up its own reactions among the élite and majority of Brazilians, these were coloured by one enormous doubt. Was the region a green hell, or was it a paradise? This doubt was sustained by ignorance, the travellers' tales of explorers (not all of them Brazilians) and proven horrors and marvels. The "green hell" view of the region was sustained by realities like the deaths of 6,208 workers during the construction of the Madeira–Mamore railway between 1907 and 1912. Indeed *Inferno Verde*, by Alberto Rangel, was published in 1917. The "green hell" image tended to focus on the health risks of the area; it helps to explain why, when the Vargas government tried to mobilize north-easterners to revive the rubber collecting industry in the Second World War, it established a special health service (Fundação SESP) to protect them. This service, inadequate though it was, was perhaps the most useful legacy of the abortive "rubber war". Yet equally persistent, both in literature and popular feelings about Amazonia, was the idea that it was an earthly paradise. Its tracts of untouched jungle, apparently luxuriant, and containing brightly coloured birds and Indians living an arcadian life, touched off similes with the Garden of Eden. Perennial rumours of cities of gold and lost civilizations nourished the dream of incalculable riches. Scarcely 50 years ago, after all, the British explorer Colonel Fawcett had lost his life in a vain search for one of these cities. Where so much territory was so little known, and those who did know it were illiterate *caboclos* or tribesmen speaking Indian languages, romance was hard to dispel. The co-existence of two such different ideas of Amazonia—for how could a green hell be equated with paradise?—endowed the majority of Brazilians with curiosity. It would strengthen the hand of any government which embarked on a vigorous programme of penetration, using modern techniques to seek new treasures.

There were two other elements in the Brazilian response to

Amazonia by the middle of the twentieth century: a tradition of exploitation and mobility, and an imagery of sexual conquest. The apparently inexhaustible forest had, ever since the Portuguese arrived, encouraged a predatory approach to its wealth. At its simplest the type of slash-and-burn agriculture that the Portuguese inherited from some of the Indians involved perpetual movement: a farmer would cut the jungle, fertilizing the ground with ash, get two or three crops of manioc and then move on when the soil was exhausted. Similarly, during the rubber boom, the tappers would just move on if the trees had become worn out, or they heard rumours of better groves, giving more latex, up another tributary. It was very rare for people to stay put and invest in long-term improvements. The atmosphere was far more conducive to a life of subsistence based on extracting the fruits of the rivers and trees, or of get-rich-quick for the few who were commercially minded.

Some of this exploitative approach blended with an overtly sexual attitude of masculine conquest. The sexual myth of Amazonia was born when Orellana baptized the main river Amazon after fighting with Indian women warriors: they were said by Fr Gaspar Carvajal, the historian of the expedition, to capture and then dispense with their husbands, bringing up their daughters as fighters after slaughtering any male children. No more reliable evidence has been adduced for the existence of such a tribe or custom, but the grasping of Indian women by subsequent Portuguese arrivals, and the undoubted hardships of men in the river valley since, have maintained a sexual imagery about the "virgin" forest up until the present. The spirit was caught by João Peregrino Junior, in his book *Panorama cultural da Amazonia* (1960) when he wrote, "But the man who fights with the land, who takes her by assault and seeks to dominate her by violence in order to rape her, is the north-eastern pioneer who, with the courage of his adventurous hands, built the rubber epic. . . . The exploitation of Amazonia always has been predatory." Its hazards had made the river basin a man's world, where venereal disease was common and any sudden prosperity, as in Manaus during the rubber era, was celebrated in brothels. When recently Brazilian governments wanted to occupy and make more economic use of the region a favourite word, both in documents and for journalists, was to describe the process as one of "conquest". President

Vargas himself had said, in Manaus in 1940, that "to conquer the land, to dominate the water, to subject the forest will be our task".

But if these sorts of attitudes were held about the region, particularly in the dominant central and southern parts of Brazil, what were the social and economic realities for people living there by the 1960s? An archipelago of settlements, linked only by erratic boats and improving but still expensive air services, was inhabited by people who were poorer, worse educated, and sicker than the majority of their compatriots. Although there was a flourishing smuggling trade along the borders, they were economically dependent on the more advanced regions of the country, and they had to pay inflated prices for goods because of the distance these had to be transported. They lacked political muscle in their dealings with the federal government because they seemed so few and so remote.

Decades of neglect and lack of investment had left Amazonia as a large undeveloped appendage of a country which classed itself as developing. In the nineteen years from 1947 to 1966 the average income per head of the two largest states in the region had kept their impoverished distance behind the national average. Whereas the average Brazilian's annual income had risen from $225 to $317 the average in Pará had gone from $146 to $207 and the average in Amazonas had moved hardly at all, from $211 to $218. Such figures were bound to be somewhat speculative where a high proportion of the rural population had only a slight participation in the cash economy. According to the industrial census of 1970 the northern region of Brazil—the states of Acre, Amazonas and Pará, with the territories of Rondonia, Roraima and Amapá—then had a mere 3,201 industrial establishments, employing only 40,332 people.[6] In terms of Brazil as a whole this amounted to scarcely 2 per cent of the industrial activity. The chief reasons why the industrial sector could be made to look at all dynamic in production indices were because manganese exports had begun from Amapá in 1957, and a new petrol refinery had been installed in Manaus in 1966. The statistics for food output looked even more worrying. In western Amazonia, for instance, agricultural output grew by only 61·2 per cent between 1947 and 1968—or less than the population growth. The extractive agriculture on which many still depended—the collection of fruits, nuts and latex—was stagnating.

By the late 1960s Amazonia was being increasingly affected round its southern rim—Acre, Rondonia, Mato Grosso, Goiás and southern Pará—by economic penetration from the south. This was particularly true of the growth of cattle ranching in these areas. The total cattle population rose from 1·2 million to 1·7 million in the north between 1960 and 1970: in the adjoining states of the centre west—Mato Grosso, Goiás and the Federal District of Brasilia—the jump was from 10·5 million to 17·2 million. Human migration into these areas, along with the high birth rate typical of an underdeveloped region in other parts of Amazonia, gave these two regions the fastest growing population in the 1960s of the whole country. Numbers in the north jumped from 2·6 million to 3·6 million between 1960 and 1970, while the inhabitants of the centre west rose from 1·6 million to 2·7 million in the same decade. Throughout both the 1950s and 1960s the population increase in Amazonia had been running faster than the Brazilian average—3·3 per cent a year in the 1950s (compared with 3 per cent for Brazil) and 3·4 per cent in the 1960s (compared with 2·9 per cent nationally). However, in two respects the demographic pattern of Amazonia was significantly different from that of the rest of the nation. While the 1960s were the decade in which Brazil became an urban country and the rural population grew by only 0·9 per cent a year, in Amazonia the rural population rose by 2·1 per cent a year. At the same time the actual picture of births and deaths was far more like that of the poorest developing countries, in the grip of a population explosion, than was true of Brazil. In the 1960s in Amazonia the proportion of births and the proportion of deaths was much higher than in Brazil: the death rate was almost twice as high, and much of that was caused by child mortality.

Public health and education services were still poor in the late 1960s. Most of the children in rural areas had worms. Malaria was still prevalent. Malnutrition persisted in a river basin rich in fish protein, fruit and nuts. In 1967 only 59 of the 143 municipalities in the region had any running water, and these were mostly near the state capitals. Only 23 of them had any sewage systems at all, though these were crucial to the control of worms and other diseases. The proportion of doctors and dentists available were less than half the national average. In 1968 Amazonia had only eighteen doctors and one dentist for every 100,000 inhabitants. But these medical services were largely concentrated in the state capitals, where the average was 54 doctors and three dentists per 100,000 inhabitants. In view of the irregularity, delays and expense of travel this really meant that much of the population of the interior was having to live and die without access to any medical services whatever. Given the poverty and lack of roads outside the bigger towns it was hardly surprising that, as late as 1969, there was only one vehicle per 81·4 people in Amazonia, compared with a national average of one per 33·1. River transport was slow, particularly upstream at times of flood or when low water revealed more rapids. To get to Manaus from Rio Branco, the capital of the state of Acre, by the River Madeira took twelve to eighteen days; to go up the main river from Manaus to Benjamim Constant on the Peruvian border took about ten to fourteen days; and from Manaus to Belem, the main point of entrance and exit for nearly all goods for the Amazon basin, was another five or six days. But the boats tended to dawdle, mixing goods and passengers, stopping everywhere along the river where every arrival was treated as a social event. Although it was technically possible to get something from Rio Branco to São Paulo via the river system and the port of Santos in a little over a month, in practice it might well take over three months. FAB, the Brazilian Air Force which had a number of bases in Amazonia, offered free flights as a social service in health and other emergencies. But much of the population was living a rather isolated life.

This isolation was compounded by the neglect of schools and a social conservatism. Schools of any sort were hard to find outside the towns in the mid 1960s and there were few secondary schools outside the state capitals. Only 43 per cent of teachers were trained and, optimistically, officials claimed that the rate of non-attendance even in urban areas was 16·6 per cent. In reality this meant that a majority of the population was illiterate, and an overwhelming majority in rural areas. In the territory of Amapá, for instance, possibly as few as 5 per cent of adults could read and write. The way of life was conservative and easygoing. In the forests many families were still tapping latex and collecting nuts just as their parents and grandparents had done, almost irrespective of the prices they received, and entwined in the same credit dependence on the landowners and river merchants that had characterized the rubber boom. In the small towns the Roman Catholic Church, often manned by Italians and other foreign priests, set a cultural tone based on respect for the family. Power here was held by those who monopolized the export and import trade along the rivers, and the poor depended on patrons in a semi-feudal way. Although much of Amazonia lived in a permanent state of illegality, simply because it took so long for news of new laws and decrees to get up-river, the communities were too small for theft to be a problem. Everyone knew everyone else and felt it safe to go out of a house with the doors open or unlocked. But there were periodic shootings when the partisans of rival factions took a feud too far, or a man who was drunk on cachaça, the cheap sugar spirit, laid his hands on a gun. When a woman judge, Maria Helena, arrived in Altamira on the River Xingu in 1969 one of her first orders was, "Anyone who fires shots within the town will have his gun taken away and be imprisoned for 24 hours without further formalities." She found this effective in stopping the shoot-outs.

The major government-inspired invasion of Amazonia was, as we shall see in the next chapter, set off by President Medici's roads programme in the middle of 1970. But the contrast between the social and economic conditions in the region, and the views held about it elsewhere in Brazil, had already stimulated an official and spontaneous response in the course of the previous decade. Humberto Castello Branco, first military president after the revolution in 1964, was himself a north-easterner who had been an army commander in Amazonia. His first impulse was to try to put more strength into the existing planning mechanism for the region, the Superintendencia do Plano de Valorização Economica da Amazonia (SPVEA). This had been set up in 1953 by Vargas's post-war government, promised 3 per cent of Brazilian income tax, and told to spend it according to a regional development plan. However, political chicanery had prevented the SPVEA from ever receiving the funds due to it. Its plan was shelved by Congress in 1955. It never established authority over the states and municipalities in its region and, although it had a hand in the construction of the Belem–Brasilia highway, such funds as it

had were frittered away without priority or subsequent eval-
uation. The military government had also inherited two other
types of economic inducement for Amazonia—a customs-free
zone in Manaus which had been introduced in 1957, and a
policy of tax incentives for investing companies which had
been launched by the overthrown government of President
Goulart in 1962–3 and extended to Amazonia as a by-product
of a similar policy for the north-east. The customs-free zone was
not prospering and the tax incentives had not had time to make
an impact.

President Castello Branco was soon informed that SPVEA
would need to be completely overhauled if it was to have any
effect on a region that was so large and so economically backward, and that its successor body would need stronger powers
and resources. Late in 1966 a series of measures were announced
which were dubbed "Operation Amazonia". SPVEA was
replaced by the Superintendencia de Desenvolvimento da
Amazonia (SUDAM) which was modelled more closely on
SUDENE, the regional development authority for the north-
east, which had been founded in 1959 and still had a good
reputation. It was made clear that SUDAM, which was to be
based in Belem, would be the main arbiter of all new federal
funds for the region. Governors of the states and territories in
Amazonia were tied into the new system, as they would comprise
the body's deliberative council; at the federal level SUDAM
was answerable to the recently established regional planning
ministry, the Ministry of the Interior. The existing government
rubber bank, the Banco de Credito da Amazonia, was simultaneously transformed into SUDAM's financial agent as the
Banco da Amazonia SA (BASA). The basic law establishing
SUDAM followed the SPVEA precedent for the area in which
it was to operate—the whole of the states of Acre, Amazonas
and Pará and of the territories (which have appointed, not
elected, governors) of Amapá, Rondonia and Roraima; furthermore this "legal Amazonia" which was wider than traditional
definitions but which made geographical and economic sense
also took in the states of Mato Grosso north of the 16 degree
parallel and Goiás north of the 13 degree parallel as well as
Maranhão west of the 44 degree meridian. (It is this definition
of Brazilian Amazonia that is being used in this book.)

While law 5.173 set up SUDAM, law 5.174 outlined the

battery of fiscal incentives it would supervise. These were extremely generous and permitted any company registered in Brazil to invest half the money it would have had to pay in income tax in projects approved by SUDAM in Amazonia; in return the investing company was given shares in the Amazonian project which, if successful, would start paying dividends after four years. The operation in Amazonia meanwhile was exempt from paying income tax for ten years and was also exempted from import and other taxes.

What all this added up to was an invitation to firms from the centre-south—and indirectly to foreign firms also, which were not dicriminated against—to do themselves a favour by investing some managerial effort in grasping the resources of the river basin. They couldn't lose, because in a sense it wasn't their money. If the scheme in Amazonia was a success—and these were often being launched by separate firms rather than as direct subsidiaries of the concerns in the centre-south—the companies from São Paulo, Rio de Janeiro and so on would have acquired a capital asset and an extra dividend income. Although these incentives were a development of those started by the Goulart government, which the military régime had attacked as being too far left, they fitted in well with the new régime's economic strategy. Castello Branco and his financial technocrats were anxious to build a stronger domestic capitalism, in concert with increased foreign investment, under firm planning supervision by the state. What this could mean for Amazonia, if the inducements worked at all, was that its economic dependence on the centre-south would be reinforced. It would become even more of an internal colony—initially of the firms in the more advanced parts of Brazil and, if they themselves were incapable of withstanding the competition promoted by the welcome for international companies, then of those too. For both in Brazil at large and Amazonia in particular the strategy was a gamble in two respects. Would the encouragement for external finance prove a stimulus to, rather than fatal for, the growth of domestic firms? Could the firms which were external to the country or region be made to serve the priorities laid down by the government or SUDAM?

By 1967–8 the Brazilian economy was beginning to recover, both from the high rates of inflation which had been inherited from the Goulart government and from the recession which in part was caused by the post-1964 financial remedies. The programme of fiscal incentives for Amazonia began to pick up momentum. By November 1968 some 1,077 million cruzeiros (roughly $317 million) had been applied to 184 projects approved by SUDAM. Of that sum 32 per cent had been raised by the firms concerned, 60 per cent was fiscal incentive money, and 8 per cent came from other public sources. So far the investment was small, but it was accelerating. But although the programme was intended to help the growth of farming and industry equally, it was clear at this stage that the firms which were most ready to take part were interested in agriculture: 64 per cent of the incentive money was devoted to cattle raising and farming. To this extent SUDAM's money was merely helping along a spontaneous movement that had already been getting under way in the 1960s as cattle ranching had begun to move up in southern Pará, Goiás, Mato Grosso and Rondonia. Although he was not getting fiscal incentives yet it was significant that the biggest foreign investor in Amazonia— the United States shipowner D. K. Ludwig who had won control of 1·5 million hectares on the River Jari—chose in 1967 to set in motion an ambitious agricultural and pulp project. In that year he took over an old trading firm, Jari Comercio e Navegação and renamed it Jari Florestal e Agropecuaria Ltda.

Simultaneously the free-trade zone in Manaus, directed by a body known as SUFRAMA (Superintendencia da Zona Franca de Manaus), was beginning to show that it meant business: between 1967 and 1970 the import of goods through the zone had doubled. The decree-law which reorganized it (no. 288 of 28 February 1967), defined it as "an area of free trade and import and export and of special tax incentives, established with the object of creating an industrial, commercial and agricultural centre in the interior of Amazonia". Initially the import-export trade was stimulated; it took longer to open assembly plants in the new industrial district, while the problems of feeding the expanding city tended to be postponed. The idea of the free-trade zone was interesting, belonging as it did to the "international" tradition of Amazonia which had opened the main river to the shipping of all nations in the nineteenth century. The new free-trade zone was to last for 30 years: it was an invitation to international firms to set up the kind of electronics and other factories which were characteristic of the Shannon Airport development area in Ireland, or of Hong Kong. But the obvious risk was that Manaus could become more closely integrated with the division of labour and trading patterns of the rest of the world than with Brazil itself. At the same time, although the customs exemptions were extended in mid 1968 to the capitals of Amapá, Roraima and Rondonia and frontier districts in Amazonia, there was a certain lack of forethought in seeking to use Manaus as an instrument to develop the entire region: it was equally possible that the city might grow at the expense of its vast hinterland, sucking labour from the smaller communities and the interior, and swallowing resources which might have been distributed more widely.

These official initiatives in the late 1960s were complemented by migration into and land speculation in the more accessible fringes of Amazonia. The bulk of this activity was by Brazilians themselves but the dialectic between international and national concerns still played an important rôle in the background. In 1967, for instance, the Hudson Institute put forward its "great lake" proposal for Amazonia while the Brazilian Congress set up a commission to investigate the sale of land to foreigners. The scheme from the US research body was distinguished by its ecological ignorance and its nil valuation of the large area that would have to be flooded to provide hydroelectric power and extensive navigation. The proposal caused some irritation in Brazil, but may have strengthened the hand of those who would advance drastic engineering projects for the river valley later. The inquiry into land sales to foreigners was, for parts of Goiás and Mato Grosso, a question of shutting the stable door after the horse had fled. Even in the 1950s it had been fashionable for Hollywood stars and others to buy land there at nominal prices, and the 1967 inquiry was followed only by ineffectual restrictions on foreign land purchase.

One further initiative of the late 1960s, which started unofficially and then became a government enterprise, illustrates the Amazon consciousness which was growing among élite opinion in Brazil. This was Operation Rondon—a scheme for sending student volunteers from the universities of the centre-south to work for a month at a time in communities in Amazonia. Their main contributions lay in teaching and health. But more important than what they could actually do in Amazonia, which was limited by their own inexperience and rapid turnover, was the awareness of the region and people which they brought back with them to their universities and homes. The scheme firmly labelled Amazonia as a backward area, deserving a sort of colonialist philanthropy; it did not include any reciprocal device by which people from the region could serve in the centre-south, although in a few cases it made it possible incidentally for young people from Amazonia to study in participating universities at reduced fees or for no payment. But it could enlist the idealism of middle-class youngsters—much as the Peace Corps, which worked in Brazil, had done for North Americans a few years earlier—and turn fresh eyes on northern Brazil. Operation Rondon was active in 21 towns by 1976, including five along the TransAmazonica highway. It adopted a nationalistic pun as its motto—"To integrate in order not to sell out to foreigners" (*"Integrar para não entregar"*).

Hence, by the time President Garrastazu Medici came to power, after his predecessor had suffered a stroke in late 1969, Brazil was ripe for a more aggressive push into Amazonia. There was a quickening of interest—military, commercial and intellectual. The federal government had planning instruments which allowed it to take the initiative in regional development and, while the poverty of a scattered population could justify almost any federal investment, the same weakness permitted Brasilia to brush aside any local objections to a federal plan. Prompted both by hopes and fears, Brazil was developing the will to "conquer" Amazonia. The opportunity to do so arose seemingly by chance, in an attempt to alleviate a catastrophic drought in the north-east, in the middle of 1970.

2

ROADS—THE SIGNAL FOR ASSAULT

" 'This road will be our salvation. Now it takes one of the ordinary launches up to 24 hours to go upstream to Manaus. Once this road is finished, you will be able to leave Itacoatiara at 3 in the morning, reach Manaus at 9, do a day's business there, and be back home at midnight.' The thought of being able to travel 150 miles in six hours could fill a man with bliss only in Amazonia." Lilo Linke, reporting the mayor of Itacoatiara in *People of the Amazon*, 1963.

BUILDING A ROAD through tropical forest requires sweat and comradeship from the workmen, however well equipped they may be with caterpillars and bulldozers, and good organization by their employers. For a prestige job like the TransAmazonica, where a dirt road had to be built to a good standard in double quick time, the organization was crucial. Barely six months of the year, from May to September, were dry enough for intensive work. The right equipment had to be in the right place—usually a river port on the line of the road, sometimes an isolated airstrip in the jungle—at exactly the time it was needed. The construction firm of Mendes Junior, for instance, needed to keep 1·5 million gallons of diesel oil by its camp on the Xingu, and was parachuting clothes, medicine and food to 300 workers who were cut off by floods in early 1971.

The procedure for making the TransAmazonica was methodical: first the route was surveyed from the air, then pioneers hacked a trail along the ground accompanied by FUNAI specialists who were supposed to contact and move aside any Indian groups, then the road builders themselves got to work. Teams of half a dozen men would work together, cutting down the trees with saws and machetes. *"Alo pau, alo madeira/pau bonito./Minha mãe/Maria Santissima/ajudai/derrubar este pau,"*[7] sang one of the groups, according to the magazine *Veja* in October 1970 as it hacked away in time to the rhythm.

Most of the cutting had to be done by hand, partly because the trees often grew so close together that they wouldn't fall unless pulled aside. Where it was possible to use a bulldozer to clear the trees the machine would keep shoving against the base, like a man trying to break down a door, until it fell over. Only a small proportion of the best timber, which could be extracted most easily, was saved: the bulk was burnt or left to rot beside the road.

The men themselves lived in simple wooden dormitories, sometimes without mosquito nets. On the whole they were well fed with the sort of food they liked—beef, chicken, rice, black beans, and farinha, the gritty carbohydrate which was manioc flour when fried. The bigger camps which were not based on existing towns had brothel areas nearby, set up with the collusion of the contractors and DNER (the federal highways authority) who knew that most of the men were dreaming of having a woman, and who did not wish to encourage homosexuality. The entry of other women was rare, and controlled. Beer was usually available but not cachaça or spirits—though cachaça was sometimes smuggled in. Different contractors had different rules, though all were quite closely supervised by DNER. One labourer who had worked for several told me in Humaita in 1976 that he believed Sebastião Camargo, of Camargo Corrêa, was the best employer, "because old Sebastião used to be a peon himself". Camargo Corrêa prided themselves on the amount and quality of heavy machinery which they utilized. Their rule, for the 600 workers on their stretch of the TransAmazonica, was that unmarried men would have 90 days in the field, followed by three days' leave in Manaus at the company's expense; married men had three days' leave every 60 days.

The various work fronts kept in touch by short-wave radio, supplemented by teenage runners. Most of the workers came from the north-east or the south, bringing with them all the traditional fears of the forest. The companies took care to inoculate them, but even so up to 10 per cent were off work for health reasons at any time. Malaria and dysentery were the chief menaces but a few also caught hepatitis and beriberi. Snake bites, drownings, accidents with machinery also added to a death toll which was never officially published, although roadside wooden crosses along the TransAmazonica mark

some of the burials to this day. *Time* magazine in July
1972 reported that there had been as many as 100 deaths
in the construction of one forest road to the west of Porto
Velho; the Porto Velho–Manaus road, much of which had
to be built up out of water, also had a reputation for fatali-
ties. The TransAmazonica itself seems not to have been so
bad.

A leading fear was of attack by wild animals or Indians. As
many as one in ten of the Camargo Corrêa men were reported
as carrying a gun; this was partly in self-defence from jaguars
or cobras, and partly to shoot duck and game in order to vary
the camp diet. The jaguars, protected animals, were not
normally aggressive to humans—but their skins fetched a high
price. As far as Indians were concerned all the contractors and
workmen were under strict instructions to behave peacefully
and with tolerance. FUNAI had warned that there were about
fifteen separate tribes between Marabá and Humaita living
near the line of the TransAmazonica, of whom about half had
had little previous contact with modern Brazilians. In fact
while the semi-civilized groups took the chance to beg for food
and other items they fancied—some even asked for a trip to
Belem—the so-called primitive groups reacted chiefly by
making themselves scarce. On the rare occasions when members
of the latter did come to see the gangs who were cutting an
ominous track through areas where they had hunted at will
their motive was curiosity. Work fronts of Mendes Junior in
the region of the River Tocantins were "attacked" three times
in a week in June 1971. The Indians involved may have been
Parakanas or Araras, but there was little hostility in these
encounters; the men surrounded the road workers with bows
and arrows while their women made off with theodolites, food
and clothing.

What was it that suddenly threw thousands of men, working
for several engineering firms, not to mention the engineering
battalions of the Brazilian army, into a frenzy of road-building
in Amazonia from the middle of 1970? The answer, of course,
was wholly political. The north-east was in the grip of one of
its worst-ever droughts. An anxious federal government had
opened work fronts for half a million men, many of them on
road-building projects, in order to provide some income in the
agricultural disaster areas. President Medici himself visited

some of the worst-hit districts in the first week of June and was sincerely moved by what he saw.

"This cannot go on, [he told an audience of governors and other authorities in Recife on 6 June]. At the end of this visit, from which I return even more determined to do my duty, I want to say to the people of the north-east that I don't promise you anything, I don't promise miracles, nor a transformation, nor money, nor favours; I'm not asking for sacrifices, nor votes, nor am I mobilizing charity. I'm only saying that all this has got to begin to change. I'm exacting a contribution from the whole nation, the determination of its governors, public spirit, the firmness of every leader. I am insisting on an austerity in all responsible persons, so that there shall be no indifference to suffering and hunger. . . ."

In his speech in Recife, Medici made no mention of roads in Amazonia, though he talked of incentives to strengthen agriculture in the north-east: the nearest he got to one of the cardinal ideas of the TransAmazonica programme was when he said that he had decided to encourage colonization in humid zones of the north-east, of Maranhão, of southern Pará, of the São Francisco valley and of the central plateau of Brazil in order to absorb people from the most hopelessly dry zones. Yet ten days later, on 16 June, the president announced the Programme of National Integration (PIN). He decreed that 30 per cent of the company income tax deductions that made up the pool of fiscal incentives should be diverted into a special fund, worth about 2,500 million cruzeiros (about $543 million), to operate from 1971 to 1974. Although part of this sum would be available for road-building and irrigation in the north-east, most of it would go on roads and colonization in Amazonia. The programme foresaw two major new roads: the Trans-Amazonica (BR 230) stretching for 5,400 kilometres from João Pessoa, the capital of Paraíba in the north-east, as far as the Peruvian frontier at a place called Boqueirão da Esperanca; and a northerly road, of 1,670 kilometres, linking Cuiabá, the capital of Mato Grosso, with the port of Santarem on the Amazon (the BR 165). At the same time the government expropriated 100 kilometres on each side of the new roads to provide lands for north-easterners. A revitalized agency, INCRA, was made responsible to the Ministry of Agriculture for an ambitious colonization scheme. In general terms the target was to plant 100,000 families along the new roads in five years; the detailed plans were for 16,000 in 1972, 22,000 in 1973 and 26,000 in 1974—which left nearly a third of the target to run the gauntlet of President Medici's successor.

Why did the Medici government plunge so suddenly into Amazonia? The speed of adoption of a major, symbolic programme of development was not unique in Brazil: Juscelino Kubitschek had stumbled into his commitment to the building of Brasilia at an election meeting in the small town of Jataí, Goiás, in 1955. A military-led government, with nearly absolute powers, had even greater freedom to embrace a new venture. But although there was a developing Amazon consciousness in the centre-south, and the DNER and Ministry of Transport were lobbying hard for an Amazon highways programme, the trigger which made it possible lay in the north-east. The north-east, with its 28 million people living at as little as half of the Brazilian average standard—the average annual income in Ceará was only 142 dollars in 1966—was a perpetual cause of unease.

If Amazonia conjured up marvels and possibilities in the minds of the centre-south, the north-east summoned up fear and guilt. Its problems of poverty, drought and an almost feudal agriculture had defeated the periodic efforts of successive generations. Its troubles had helped to fuel the 1930 revolution which brought Getulio Vargas to power. In 1964, with peasants' leagues agitating for land reform and a socialist governor of Pernambuco, Miguel Arrais, calling for justice, the region had frightened the middle class with the fear that a Cuba could happen in Brazil. Its unrest helped to precipitate the military revolution. By 1970, of course, there was no risk of a change of régime: in spite of some publicized kidnappings and robberies by small groups of urban guerrillas the army and local military police forces had a firm grip on the country. The photographs of starving people, leaving their homes and taking to the roads, had a different effect in 1970. Once more they touched a generous chord of sympathy in other Brazilians. This time, however, they stimulated fears of an invasion of the towns

and cities, including those of the centre-south like Rio, São
Paulo and Belo Horizonte. Desperate people, looking for work,
would add to the slums which were already beyond the capacity of the municipal services: wrongly these slums were seen
by the better-off as hotbeds of social disorder; rightly they
were seen as a reservoir of diseases which could prove contagious
to other citizens. Headlong urban growth had been characteristic of Brazil in the 1950s and 1960s, propelled by the
numerous attractions of the cities, and the stagnation, low
incomes and in some places mechanization of the countryside.
But attitudes to this migration were beginning to change,
particularly among the educated. International publicity had
defined the Brazilian slums as eyesores and a source of national
shame. In the 1960s campaigns to rehouse the slum dwellers
and remove the shanty towns were under way in every major
city. By 1970, when of course the bulk of Brazilians were now
living in urban areas, city growth was beginning to be perceived
as a threat to better living standards and amenities. A scheme
to divert migrants from the north-east into Amazonia could
count on a lot of implicit support in the centre-south.

North-eastern droughts had several times justified a political
initiative or administrative reshuffle in the past. As a general
rule, whichever body was supposed to be in charge tended to
be blamed for its lack of preparedness or reaction, and suffered
an eclipse as the new remedy was promoted. This had occurred
most recently in the drought of 1958. In that year the Kubitschek government had criticized the federal drought agency
(DNOCS) and had set up SUDENE to see whether regional
economic planning could not put agriculture and industry in
the north-east on a sounder footing. SUDENE, which employed
some leftist economists, was slightly suspect to the military after
1964; more seriously its chief impact on the region seemed to be
to stimulate capital-intensive industries which provided too few
jobs. After 1967 its efficiency declined, its budget fell in real
terms and its influence over other federal agencies slipped.
In 1970 it appeared unable to react to the natural disaster
and it became a scapegoat. The Programme of National
Integration involved switching resources, which might have
tackled the problems of the north-east in the north-east
itself, into Amazonia instead. SUDAM waxed as SUDENE
waned.

If the drought provided a trigger for the TransAmazonica programme, there were at least two groups who were quick to persuade Medici to squeeze it—close military advisers who were concerned with his image, and transport officials and their associated contractors. Medici was the first of the three military presidents after 1964 who was virtually unknown when he took office and who wished to cultivate a good public image for himself and his régime. He had not become well known at the time of the 1964 coup and his more recent work as head of intelligence had kept him out of the public eye. Hence he included army public relations experts in his immediate entourage. Although they were anxious to influence three rather different audiences—the army itself, the Brazilian public and western countries which were worried about some political aspects of Brazil, including allegations of torture, but whose investments were needed—their message was essentially the same. Under Medici Brazil was politically stable and developing fast towards great power status; all Brazilians were taking part in this effort. While a steady inflow of foreign investment was a cornerstone of the economic strategy being pursued by Delfim Netto, Medici's skilful finance minister, the government also wished to present a more nationalist image at home than some of its military predecessors. A popular slogan which was circulating on car stickers said simply, "Brazil—love it or leave it".

From a public relations view, the march into Amazonia could hit several targets simultaneously. It would remove fears in the army about the weakness of Brazilian control in the region. These had been expressed not only by General Golbery but by the ex-Director of the Escola Superior de Guerra, the army's "Sorbonne", Rodrigo Octavio Jordão Ramos. This current thinking had been given sharper point by two recent events. The first was Che Guevara's abortive attempt to start a revolutionary *foco* in Bolivia in 1967. Although Guevara had been killed his strategy might be repeated: he had sought to launch a guerrilla war in Bolivia's share of the rainforest and, once his army had grown, he had planned to spread the continental revolution into Brazil via its Amazon region. The second was the actual existence of small groups of Maoist guerrillas in southern Pará. They had appeared near Marabá after fleeing there from São Paulo in the crackdown on urban terrorism during 1968. After a period of quiescence they had begun to propagandize among the peasants and labourers. Their three small fragments coalesced. They were not a security threat as such, but they were a warning, for their area of operation was not too far from Brazil's 18,000 million tons of iron ore reserves in the Serra dos Carajas which were now awaiting exploitation. The Amazon highways programme, with its concept of physical occupation, would reduce the danger from guerrillas just as it would reduce the risk of the illicit extraction of mineral and other resources by foreigners. The army itself would have a rôle in the programme: it would build the whole of the Cuiabá–Santarem highway and certain other road sections, mostly in the west; the TransAmazonica itself would be declared a national security zone with barracks built in all the towns along it.

The programme also had attractions for the general Brazilian public and the overseas audience. It could be presented not only as relieving suffering in the north-east but as unlocking the resources that would make the country strong—the second was a thought which was forcefully presented to foreign journalists. This could be a Brasilia-style operation which could catch the national imagination, putting the Medici government firmly in the Vargas and Kubitschek tradition as a builder of national development. (Six years later, when many cafés along the TransAmazonica still hung portraits of Medici, this opinion was widely accepted; many described him as "far-sighted".) The title of Programme of National Integration also stressed that this was a unifying project—even if a few might recall with embarrassment that Integralismo had been the creed of Brazil's fascist movement before the Second World War. The military governments after 1964 had steadily appealed to a spirit of national unity. They believed that the services themselves were the best expression and instrument of this and, even when the electors took their small chances to express some opposition, it was one justification for their political intervention. The TransAmazonica programme could give the wider Brazilian public some tangible examples of national progress which might justify the low level of political involvement, which could shade into a brutal repression, which was a structual feature of the régime. They might also justify the heightened concentration of upper incomes and the loss of purchasing power by the majority of Brazilians which was a critical element in the post-1964 economic model. Statisticians of the Fundação Getulio Vargas, for instance, were reporting that the richest 10 per cent had increased their share of national income by 20·5 per cent between 1960 and 1970 so that they now took nearly 48 per cent of the whole. The 10 per cent who were most poor, who took only just over 1 per cent of national income in 1970, had lost over 5 per cent of their share in the same decade. The biggest losers relatively were not the very poorest but those who were skilled workers, or who had aspirations to join the lower middle class. The fifth, sixth and seventh deciles in the population, by income distribution, had all had an average loss of over a fifth of their real incomes. There was therefore a psychic gap, a hunger to see some results for these sacrifices, which Amazonia might help to meet. Although Delfim Netto was to compare Brazil's process of capital accumulation with that of nineteenth-century Europe, in arguing that political democratization could follow but not accompany a period of enrichment, it is doubtful whether he or anyone else close to President Medici consciously noted another comparison: that the economic conditions which stimulated nineteenth-century Europe into colonial adventures bore a similarity to those which were leading Brazil into a contemporary essay in internal colonialism.

But the public relations impetus was not the only one which helped to convert the north-eastern drought into the Trans-Amazonica. There was also a growing technical lobby among transport officials, which could count on the sympathy of the road construction firms, that was ready to seize its chance. This was much more a pressure from within the DNER, the Ministry of Transport and regional planners in the Ministry of the Interior rather than from the capitals of the state governments of Amazonia, some of which still gave priority to improving the river transport for their riverside communities. And the leading individual advocate of an Amazonian highways programme was the director of the DNER, Eliseu Resende. By 1969, when he published an article in the *Jornal do Brasil* calling for a TransAmazonica, work was already well advanced on the difficult Porto Velho–Manaus road (the BR 319). Both this, and its northward extension to Boa Vista and the Venezuelan frontier (the BR 174) on which work had also started, had been conceived as roads to promote colonization under the brief government of President Costa e Silva. When Costa e Silva took his ministers to Manaus in August 1968, to symbolize their interest in the problems of the region, they were greeted with a request to declare the BR 319 "a priority work of integration" and to secure international funds for a scheme to plant 3,500 families along that road. At about the same time a special Amazon study group was set up in the Interior Ministry which was also working on the idea of territorial occupation, this time using the BR 174 as its focus. Neither of these projects came to fruition at the time: CRASA, the mixed state and private entity which was to colonize the Porto Velho–Manaus road, could not get the necessary finance, while the Amazon study group was wound up when a stroke removed Costa e Silva from office.

Nevertheless, Eliseu Resende, who deserves better than anyone else recognition as the father of the TransAmazonica, was able to assume some administrative sympathy for his ideas when he decided to put his scheme before the middle-class readers of *Jornal do Brasil* on 28 March 1969. To an astonishing degree—both in the name, route and justifications for the road—his article prefigured the programme which was adopted fifteen months later. This TransAmazonica, he wrote, would be built in a westerly direction to attract north-easterners to populate the empty areas of Amazonia in a rational fashion. It would link the navigable heads of the rivers and would therefore be complementary to the river network. It could be built by degrees, as resources became available. Its line would be, from east to west, via Estreito, Marabá, Tucuruí (thereby allowing the closure of the loss-making Tocantins railway), Altamira, Itaituba, Jacareacanga to Humaita on the Porto Velho–Manaus road. Beyond Humaita, he wrote inaccurately, there was already a link to Labrea. Labrea could then be joined to Boca do Acre and Rio Branco which, within a foreseeable future, would mean that the TransAmazonica was tied into the Bolivian and Peruvian highway networks also. The TransAmazonica's road number would be the BR 230: "further in the future still the road could carry on north-west of Labrea until it reached Benjamim Constant, at the frontier with Peru and Colombia". The Ministry of Transport, Resende was able to

report, was now planning just such a transverse road through
Amazonia. (In fact his own roads agency, DNER, had begun
thinking about it in 1968.)

Although the TransAmazonica was supposed to induce
development rather than link numerous established centres, it
was still very much an engineer's road. Just as Peruvian
President Belaunde Terry's development road through Peru's
eastern jungles in the mid 1960s was to run parallel to the
Andes, so Resende's scheme involved a course roughly parallel
to the Amazon. His article made no mention of soil conditions,
although agricultural colonization was one of his main justifications for the road; nor did he refer to the part it could play
in the development of any specific mineral or natural resources.
He did stress, however, that the details would have to be worked
out in close collaboration with other public agencies concerned
with colonization and agricultural and industrial development.
Two other features of his article were interesting. The first
was where he called for a rational and conservationist approach
to the Amazon rainforest. "We cannot allow a repetition in
Amazonia of the predatory occupation which occurred in
nearly all the centre-south of the country in the last century.
The devastation of the forests which took place in that region
brought, in consequence, sharp and irreparable climatic
changes, enormous losses through erosion and, further, the near
exhaustion of the timber resources which were closest to markets
for consumption or centres for export." The second was where
he called on the authority of Brazil's great writer of the turn
of the century, Euclides da Cunha, who had proposed a
railway line in Acre which could cut from river valley to river
valley.[8]

Eliseu Resende seems to have been the originator of the
TransAmazonica but he was lucky in winning the support of
his Minister of Transport, Mario Andreazza. He was luckier
still because Andreazza was one of Costa e Silva's ministers who
were taken over by President Medici. By 1970, when drought
hit the north-east, both men were well versed in their case for
a major road-building initiative in Amazonia. Resende decided
to strengthen this by commissioning a study of the effects of the
Belem–Brasilia road, by then exactly ten years old. This
appeared to prove beyond doubt the potential benefit of a
major road in attracting colonists and stimulating economic

development. The population within the area of influence of this road had grown from 100,000 to two million; the number of towns had grown from ten to 120; the cattle stock had grown from virtually none to five million head; maize, beans, rice and cotton were under intensive cultivation; and average daily traffic was 700 vehicles on the southern stretch and 350 vehicles even on the emptier central stretch. Resende's case was timely for a government which wanted to do something for starving people in the north-east. The fact that the Trans-Amazonica was an east–west road that would not be linking such obvious generators of traffic as Belem and Brasilia, nor coinciding with existing lines of economic penetration, was easily overlooked. The population analysis, which might have shown that some of the growth could be explained merely by the concentration of more scattered settlers, was not subjected to rigorous analysis. In May the Ministry of Transport sent a party of experts to Amazonia to check the final details of the TransAmazonica scheme. It was therefore not surprising that, within ten days of his speech in Recife in June, President Medici had bought and promulgated the whole package.

The first task was to confirm the line of the TransAmazonica and to call in tenders from construction firms. Ivan Gomes Paes Leme, now the head of DNER's Institute for Road Research (Instituto de Pesquisas Rodoviarias) was heavily engaged in early studies of the route. He says that DNER and the ministry had a choice of three possibilities: a northerly line along the highest navigable points of the Amazon tributaries, which would have the merit of joining existing settlements like Altamira on the Xingu or Itaituba on the Tapajos; a more direct east–west route which would run to the south of those towns, probably running straight from Maraba on the Tocantins–Araguaia to Jacareacanga, the air-force base on the Tapajos; and a much more southerly route, which might have been more help in the extraction of the iron-ore reserves of the Serra dos Carajas, which would be almost identical with the BR 235 as it is now projected on DNER maps. The two fixed points in the planning were Tocantinopolis at the eastern end and Humaita on the Porto Velho–Manaus road and the River Madeira, at the west. In the event the crash nature of the plan confirmed DNER's preference for the northernmost route: if the road was to be built in a hurry it was essential to use any

existing ports and settlements to provide support. But in a
number of respects the detailed planning caused the Trans-
Amazonica to depart from its general prescription. At two
places, Marabá and Altamira, the engineers had to choose
between including the town or crossing the river at a point
where it was navigable from the sea. On the Tocantins–
Araguaia the major port was Tucuruí, downstream from
Marabá, where the government was planning a major hydroelectric dam which would have the incidental advantage of
making the river navigable up to Marabá. Marabá was
included on the TransAmazonica and a spur road was sent
north to Tucuruí, which was excluded from the main road. A
similar decision was taken for Altamira, on the Xingu, which
was linked to a new port to be built downstream at Belomonte.
Further west, between Altamira and Itaituba, there was a
further anomaly in that the TransAmazonica would overlap
for roughly 120 kilometres with the north–south road from
Cuiabá to Santarem (BR 163). The explanation here seems to
lie more in the terrain and delays which attended the army-
built BR 163 than in the TransAmazonica as such: it was
simply easier to launch its long southward sweep from closer to
the River Tapajos than from the obvious crossroads point at
the Ruropolis President Medici. Although the theory of the
TransAmazonica was that it should complement and not
duplicate the river network it nevertheless ran parallel to the
River Tapajos for several hundred kilometres between Itaituba
and Jacareacanga; this deviation from theory was inevitable
once it had been decided to connect the two towns. Itaituba, in
fact, was the site of one of the few substantial changes of route
which occurred during the course of construction. The original
plan was for the TransAmazonica to bypass the small town
itself, crossing the Tapajos about twelve kilometres away. But
closer inspection revealed that there were dangerous rocks in
the river at the spot where the ferry would have to cross and,
as a result, the TransAmazonica was routed through Itaituba
itself.

The engineering specifications for the road were those of a
pioneer highway which could be improved as the growth of
traffic warranted. The trees were cleared to a width of 70
metres and there was a seven-metre gravel surface on a nine-
metre roadway. Unlike the situation in the state of Acre, where

road-building stone had to be shipped or trucked in at enormous expense, suitable rock for strengthening the carriageway
existed at intervals along the TransAmazonica. The engineers
compared their problems—in carving a road across laterite
soils through the heavy rainfall of a tropical forest—with those
that had been successfully overcome in Burma: more originality
was required on the Porto Velho–Manaus road where 3 per
cent of cement was added to the top covering to protect the dirt
road from the heavy rainfall. The maximum gradient was
9 per cent. Huge galvanized metal pipes were inserted under
the roadway to permit the smaller streams and floodwaters to
pass through. Wooden bridges, usually only of one lorry width,
were constructed over the smaller rivers. For the major
tributaries of the Amazon, like the Xingu and Tapajos, DNER
would provide ferries. The result aimed at would be a good
quality dirt road—not quite what the word "highway"
conjures up in countries that take four-lane tarmac motorways
for granted, but a year-round, all-weather route which would
be passable for traffic. Compared with the arrow-straight Porto
Velho–Manaus road which was already under construction the
TransAmazonica was an interesting road, designed with curves
and gradients. Compared with the Belem–Brasilia it was built
to a better standard, more expensively: as much as 30 per cent
of the Belem–Brasilia had had to be "rectified" afterwards,
with adjustments to the line and carriageway.

Although the TransAmazonica started in the north-east and
would continue west to the Peruvian border the jungle section
which was the focus of priority and publicity was of 2,322
kilometres, between Estreito and Humaita. The stretch between
Estreito and Itaituba, 1,252 kilometres, was started in October
1970[9] and finished in September 1972. The stretch between
Itaituba and Humaita, 1,070 kilometres, began in March 1971
and was finished in 1974. From Estreito to Itaituba was completed on time; the link between Itaituba and Humaita ought
to have been opened in 1973 according to the original plan.
Altogether eight construction firms were employed between
Estreito and Humaita, all of them among the biggest in Brazil;
four of them were to win the lion's share of contracts for the
Perimetral Norte, on the north side of the Amazon, when the
Medici government decided to extend its highways programme
in the region. Going westward from Estreito the firms which

got the TransAmazonica contracts were Mendes Junior (252 kilometres from Estreito to Marabá); S. A. Paulista (117 kilometres from Marabá to the spur road to Tucuruí); Mendes Junior again (342 kilometres from the Tucuruí crossroads to Altamira); Queiroz Galvão (255 kilometres from Altamira to the turning to Santarem); EIT (237 kilometres from the Santarem turning to Itaituba); Rabello (350 kilometres from Itaituba to Jacareacanga); Camargo Corrêa (407 kilometres from Jacareacanga to the River Aripuanã); and Paranapanema (306 kilometres from the River Aripuanã to Humaita). There was nothing particularly surprising in this outcome of the tendering procedure. The absence of one of the biggest contractors, Andrade Gutierrez, could be explained by the fact that it was up to its ears in the task of completing the Porto Velho–Manaus road. It was suggested that perhaps Paranapoema had put in an unusually low bid to make certain of getting its section of the road, largely because an associated company was extracting tin nearby.

What sort of firms were these, and how important was the TransAmazonica to them? The biggest was Camargo Corrêa, one of Brazil's largest companies, which had been founded in 1938 in São Paulo by Sebastião Ferraz de Camargo. Old Camargo came from a peasant background in the interior of the state; both his parents had died by the time he was nine and he had fought hard to get where he was, founding the firm on a tiny investment and growing with Brazil's construction and engineering needs. Personally he was autocratic, but he believed in hiring the best men and the best machines and had a paternal attitude to his workforce. Politically he was conservative and a furious anti-communist, one of the tough group of industrialists and army men in São Paulo which believed in using all measures to crush urban terrorism in the late 1960s, and therefore particularly sympathetic to President Medici who had risen to power on his security record. In São Paulo it was alleged that Camargo himself had attended sessions where suspected urban guerrillas had been interrogated. Industrially his firm had diversified widely: it built dams, roads, railways, the Manaus airport and the São Paulo metro; associated companies processed jute and cotton, made cement and—what became a particular interest of the old man in the 1970s—raised cattle. Real take-off for the firm had come after the 1964 revolution the number of employees had multiplied sixfold, from 4,200 to 25,200, in the following decade. But the sharpest rise, especially in asset values and profits, occurred during the Medici years. In real terms the profits had risen nearly tenfold between 1969 and 1974; by that year the holding company's net assets were worth more than 200 million dollars. For Camargo Corrêa therefore the TransAmazonica contract was welcome but in no way economically crucial. What was important was for the company to be associated with a symbolic national development project which was dear to the heart of a government which was stimulating all kinds of other construction works and an annual growth rate of 10 per cent or more each year.

Two of the other firms involved in the highways programme, Andrade Gutierrez and Mendes Junior, were based in Belo Horizonte, Minas Gerais, and had cashed in by their proximity to the great building sites of Brasilia in the late 1950s. Both firms had diversified, though Andrade Gutierrez was only about half the size of Camargo Corrêa, and Mendes Junior was only about a quarter. Andrade Gutierrez was perhaps more involved in highways, though it too was building a stretch of the São Paulo metro and it even had an associate company looking for gold in Rondonia. Mendes Junior, which reckons that the TransAmazonica accounted for about 20 per cent of its turnover in 1972, had interests in steel, kaolin, offshore oil platforms and rail building in Algeria and highway building in Mauretania by 1976. Although neither of these companies were as powerful or nationally visible as Camargo Corrêa their managements too had a strong patriotic feeling about their work. They firmly equated the physical construction they were engaged on with the development of Brazil. This convergence with the government's own philosophy percolated down to the engineers actually involved on the Amazonian roads; it helped to develop close relations between the company men and the DNER personnel who were supposed to supervise them. In practice this could become an equal relationship, even involving family friendships, in which DNER and company engineers united against their technical and bureaucratic difficulties. Although the best DNER men took care to avoid anything that could be construed as corruption the companies were able to help DNER officials to cut red tape—for instance by laying on public-relations services, or providing compassionate flights

C

for a DNER employee who had a family crisis at a weekend. For the smaller companies engaged on the highways programme it was obviously more important. The price of the TransAmazonica itself was around $51,000–$60,000 per kilometre; the price of the more difficult BR 319 was 600,000 cruzeiros (about $66,000) per kilometre. The DNER and companies made regular adjustments to cover cost escalations and inflation.[10]

How much did the whole TransAmazonica programme cost, and how was it paid for? The facts here are not easy to establish, partly because the prices changed over time and partly because the heavy political commitment of the Medici government discouraged too many questions. In July 1970, for example, the price of the whole TransAmazonica was expected to be 350 million cruzeiros ($77 million); by 1972 an authoritative DNER publication (*TransAmazonica: uma experiencia rodoviaria nos tropicos*) was putting the cost of the section from Estreito to Humaita at 510 million cruzieros ($86·4 million); unofficial DNER estimates and the *New York Times* put the cost of that section at 810 million cruzeiros ($119 million) when it was finished two years later. Of the original 2,500 million cruzeiros set aside for PIN from the fiscal incentives pool it had been expected that only a fifth (or $108 million) would go on the roads (the TransAmazonica, the Cuiabá–Santarem and the Porto Velho–Manaus) and approximately the same sum would go towards the costs of the associated colonization programme. According to Delfim Netto the cost of the Cuiabá–Santarem road would be borne by an earmarked loan from the World Bank and the natural buoyancy of company taxation in Brazil would cover something like 80 per cent of the PIN programme without inflationary pressure or the need to raise more than 400 million cruzeiros (nearly $87 million) in foreign loans. In fact the great inflow of foreign investment during the Medici term, and the high growth rate achieved, did mean that the roads and colonization programme was much less inflationary than the construction of Brasilia. For the same reasons, although PIN initially meant a cutback in the availability of fiscal incentives for companies in Amazonia and the north-east—a switch of resources from industrial and agricultural developments to infrastructure—the general power of the boom meant that this effect was relatively shortlived, and more than compensated for by the fresh investment attention which it focused on Amazonia. Delfim Netto, a prematurely stout financial expert from São Paulo, was a public advocate of PIN: in private he said that he had been landed with the project by the military. Nevertheless he used it as a sales tool for the prospects of the Brazilian economy. In terms of the roads budget alone the spending on highway construction and paving in the north averaged less than 17 per cent of the total for Brazil between 1972 and 1975, a smaller proportion than went to the south, south-east or north-east.

Nevertheless the era of relatively straightforward financing for PIN ended in the course of 1973, just after the roads programme had been extended to include a commitment to the 3,900-kilometre Perimetral Norte along the northern border of Brazil. Rising costs and doubts about its effectiveness were causing cuts in the colonization programme; the Yom Kippur war and the consequent rise in oil prices caused a rapid rise in the real cost of highway construction, as well as questioning every nation's dependence on road transport; and the shock effect to oil and the world economy meant a sudden leap in Brazil's domestic inflation rate, which jumped from 15·7 per cent in 1973 to 34·5 per cent in 1974. Altogether these factors meant that the incoming government of President Ernesto Geisel, the former head of Brazil's state oil concern, Petrobras, would have to pick up some rather expensive pieces when it came to power in March 1974.

In the meantime, how much of the TransAmazonica programme had been paid for by foreign loans? Since the 1964 revolution Brazil had been quite successful in attracting foreign loans—from the World Bank, the Inter-American Development Bank and USAID—for road-building in the centre-south and north-east. Delfim Netto's claim that the roads element in PIN was being paid for by the Brazilians themselves seems to have been justified only in part. Between April 1970 and February 1976 the World Bank, for example, loaned Brazil $400 million for highway construction of all sorts—and a loan for a project in the north-east, for example, could release Brazilian funds for Amazonia. At least two specific Eurodollar loans were raised for Amazonia: in 1972 the DNER was authorized to raise a loan of $15 million to pay for some of the Itaituba–Humaita stretch of the TransAmazonica, and in August 1974 the Banco do

Brasil raised $150 million for Amazonian highways, particularly for those being built towards possibly oil bearing regions by the Peruvian and Colombian frontiers. Depending on the mode of accountancy it would be possible to argue that the whole of the Estreito–Humaita stretch of the TransAmazonica had actually been financed by foreign loans. Yet when all this is said the direct foreign investment in the Amazon highways, particularly under Medici, seems to have been supplementary rather than decisive. It was not sufficient to rescue the programme from its difficulties and postponements after 1974. Although the Cuiabá–Santarem road (BR 165) was being made by the army—which tended to be cheaper, slower but possibly more thorough than the civil contractors—it did not complete the road until the end of 1976; one of the reasons for this delay quoted by the army engineers was that, even if it had received a contribution from the World Bank, the DNER had not made sufficient funds available regularly. (When the army was contracted to build a road it always did so at cost price to the services; although the military built barracks and other facilities on the proceeds its prices were relatively low because it often already had the necessary equipment and could regard the work as a type of training.) Another sign of strain in the later years of PIN was that the federal roads in Amazonia were eating up more of the resources which could have paid for local road improvements under the jurisdiction of the states. The DNER always had the final say over state highway plans and the poor Amazon states were particularly dependent on contributions from federal transport funds. It was with some irritation that Roberto dos Santos Vieira, planning secretary for the state of Amazonas, pointed out to the author that the price of asphalting the Porto Velho–Manaus road (BR 319) after 1972 was such that the state was precluded from any road-building of its own for the following four years.[11]

One of the main arguments for the TransAmazonica was that building it would provide lucrative employment for north-easterners. Yet this was only true for the north-eastern section of the road itself, east of Estreito, where the two roads leading from Picos to Recife and from Picos to João Pessoa were both considered part of the TransAmazonica. On the Amazonian stretch from Estreito to Humaita it is doubtful whether there were more than 12,000 men working at any time, and many of these were from the centre-south or Amazonia itself. Mendes Junior, for example, employed 1,800 on their longer stretch and 1,200 on their shorter one. Camargo Corrêa, on the other hand, had only 600 men on a stretch that was 69 kilometres longer than Mendes Junior's longest. Engineer Luis Claudio Nolasco of Mendes Junior explained in 1970 why his firm was taking on so few of the drought unemployed for work on the forest sections of the road. "If we picked an unemployed north-easterner, accustomed to the dust, and put him down in the middle of the forest, we are committing a crime," he claimed. Engineer Mario Coutinho of Andrade Gutierrez estimated with hindsight that, during the construction period of the Porto Velho–Manaus (BR 319), "about 70 per cent of workers came from the south, 20 per cent from the north-east and 10 per cent from the north—Amazonia".

If it was a crime for north-easterners to be set down in the forest, this was a crime that the north-easterners themselves had been knowingly committing since the nineteenth century. The real reason for the rather moderate use of north-easterners was rather different—they tended to be less educated, less experienced where skills were necessary, as with driving bulldozers, and less healthy than other people the firms could get. But in fact the construction firms were only partly in control of their labour recruitment. Much of this was subcontracted to "*gatos*" (cats) as the labour recruiters were called. These men were paid to round up labourers; sometimes they started with their own family and friends; sometimes they stored up discontent for later by overselling the merits of the Trans-Amazonica to the ignorant and unemployed. Costs of transport to the site were deducted from subsequent wages. There was indeed some labour unrest along the TransAmazonica, often involving subcontractors rather than the big companies. In the absence of trade unions the local priests and the Roman Catholic Church took it on themselves to air the grievances. Late in 1970, for instance, the bishops of Pará complained that some workers were only getting four cruzeiros a day—less than the minimum salary laid down for the region. But the then Labour Minister, Julio Barato, replied that the firms criticized were paying 134 cruzeiros a month and making up the difference with food and payments in kind. The *Estado de São Paulo* reported in October 1970 that sub-contractors near Itaituba were not complying with the labour laws and that local police had sided with the employers and were trying to persuade the protesting workers to go back to their homes. The local public prosecutor then took the matter up in Belem. He returned warning the Itaituba police that he would charge anyone who tried to prevent workers from claiming their lawful rights. Again in 1971 the Church claimed that there had been clashes between employers and their workforce along the Trans-Amazonica: Medici's new Labour Minister, Armando de Brito, answered that he could find no evidence of these.

Wages in fact were far from uniform along the Trans-Amazonica. If in some cases the deductions for food and transport made them seem too low, in others their apparent generosity completely disrupted the economics of the small towns through which the road passed. Mendes Junior, for instance, had a formula of paying 30 per cent more than the minimum salary, and then making deductions for the cost of food. In 1970 the best salaries in Altamira were paid by the *Prefeitura* (the town hall), and they were only 70 cruzeiros a month. Then along came Mendes Junior and Queiroz Galvão paying a minimum of 500 cruzeiros a month to simple workmen. The earnings of all grades of public-sector employees were actually higher than they were in other parts of Brazil. A presidential decree of October 1970 provided for special bonuses, ranging in seven categories from an extra 800 cruzeiros a month to an extra 3,600, which were payable to public employees working in the neighbourhood of the road. This inducement affected considerable numbers for one of the main features of the TransAmazonica operation was the sudden descent of federal agencies on places like Altamira and Itaituba. These were not only DNER and Incra, the colonization agency, but also bodies like Rondon, IBDF (Instituto Brasileiro de Desenvolvimento Florestal) the agency supposed to conserve forest resources and wild life, SESP the health service, and of course the army itself which stationed its jungle battalions, BIS (Batalhães de Infantaria de Selva) in every town along the TransAmazonica.

The extent to which either the building contractors or these federal agencies felt obliged to offset the disadvantages of life at the work fronts or support bases obviously varied considerably. On the whole the conditions of life during the construction phase of the TransAmazonica were spartan, with food and a shower seeming the best luxuries. Even then, however, a contractor like Mendes Junior was building the odd school for the children of employees and in some cases to provide literacy instruction for adult workers. As the road became consolidated, and as later stages of the Amazon highways programme commenced, more attention was given to these aspects. Although facilities were strictly stratified according to the rank of employee the various employers recognized a need for some non-financial inducements to keep people happy in isolated places. The DNER, for example, built swimming pools at each of its big encampments; these were usually restricted to use by engineers, their families and more senior employees.[12] Nearly all the agencies and big firms had football and volleyball teams. More thought too went into the construction camps as it became appreciated that today's wooden shanty town for roadworkers might well become the basis for tomorrow's city. Prainha, a dot on the map between Humaita and Jacareacanga, was an early example of this kind of spontaneous development and by the time the Perimetral Norte started in 1973 the constructors were encouraged to plan for it. Andrade Gutierrez then built a support camp at Cachoeira Porteira, by some attractive rapids on the River Trombetas, which was not only a town in miniature but a potential tourist centre. There was nothing provisional about the mode of construction of housing, hospital or church; the layout, around a hill overlooking the rapids, was planned as a town from the start.

How much of the roads programme was actually completed by the end of 1976? The Porto Velho–Manaus (BR 319) which was open for traffic in 1972 had been entirely asphalted by early 1976. The Cuiabá–Santarem road (BR 163) and the Manaus–Boa Vista (BR 174) were both just opened at least two years behind schedule. (The formal inauguration of the BR 174 did not occur until April 1977.) But neither the TransAmazonica (BR 230) nor the Perimetral Norte (BR 210) were open for their full extension. The BR 230 had two gaps: one, rather surprisingly, was east of Picos on its north-eastern section (though Picos was linked to both Recife and João Pessoa, but by other roads); the second, more predictably, was west of Humaita, where the BR 230 had only just reached Labrea. A certain confusion has been caused for those who are interested in the TransAmazonica by its transmogrification west of Humaita. Early maps of the road suggested that it might be coextensive with the BR 317 from Labrea to Rio Branco, though hinting at a continuation of the BR 230 from Labrea to Benjamim Constant on the frontier with Peru and Colombia. However, quite soon after the PIN programme was under way— and the real costs and difficulties of building jungle roads were more vivid in the minds of DNER and the Ministry of Transport—the TransAmazonica was redefined as being the BR 319 from Humaita to Porto Velho, and the BR 364 from Porto Velho to Rio Branco and Cruzeiro do Sul. This change made sense in that the BR 364, linking more towns and a region that was already awakening economically, deserved a higher priority than a road through almost empty forest from Labrea to Benjamim Constant. But even this BR 364 TransAmazonica did not go much further west than Sena Madureira by the end of 1976, leaving some 300 kilometres still to be built by the army's fifth engineering construction battalion. The main section of the BR 317 from Labrea to Rio Branco—from Labrea to Boca do Acre—had no target date for completion, while it was with considerable disbelief that the author heard Acre highway officials forecast that the army road from Cruzeiro do Sul to Benjamim Constant (BR 307) would be finished by 1978.

The Perimetral Norte looked likely to be worst hit by the rising costs and delays. Its 2,618 kilometres were due to be open in 1977 but by mid 1976, when only 976 kilometres were ready the price had gone up so much that work was halted for some six months and the contracts were put out to tender again. This procedure was forced on DNER by the federal auditing authorities because the forecast cost had trebled to an actual expenditure of one million cruzeiros ($95,000) per kilometre; DNER personnel explained that it would nevertheless be more expensive to employ new firms to complete the sections because of the time they would take to bring in their equipment, so the fresh tendering was really a device to satisfy the auditors of the new price levels. DNER did take the opportunity, however, of abandoning the most westerly section of the road altogether— from São Gabriel da Cachoeira to the Colombian border. The contractors Queiroz Galvão had hit an area of virtual quicksands less than 20 kilometres west of São Gabriel where it was

overlap between foreign and domestic criticism, and awareness of environmental arguments grew steadily in Brazil in the 1970s. The special October 1971 edition of the magazine *Realidade* quoted two German scientists, Harald Sioli and Wilhelm Brinkmann, as fearing that destruction of the forest could have lasting and far-reaching consequences; the same issue also quoted Brazilians like General Mourão Filho and the then director of INPA, Paulo de Almeida Machado, in the same sense. Brazilians had, after all, seen forested areas like Bragantina lose their fertility and were familiar with the "slash-and-burn" cycle which could reduce crops on Amazonian soils to almost nothing after the third year. Questions about the depredation of Brazil's last big forest resource, and about soil fertility, were raised almost automatically by the PIN project. The same issue of *Realidade* also raised the biggest environmental question of all, by reporting that Paulo de Almeida Machado had been given a speculative calculation that as much as 50 per cent of the world's oxygen could be produced by photosynthesis in Amazonia. This theory is still far from substantiated—instead the balance of scientific opinion would regard it as exaggerated—but it electrified critics of PIN. A young barman in Manaus, for instance, still gave it me as an established fact in mid 1976. The UN's environmental conference in Stockholm in 1972, and the year of the rainforest declared in 1975 by the World Wildlife Fund and the International Union for the Conservation of Nature, helped to maintain both foreign and Brazilian interest in the vulnerability and significance of the Amazon rainforest. This combination appeared by the mid 1970s to be having some effect on government policy and the policing of measures to protect the environment.

Most of the criticism discussed so far was a response to Medici's political decision and, in the case of some of the environmental critics in particular, they were open to the charge that they only began to value the tropical forest when it was threatened. Both in Brazil and the exterior this value was only rising, of course, in as much as other temperate and tropical forests had already disappeared. More immediate in its results would have been criticism from the political leaders of those whom PIN was supposed to help: the governors of the north-east and Amazonia. In fact both Nilo Coelho, the governor of Pernambuco in 1970, and João Agripino, who was the governor of Paraiba, complained publicly of the diversion of resources from the north-east into the Trans-Amazonica. Nilo Coelho said, "We are all front-line soldiers for the conquest of Amazonia, but not at the price of the destruction of a developmental movement . . . for the construction of a new north-east". João Agripino pointed out that SUDENE would lose a potential 1,900 million cruzeiros ($41 million) between 1971 and 1974 to PIN, a sum equal to the total which that institution had invested in both industrial and agricultural sectors between 1963 and 1969.

However, at the height of the north-eastern drought it was not too easy for north-eastern governors to oppose anything that might seem to provide immediate work and hope. In any case the interests of the north-eastern states differed. While coastal ones like Pernambuco stood to lose, interior states like Piaui and Maranhão—which had respectively obtained only 24 and 18 SUDENE projects out of a total of 883 up to December 1969—were likely to benefit from the Trans-Amazonica roadworks. In Amazonia proper the political leaders, who were much weaker in relation to the federal government than the north-eastern ones anyway, tended to welcome Medici's initiative even if the TransAmazonica would not automatically have been their first priority. The three territories—Rondonia, Roraima and Amapá—were in any case ruled by service officers appointed by the federal government; by tradition Rondonia had an army governor, Roraima which was only accessible from the rest of Brazil by air for much of the year had an air-force man, and Amapá had a naval governor.

Adoption of the roads programme in mid 1970 was sudden, and political. Domestic criticism was slow to develop, occurred after the decisions had been taken, and was frequently labelled unpatriotic. In the chapters which follow we shall trace some of the consequences of the assault which the roads represented.

3

ORGANIZED COLONIZATION

THE PLACE WAS the Agrovila Boa União, thirteen kilometres up a side road from the TransAmazonica in the Altamira region and eight kilometres from the River Xingu. Compared with many of these side roads, which tend to be muddy, sandy, or broken up, this was at least passable for a high wheel-base Chevrolet van. On the way you pass fields of manioc and rice, and small cleared areas of pasture where burnt tree stumps are still visible and the humpbacked Zebu cattle graze. Even by the road parts of each lot, as the 100-hectare farms are called, remain covered with trees. Suddenly the narrow road emerges by a row of wooden buildings. You get out and realize that they form one side of a three-sided square of 45 houses—though the central square is so thickly covered with tall grass and scrub that you can't see across it. Amazingly in Amazonia no part has been cleared to make a football pitch. The water tower, designed to collect rainwater for the *agrovila*, is out of use and people have to fetch their water from the *igarapé*. The houses are built to the standard Incra specifications, raised from the ground on low stilts, with some three or four good-sized rooms to accommodate families which are often of eight or more people. Inside such a house there are pin-ups, holy pictures, a wood fire, a rifle and a thermos of constantly available coffee. Outside one house in a previous *agrovila* there had been a smart new privy. Although Incra is supposed to be encouraging outdoor lavatories—there is none indoors—none are yet to be seen at Boa União.[14] The houses are close together, one or two have flowers and banana trees growing; most keep chickens and a few have pigs. Here the houses which are to be occupied by SESP, the health service, and COBAL, the government's cheap food service, are both empty. Mobral, the literacy service, has been operating here for a year. The teachers running it say that 60 per cent of the people are illiterate, that there is a high incidence of worms among the children, and that there is a shortage of vegetables which the families are not used to growing or eating. Only three farmers here keep any cattle, and only their families have milk. Fresh meat, apart from anything that is shot in the woods, is almost unknown.

But the people, as so often, are friendly and willing to talk about their problems. "Incra doesn't do much for poor people here," says Francisca Nascimento da Silva, complaining particularly about the lack of transport and its expense. It costs 40 cruzeiros ($3·80) to hitch a round trip on a lorry to Altamira and 10 cruzeiros ($0·95) a sack to get rice transported as far as the TransAmazonica. With rice only fetching 50 cruzeiros ($4·75) for the 60-kilo sack—five cruzeiros less than a kilo of coffee—some farmers are wondering whether it's worth growing it any more. But Geraldo Lucindo Nobre says, "Each year the position of the colonists is tending to improve." In 1975 he grew six sacks of beans worth 200 cruzeiros (nearly $25) each and 50 sacks of rice—a total income of 3,700 cruzeiros (nearly $457) which is spent on clothes, utensils, seeds and in repaying agricultural loans. In this *agrovila*, populated mostly by north-easterners from Ceará, there is little communal sense. Why, I asked Antonio Paulino Vieira, a 51-year-old Cearnese, didn't people co-operate to buy a lorry for the *agrovila*? "People here are too individualistic. They would ask, 'Who would drive it?' or 'Who would pay for the petrol?' " Psychologically many of the inhabitants still feel dependent on Incra or the government. A lot say, "Incra is my father." Vieira, who protests that the government does not do enough, remarks that it has "opened one eye" to the situation of rural families. Prices for 100-hectare farms, bought for as little as 2,000 cruzeiros ($377) with payment over more than ten years, now vary between 10,000 cruzeiros and 25,000 ($952–2,380), according to their condition: Incra is chiefly concerned that incoming purchasers clear any bank debts attached to the land.

Incra was set up to replace an earlier ineffective body, the Instituto Brasileiro de Reforma Agraria (IBRA). Although agrarian reform had been much discussed under the Goulart government—when it was proposed to expropriate land along-side existing federal roads—the coming of the military régimes after 1964 had virtually stopped any takeovers of this sort. From then on IBRA's function had been to carry out a landownership survey of Brazil, and to attempt to arbitrate on the numerous conflicts between different owners, and between owners and *posseiros* (squatters). Hence when President Medici wanted a government agency which was capable of organizing the large-scale transfer of settlers from the north-east to Amazonia a substantial overhaul was necessary. Much of the chaos and many of the mistakes which surrounded the transfer operation, which really got under way in the middle of 1971, can be put down to the fact that an effectively new body was having to improvise its services in the middle of a stampede. At the beginning of that year over two-thirds of the staff which Incra had inherited lived in Rio and Brasilia and almost no one in Amazonia. Incra was given two decree laws in 1971 to operate. The first, in March (decree 68.443) expropriated 64,000 square kilometres in a polygon between Altamira and Itaituba; this area did include one of the few patches of really good soil in Amazonia, the red soil area near Altamira, and it was given top priority in the colonization programme. The second decree in April (1.164) declared as "indispensable to security and national development" the land 100 kilometres on either side of the planned federal roads in Amazonia. The effect of this second decree (which was far less threatening to private interests than the Goulart proposal, for the land was virtually unoccupied) was to make Incra master of 2·2 million square kilometres. This was an area which, on its own, would rank as the eleventh largest country in the world—and included the great bulk of Amazonia. In principle Incra aimed to settle colonists on 100-hectare plots up to ten kilometres on either side of the roads; in the remaining 90 kilometres on either side it would begin by trying to establish whether there were any legal owners (not at all easy given the number of forged titles) and how many squatters there were; after that it intended to sell the unowned and unoccupied lands, giving preference to purchasers who could make early use of them and settle a population there.

In 1971 and 1972 therefore Incra personnel were active in four areas particularly, soliciting recruits for the Trans-Amazonica agricultural settlements: in the coastal sugar belt of the north-east and in the dry *sertão* land further inland; in the overpopulated and agriculturally decaying valley of the Paraíba in the state of Rio; and in the north of Paraná where there was also a land hunger. In each case the potential colonists were offered a wooden house, at least 100 hectares of land with a provisional title, guaranteed money for six months at the current minimum salary, and guaranteed minimum prices for their crops for two years, whether or not they were actually able to sell them. Typically, of course, the recruiting agents went further. They made it look as though more land would be cleared in advance for the colonists, the schools and health clinics would be built by the time they arrived—and credulous and desperate people believed them. As one peasant remarked in December 1972 to a reporter from *Jornal do Brasil*, "My children, my family . . . they were always OK. I had my land. I came from there, believing the promises. I brought seven children to die of hunger here. My family is very hungry. It's bad to trick people. Why won't they speak the truth?"

Incra adopted a system of colonization which looked fine on paper. It allowed for virtually continuous 100-hectare farms along the main roads, broken occasionally by 25-kilometre tracts of forest which would be left untouched for ecological reasons, with the standard Incra houses built close to the roads and within sight of one another. Altamira, Itaituba and Marabá were each made the centre of an "integrated colonization project" (PIC) which was supposed to organize the process of settlement and provide seeds and technical services. Only on the TransAmazonica itself would families actually live on their plots. The majority up the side roads would live in *agrovilas*, serving about 50 families. The *agrovilas* would be between five and ten kilometres apart and would contain a primary school and health post. Every 40 kilometres or so there would be an *agropolis*—a bigger administrative centre serving around 20 *agrovilas*, designed to develop a secondary school and some industry. Every 140 kilometres or so there would be a *ruropolis*, which would be a town. In fact not much attention was ever paid to the *ruropolis* idea. The only one specifically designed as such was the Ruropolis President Medici, at the junction of the TransAmazonica and the Cuiabá–Santarem, which was opened by the president in one of his last official functions in early 1974. From the start it was felt that the existing towns along the TransAmazonica would serve this purpose, leaving open the possibility that some of the *agropolises* might grow from being merely administrative encampments to full-blown towns. Incra's plan looked tidily bureaucratic. If it succeeded it would indeed "fix the man to the land" in Amazonia, pepper the TransAmazonica with small towns, and use that main road as a basis for occupying a swathe westwards from Marabá.

In reality the paper plans bore too little relation to what was actually happening in 1971 and 1972 so that they became discredited. The effect of government propaganda and Incra's own recruiting was to launch a rush which the administrative processes along the TransAmazonica were not ready to receive. In mid-1971, 50 families a day were being brought in, often by plane. By September, 1972, Incra said there were about 7,000 colonists along the road, but only 1,511 were installed on their lots. The houses were not ready for them; the schools and health posts did not exist; the ten hectares on each lot which were supposed to be cleared ready for planting were still trees and bush; the families had to be fed until they could get their first crops, and there was not always enough food; there was no attempt at first to select the colonists from the north-east and those who came were often bad subsistence farmers, expecting Incra to do everything for them. The difficulties were compounded by friction between the middle-class agricultural experts of Incra, who were often ignorant of the real possibilities of the Amazon soils and who were frequently unwilling to get their hands dirty, and north-eastern peasants whose own techniques were often inappropriate. Corruption in some cases, where Incra men sold off good seeds and distributed poor ones to the colonists, did not help. The lots were not always properly marked out in the rush. Colonists who were eager to see a rapid return planted crops in the wrong season. (A family who arrived at the Agrovila Vale Piauiense from Ceará told me that they had planted rice in November and had had to burn it all.) There were deaths from malaria and even measles. North-easterners were decanted into lots and *agrovilas* with little choice; significantly, however, two researchers from Florida University (Emilio F. and Eve de Moran of the Center for Latin-American Studies) found that none of the colonists who had come from the Amazon state of Pará had got bad soils. In a survey they did near Altamira they reported, "We didn't find a single Paraense with soil which was poor or of moderate quality. The Paraenses know that it's not the big trees which indicate the better land: on the contrary they are a sign of poor ground."[15]

The big questions, right from the start, were agricultural and social. It was tragic, of course, if anyone went hungry along the TransAmazonica or died for want of medicines or doctors; but the unpleasant truth was that in each respect the situation in the north-east was probably worse. More important was whether the settlers were able to establish a viable and economic agriculture, and whether it was the poorest and landless north-easterners who were benefiting from the organized migration. In both regards the mixture of national euphoria and administrative haste augured badly.

Agriculturally the TransAmazonica was a gamble in the dark. Such knowledge as existed in 1970, when its route was chosen, suggested that most of the firm higher ground was poor. Only on the flooded *varzea*, where the rivers deposited fertile silt at regular intervals, could one be certain of raising short-cycle crops like rice or maize perennially without ruining the soil and reducing the crops. But the TransAmazonica was designed to lead settlement away from the river banks. It was not until after the line was already a road and colonists were already being given plots and houses that RADAM yielded its information about the soils. It was not until 1972 that a soil scientist from IPEAN (Instituto de Pesquisas e Experimentação Agropecuaria do Norte) made a detailed survey of soil conditions along the TransAmazonica. He confirmed that, apart from the belt of red soil near Altamira, most of the soil beside the road was indeed the poor laterite soil which was so common throughout most of the basin. By then, of course, it was much too late. The problem of basic fertility was serious because the forest soil had only a thin layer of humus, and artificial fertilizer, of which Brazil had a national shortage anyway, was quite beyond the pockets of the bulk of colonists. What chance was there that they would have the patience to wait for native long-cycle tree crops, like cocoa and rubber, or the skill to nourish poor soils with every scrap of chicken dung or leaf mould that they could conserve?

The trouble was that the north-easterners brought the agriculture they knew: predominantly they knew how to grow manioc, rice and maize. A few from the interior of the north-east were familiar with cotton; some from Bahia were used to growing cocoa which indeed stood a chance along the Trans-Amazonica; many from the coastal strip of Pernambuco grew sugar, which came in useful when Incra built a sugar mill to serve the red-earth district round Altamira. Almost none of them, for instance, understood how to grow black pepper, the long-cycle crop which Japanese colonists had successfully pioneered on poor soil at Tomé Açu in Pará. In the early years along the TransAmazonica, therefore, the main crops were manioc, maize and rice; rice was the crop which Incra encouraged as a commercial product for sale; all of them were short-cycle crops which tended to impoverish the soil. Philip M. Fernacite, a soil scientist from Michigan University who has been studying 500 fields near Altamira, told me that there was no doubt that by the end of three years the size of crops was substantially reduced, in some cases by 50 per cent.[16] No colonist I spoke to in 1976 would ever admit this, and of course they need not necessarily have been aware of the trend as they were still extending the area under cultivation. Although by 1976 Incra officials were trying to persuade the colonists to switch to long-cycle crops, and a rice glut with relatively poor prices was dissuading them from placing so much reliance on that crop, Incra has not yet been very successful in re-educating them. Two other factors held back the agricultural success of the colonists: the cost of bank loans which they could not always pay back, and which depended on land titles which Incra was slow to distribute; and the appalling condition of the side roads off the TransAmazonica which meant that crops could either not be brought out at all, or only at prices that gave little encouragement to the farmers.

And who in any case were the colonists? The government's belief that unemployed men would be hired from the drought zones of the north-east to build the TransAmazonica, and that a good number of those would then settle beside it, was falsified early. The road-builders were relatively few, often skilled, and of a nomadic nature. Mendes Junior, for example, found that the bulk of their TransAmazonica workers switched to asphalting the Belem–Brasilia highway after the road was finished. Even in the chaos of the early months, few landless and unskilled labourers from the north-east were able to get plots by the TransAmazonica. José Francisco de Moura Cavalcanti, president of Incra at the time, laid down the principle that potential colonists must have "entrepreneurial capacity". This meant checking with Banco do Brasil branches in the north-east to get the names of people who had received bank loans, and had been able to repay them. In the conditions of the north-east this meant a strong preference for the richer, better-organized peasants. In so far as health checks for intending colonists were effective, these too tended to weed out the poorest. Far from providing an escape for the most benighted agricultural workers in the north-east, the PIN scheme from the start was aiming to convert the more capable peasants into a sort of rich *kulak* peasant class along the TranAmazonica. This tendency was strengthened by two other factors: a kind of natural selection among the colonists themselves, and a gradual cutback in the financial support for new colonists from Incra, which required newcomers to bring more initial capital with them.

Not all the potential colonists could afford to hang about, waiting for their plots. In October 1971 the *Estado de São Paulo* reported that, of a group of 78 agricultural workers from Rio Grande do Sul, only 29 were now left to get farms by the TransAmazonica: sixteen went home almost at once, only venturing out of the *agrovila* to see the land destined for them; another seventeen waited for a while, then left, saying that they didn't like the food and the heat; another sixteen, who would have stayed if Incra had given them titles of possession instead of just showing them the land, also went. There was also a turnover, perhaps as high as 10 per cent in the first four years of occupation, among those who actually obtained their lots. Incra found its settlement operations costly and it met increasing criticism elsewhere in Brazil. In 1975, for instance, the total cost of Incra operations in Itaituba, Altamira and Marabá was 107·1 million cruzeiros ($12 million). For these reasons it began to cut back its aid to new colonists. Richer men from the centre-south started buying lots in the PICs. At the same time the more successful farmers found ways of adding to their 100-hectare lots, by buying adjoining ones in in the names of fathers-in-law and similar devices. By mid 1976 Incra at Altamira was using this differentiation— which also included the appearance of some landless labourers, working for hire on what were intended as the family-run plots—to justify selling 1,500-hectare farms to its better, existing clients.

By then, also, it was easier to see what Incra had achieved and how it had failed along the TransAmazonica. Incra itself had been fiercely criticized in reports from SUDAM, SERFHAU (a housing agency linked to the Ministry of the Interior) and one from its own officials. SUDAM, for instance, in its second Amazon development plan (1975–9) pointed out that the spontaneous migration encouraged by all the Trans-Amazonica publicity had been much greater than Incra's organized colonization; that the region was short of good soils and the colonists were using a destructive form of subsistence agriculture; and that the colonization required huge resources for education and training which had never been allowed for. However, the same SUDAM document illustrated how Incra had become a whipping-boy in the reaction against PIN: it exaggerated the extent to which migrants and local inhabitants had swapped diseases, specifically mentioning the "black fever" of Labrea, which can be fatal to children, as something that new arrivals have caught. In fact the Labrea fever appears not to have spread from its home town and, though this kind of disease exchange was widely feared, it has yet to occur outside the Amerindian communities on any significant scale.

The most effective criticism was that the numbers which had been settled under Incra's aegis had fallen far short of the target of 100,0000 families in five years. Indeed the three PICs of Itaituba, Altamira and Marabá had only transferred 7,482 families between 1971 and 1975: from the fact that only 656 families had been settled in 1975 it looked pretty clear that Incra, under the Geisel government, was running down its TransAmazonica programme. However although these numbers were nothing like what had been aimed at, they were not as unimpressive as they might first appear. In Altamira, where 3,854 families had been given farms, Incra estimated in 1976 that the total population living in the area of the project amounted to 18,000 people. This excluded the population in the town of Altamira itself which had shot up from about 3,000 in 1971 to around 18,500 in 1975. In all perhaps the migratory movement of which Incra was the spearhead had led to some 100,000 people moving westward into Amazonia from the north-east, or little more than 10 per cent of the population increase in the north-east each year between 1970 and 1975 and hardly a seventh of the original target for the TransAmazonica. As an immediate relief for the north-east this was trivial, but if a viable agriculture and industrial undertaking with a large potential for employment had been made possible either directly or indirectly, then the TransAmazonica might continue to be a magnet. One thing that Incra had persisted with was a preference for north-easterners among its TransAmazonica colonists. In 1975, 200 out of the 266 families it settled at its Itaituba project came from the north-east; at Altamira the number was 112 out of 192, and at Marabá the north and north-east accounted for 131 out of 198.

By 1976, however, it was still far from clear whether Incra had succeeded in establishing a viable small-scale agriculture along the TransAmazonica, although there was talk there of establishing two more PICs. Many of the colonists had yet to harvest their third crop, after which so many scientists had warned that returns might decline steeply; many had still only cleared a quarter of their lots, though all seemed to be observing the SUDAM rule that for ecological reasons half their area should be left with trees. There were scattered signs of prosperity—one 100-hectare lot near Altamira went for 250,000 cruzeiros ($23,890)—and many of the colonists felt themselves to be better off; at one *agrovila*, the Agrovila Nova Frontera 80 kilometres from Altamira, a southerner had organized a co-op which had been buying machinery for general use; but the ambition of many of the colonists who were living in *agrovilas* was to build a house on their own plot—the families did not like husbands having to walk home for up to fifteen kilometres at weekends to rejoin them, and it was chiefly the presence of primary schools that kept them in the *agrovilas* at all. In 1976 it was estimated that the saleable rice harvest along the TransAmazonica would amount to as much as 9,000 tonnes. But this was an embarrassment to the growers who had to pay lorries for the waiting time as they queued outside bursting granaries in places like Altamira. It was an embarrassment also to Incra, which was having to underwrite the prices and had failed to dispose of a considerable part of the 1975 crop also. Incra had lost a great deal of money on the Abraão

Lincoln sugar refinery near Altamira, built in 1973 to process sugar and alcohol. Although sugar seemed a successful crop the factory was working well below capacity; an Incra official suggested that it would not be until 1980–81 that it would have enough of the raw material to operate economically.

What Incra had achieved, with the support of the army and other federal agencies, was a settlement programme along the TransAmazonica which was almost totally lacking in crime or shoot-outs. Chaos and broken dreams, yes: deaths and lawlessness, as in the North American wild west, no. In this the experience of the TransAmazonica was significantly different from that of parts of Mato Grosso, Rondonia and other parts of Amazonia over the last decade. In all the Brazilian criticism of Incra this was a positive point which was rarely recognized. Nor were there many scandals in the organization. One nasty exception occurred in February 1974 at the Ruropolis President Medici. Nine days before its official opening by the outgoing president, Incra ordered the destruction of 150 simple wooden shacks, on the inhumane excuse that they did not fit in with the town plan. As soon as their menfolk had gone to work Incra personnel ordered the women and children out and burned down their homes: the great majority were then driven 60 kilometres away to the barracks of the eighth army construction battalion.

Even before President Medici was succeeded by President Geisel, however, it seemed as if Incra was changing direction. From being concerned with the small 100-hectare plots it was turning its attention to areas of 3,000 hectares or *glebas* of several hundred thousand; from concentrating on the band alongside the TransAmazonica it was paying increasing attention to Rondonia, Roraima and other parts of the Amazon basin. In fact Incra had been set up to look at the whole of Amazonia and its job of settling ownership and selling federal land to private firms had been implied by decree 1.164 of April 1971. What happened in around 1973, partly as a result of the disappointments with the 100-hectare programme beside the TransAmazonica and partly because Incra was beginning to develop the necessary administrative capacity, was that this aspect became predominant. In view of its importance for the occupation of Amazonia as a whole it is worth discussing this in more detail.

Along the TransAmazonica itself Incra had always talked about collaborating with private enterprise, both in colonization schemes and general agricultural developments. It was quite possible that such private colonization would work better than Incra's—because it might be less bureaucratic, better organized and less rushed. One of the first such private schemes involved a large agricultural co-operative firm from the southernmost state of Rio Grande do Sul, the Cooperative Triticola Serrana. Incra ceded this firm 400,000 hectares at a distance of 85 kilometres from Altamira and, with funds from the Interamerican Development Bank, it planned to move 2,000 families there from Rio Grande do Sul in 1985. They would come from a place called Ijuí where problems of *minifundio* (the endless subdivision of plots) were acute and land-hungry farmers were trying to scratch a living from a mere five or eight hectares. Along the TransAmazonica instead they would get 100 or 200 hectares, to be paid for over 20 years at only 7 per cent interest, with no repayments for the first three years. This scheme suited Incra in several ways: it involved bringing fresh international aid money along the Trans-Amazonica; it made use of energetic *gauchos* from Rio Grande do Sul, whom Incra somewhat favoured in its disillusion with the more limited north-easterners; it was organized with enough time to allow for the houses, silos and access roads to be built before the colonists arrived, and for detailed soil research to be complete; and it allowed Incra to claim that its colonization process was relieving social tensions in an already settled area—something that it could rarely do so precisely as it had almost totally opted out of "agrarian reform" as that is usually understood.

By 1976 Incra had permission to sell land in slices of up to 500,000 hectares—which led some of its own experts to complain that "there will have to be an agrarian reform in the agrarian reform". The maximum holding for an individual rose from 3,000 hectares to 72,000. This was partly a response to the pressure of agricultural interests who wanted to buy land in Amazonia, and who felt Incra was being incredibly slow about putting it on the market, and partly due to a swing of policy within Incra and the Geisel government which had adopted its more selective Polamazonia strategy. Whereas small colonists along the TransAmazonica could only laugh or protest fruitlessly about the organization—a café near Marabá kept an incredibly twisted piece of wood on show simply labelled "Incra"—the Association of Amazon Entrepreneurs based in São Paulo had a lot more leverage. Whereas from 1972–4 Incra had distributed little over one million hectares out of 250 million at its disposal, in 1975 alone it sold 1·7 million.[17] But this change did not simply reflect outside pressure or the greed of intending purchasers: Incra and the government themselves, after the early disappointments and criticism along the TransAmazonica, had concluded that agriculture and colonization would only work where it was supported by big capital and careful organization.

Even along the TransAmazonica it was possible to see the difficulties for Incra in sorting out land title and acting as land salesman. As soon as it had launched its plan to colonize the red-earth belt near Altamira, for instance, it was perplexed to discover that a wealthy syndicate in São Paulo claimed a property of 70 lots of 4,356 hectares each in exactly this district. They had even put up a cattle scheme for approval and grants to SUDAM. After a little investigation Incra discovered that the land title had been forged using a bogus book from the property register in the small town of São Felix de Xingu. As well as the swindles, of course, Incra also had to deal with the defective documents and titles which were based on memory, occupation and place and river names which were ill-defined. Property claims which were based on rubber-collecting—where the tappers constantly varied and extended their tapping circuit—were notoriously vague. Even along the TransAmazonica too, Incra came face to face with the squatter problem—the *posseiros*. Under the Brazilian constitution every *posseiro* was entitled to 100 hectares, itself an application of the *uti possidetis* principle. But this never stopped private land-owners from trying, with the most violent means, to clear them off their land. For Incra itself the problem was more delicate as it was bound to try to preserve the rights of the *posseiros*, yet at the same time their existence tended to lower the value of federal land and make its sale harder. And fresh *posseiros* might be arriving all the time. In 1976, for instance, Incra's land project at Marabá was trying to survey and sell for public tender four *glebas* (large areas outlined on a map). One of 167,000 hectares was found to contain 336 people; a second, the Gleba Carajas of 942,000 hectares, was found to contain 89; a third, of 135,750 hectares, had 106; and the fourth, of 396,000 hectares, had 127. These were small numbers, grubbing a living from about 50 hectares to about 150, but they immensely complicated a rational sales policy that was intended to prevent land friction. In seven months the number of *posseiros* on the Gleba Carajas more than doubled as another 99 arrived.

Matters which were difficult along the TransAmazonica, where penetration only began from 1970 onward, were well-nigh insoluble in southern and western parts of the river basin where the land rush had begun up to a decade earlier and Incra was expected to create order out of conflict. The problems there came in four kinds—the violence of the land tensions which could arise, the speed of population growth, the complexity of land ownership, and the varied policies of the local state governments which often (as in Mato Grosso and Pará) had their own state development bodies and where politicians (as in Mato Grosso) could be deeply implicated in land speculation.

At its worst, the war between the landowners and *posseiros* could be exactly that: the owners sent in armed men, *pistoleiros*, to shoot up the families and burn their shacks. The purchasers of the Niteroi rubber groves in Acre, among them a prosperous lawyer from Parana, named João Tezza Filho, adopted a technique of "psychological pressure". A plane buzzed the huts of the *posseiros*, while his men cut timber nearby and threatened to knock them down. Purchasers of another rubber property, Porvir, used a more drastic method. Besides setting fire to the homes and gardens of the *posseiros* and colonists who got in their way they also burned the surrounding forest in order to put a stop to any rubber tapping. A third technique (reported by a commission set up by CONTAG, the Confederação Nacional dos Trabalhadores na Agricultura in Acre) was to prevent the collection of rubber from the homes of the tappers, or the delivery of food or materials. This last method was something known as the *"castanha"* (Brazil nut) approach, because its victims would have to survive on nuts alone. Acre of course was unusual in that, as well as having squatters and speculators pouring in from the centre-south, it still had the remains of a rubber-collecting industry and few districts were totally devoid of people. It was not surprising, given the pressures, that many of the *seringueiros* simply crossed the border into Bolivia where they could continue to tap rubber in the traditional way. In March 1976, Padre Peregrino Carneiro de Lima, a priest of Vila Placido in Acre, estimated that as many as 45,000 Brazilian rubber tappers were now collecting latex in Bolivia. They had been displaced by purchasers who had no sympathy with this way of life, who were setting up ranches or cashing in on the land hunger of labourers and small farmers from Paraná, or Rio Grande do Sul.

The second problem for Incra was the speed with which migration and land speculation was occurring. Every day lorries were trundling into Porto Velho and Rio Branco, piled high with families and belongings. They had come up the BR 364 from Cuiabá and the south. Throughout the 1970s the population of Acre was estimated to be growing at the rate of 15 per cent a year. In Rondonia in 1976 officials told me that they honestly could not say how many people were now living in the territory. The 1970 census had given a total of 116,610: using the conventional annual adjustments this would produce an estimate of 141,251 on 1 July 1976. But in fact the office of IBGE (Brazil's statistical institute) in Porto Velho estimated that there could be as many as 220,000 living in Rondonia on that date—that is to say, the population had almost doubled in six years. Most of this growth was due to migration and, although the towns had grown just as rapidly, many of the incomers had set their hearts on a plot of land. Acre and Rondonia were extreme cases of a phenomenon that was also common to parts of Mato Grosso, Goiás and southern Pará. Only in Roraima and those parts of Amazonas and Pará north of the main river was it possible to plan for population and agricultural growth with a certain tranquillity, and that would evaporate when Manaus was joined to Boa Vista by road and the Perimetral Norte was filled in.

The muddles over land title were exacerbated by speculation, and the need to present some kind of documents of ownership to SUDAM when an owner was applying for fiscal incentives had created a minor industry of forgery. Many of those who knew the real state of occupation on the ground, the *posseiros* and *seringueiros*, were illiterate and were not consulted when the paper boundaries were fixed. By the mid 1970s firms dealing in land were represented on every commercial street in Cuiabá, the capital of Mato Grosso, and in November 1975 Incra estimated that only 152 landowners in Rondonia had land titles which were not obtained fraudulently. The sort of thing that could happen was illustrated to a reporter of *Estado de São Paulo* by Silvio Goncalves de Faria, co-ordinator of Incra's land title project in Rondonia. A man named José de Souza Martins left as an inheritance to a certain Maria Amorim some land which he had not bought from anyone, nor registered anywhere. She sold it to a Raimundo Souza Duarte in 1973 and, all of a sudden, the property appeared in a document as having 79,875 hectares. Not satisfied, José da Silva Pinto, who bought the land from Raimundo, resolved to add a further 50,000 hectares to his estate. Of this total of nearly 130,000 hectares he sold 20,000 to the Fazenda Santa Julia of Muniz Felicio, who managed to get SUDAM support for a cattle project on "his" property. In April 1974 he declared its value as being one million cruzeiros ($147,590). A year later although he did not declare any cattle and claimed only to have put 200 hectares under hay he declared its value as 1·8 million cruzeiros ($222,220). The combination of doubtful title, apparent land-grabbing, and SUDAM-related speculation was all too common. Incra somehow had to verify the situation on the spot and halt the trade in paper titles and the real processes of forest clearing and squatting for long enough to establish everyone's rights.

Finally, of course, Incra was only one of the official parties to the land problem: others were SUDAM, FUNAI where traditional Indian lands were involved, and the state governments which had lands of their own to sell. Shrewd owners tried to play these bodies off against each other. The state governments were often the least disinterested. (All public land in the territories belonged to the federation and was therefore available for sale by Incra.) Not only did the states have legitimate interests in stimulating their own settlement and development, but land dealing was open to the patronage of state politicians whose powers in other respects were somewhat curtailed by the military-backed federal government. In some states, such as Pará and Mato Grosso, it was the state which largely influenced the price of land in the areas of rapid occupation. It did this by the price it put on its own land and the timing of its sales. In Pará, for example, the state government of Aloysio Chaves banned all sales of its own land between April 1975 and January 1977 and announced in July 1976 that the minimum price was going up by 25 per cent and by much more in the most coveted areas. One of the effects of this was to make the federally-backed iron-extraction project at the Serra dos Carajas a great deal more expensive. Amazonia Mineração SA, the company involved, in which a majority holding effectively belonged to the Brazilian government, had applied to buy 450,000 hectares of state land. Overnight therefore the value of that land rose from 45 million cruzeiros ($4·38 million) to almost 115 million ($10·9 million), or about an eighth of Pará's state budget for 1976.

How well was Incra performing, faced with this set of problems? By the mid 1970s it seemed as if the organization had established a notional authority over land dealing, but the reality varied enormously in different parts of Amazonia. There was a strong feeling that often it was merely providing a bureaucratic delay for ted tape in a process that was largely out of its own control. By espousing the desirability of big properties and large projects for much of the region it was no longer trying to enforce a system of small farming, except alongside the main roads and in the areas of its integrated colonization projects. (This of course did not mean that other federal agencies did not also have enormous influence over the pace and nature of the big agricultural schemes: SUDAM and the federal funds behind the Polamazonia strategy ensured that.) It was slow in discriminating between the claims for land title, and there was often a considerable delay between granting a "provisional" and a "definitive" title. On the other hand there was a strong impression that Incra was now giving top priority to areas where the pressures were strongest, such as Rondonia and Acre, and in making adequate preparations in Roraima ahead of the expected influx. By 1976, for instance, Incra had seven integrated projects in Rondonia: these then contained some 13,000 families—or almost twice the number settled along the TransAmazonica. Furthermore this group of projects included the brightest jewel of Incra's boasts at Ouro Preto. Here the PIC, on 450,000 hectares, had increased the value of output from 1·1 million cruzeiros ($239,100) in 1970 to 23·6 million ($3·9 million) in 1973: rice, cotton and cattle were all being raised by the colonists and people familiar with cocoa were being flown in specially from Bahia to pioneer that crop also. Incra in Rondonia was aiming to settle and regularize the ownership of 50,000 families by 1980: if this target was met the organization would really have gone a long way to solving the problem raised by migration into the territory in the 1970s.

But even in Rondonia and Acre Incra's record was far from perfect. A colonization project at Xapuri in Acre was virtually abandoned, apparently due to staff mismanagement of the type which had sometimes occurred along the TransAmazonica, most notably at the Marabá PIC. Manoel Augusto da Silva Nascimento, dumped down in Xapuri from Maranhão, was a colonist who had been shown pictures of the handsome houses which the new settlers would receive. "But the best house we could use when we arrived here was the cover of a Brazil nut tree," he said laughing. His wife added, "But that sort of house is no better. When there is a strong wind we have to go out, afraid it might fall."[18] The same inadequate maintenance of access roads, which bedevilled the TransAmazonica colonies, recurred in the west. Large crops of rice were lost in the Vilhena PIC in 1975, where 1,450 families were settled, because the rains coincided with the period of harvest and marketing, and the road to Vilhena itself was impassable. Although Incra was expected to build access roads it was not supposed to maintain them indefinitely. By the end of 1976 it had built about 3,000 kilometres of such roads in Rondonia, but the territory's government could not afford to take over responsibility for them.

Above all, perhaps, it was significant that the Incra colonies in Rondonia and Acre contained almost no north-easterners. Forty per cent of the colonists in the Ouro Preto PIC came only from Mato Grosso, a neighbouring state with its own expanding frontier into Amazonia. Although it was obviously expensive to fly north-easterners to the western side of the country, their absence symbolized both the declining importance of the north-east in Incra's priorities and a recognition that land hunger pressures to incorporate new lands existed in many other regions also. In an historical perspective, however, their lack was surprising, for north-easterners had provided most of the original population of Acre at the beginning of the twentieth century. Incra officials tend now to disparage the usefulness of north-easterners as agricultural colonists, at least by comparison with those from states like Paraná or Rio Grande do Sul. There had always been a question about the utility of colonization on fresh land as an alternative to an agrarian reform in areas of existing settlement. One calculation in 1972, for instance, by Lourdes Pimentel, a sociologist of IBGE, suggested that even if all the targets for colonization beside the Trans-Amazonica were to be reached by 1980, they would only mop up a fifth of the landless rural population of Brazil.

The modest contribution of Amazonia to relief of pressures in the north-east was important because more direct attacks on land hunger in the north-east have still not achieved much. In July 1971, the Medici government launched the Programa de Redistribuição de Terras e Estimula a Agro-industria do norte e nordeste (PROTERRA) with 4,000 million cruzeiros ($754 million). Incra then chose 150 municipalities in Pernambuco, Paraíba and Ceará as top priorities because of their social pressures; the idea was to buy and distribute lands to the landless there, but by the middle of 1974 only 480 property titles had been given out. Taken in conjunction with Incra's option for larger holdings in Amazonia this suggested that the body was not so much a force for altering Brazil's unequal existing land distribution as a means of extending it into freshly occupied areas. Although Amazonia might continue to be perceived as an escape valve this meant in practice that the problems of the north-east, in particular, were being left to solve themselves: as any kind of agrarian revolution was out of the question because of the strength of Brazil's military régime, this meant that the main avenue for change left would continue to be a spontaneous migration to the cities.

But it would be a mistake to exaggerate Incra's direct rôle in colonization. Private enterprise and the public development companies of the Amazonian states are playing a part which is arguably quite as significant. Take for example the case of Aripuanã in northern Mato Grosso, which in 1976 was the second most extensive municipality in Brazil. It covered an area of fourteen million hectares, nearly all uncleared forest, which was equivalent in size to three-quarters of the state of São Paulo. Of this in 1976 six million hectares had been set aside for colonization under the auspices of the

D

state-backed CODEMAT (Companhia de Desenvolvimento do
Mato Grosso) and at least a million hectares on the eastern side
were being colonized by a private firm, Indeco SA. Guilherme
de Abreu Lima, the director of CODEMAT, claims that 30 per
cent of the land it is developing in three blocks of two million
hectares is "of high fertility". (Ariosto da Riva, the head of

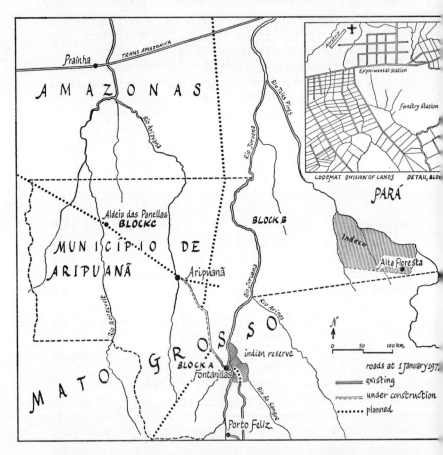

Indeco, tells prospective purchasers that all of the land in his
concession is fertile.) CODEMAT's first scheme adjoining the
tiny settlement of Fontanillas, is financed half by the state of
Mato Grosso and half by the federal Polamazonia programme.
It has got seriously delayed due to problems of health, electrical
energy, rural roads and of piped water. Originally CODEMAT

had hoped to have over 5,000 families on the site in 1976 but halfway through the year it looked as though there would only be around 2,000. Fewer than 1,300 families out of the ultimate total of over 5,200 would actually be farming the land. The rest would be scattered around five townships. As with Incra's own schemes CODEMAT allowed for some stratification between the farmers, though on a slightly narrower scale. The plan was to divide this first block as follows: there would be 716 small properties averaging 118 hectares, covering 19·9 per cent of the site area; 153 medium properties averaging 638 hectares, covering 22·8 per cent of the area; and 90 larger properties averaging 2,080 hectares, covering 43·8 per cent of the area. In reality, of course, a farm of 2,080 hectares is not that huge.

CODEMAT's second scheme, due to begin in 1977, was conceived differently. The first required CODEMAT to spend considerable sums on roads and infrastructure—estimated to come to 25 million cruzeiros (perhaps $2 million) in 1977 alone. But in other ways the first scheme (and probably the third also) was designed to be rapidly self-sustaining: competent farmers would be selected for the plots, chiefly from among the rural areas of Paraná which had had their coffee crops ruined by frost, and they would buy their new land with the aid of loans from the Bank of Brazil. The second scheme was more philanthropic, and closer to the original intention behind the Incra projects beside the TransAmazonica. The idea here was to settle 8,000 families, 70 per cent of whom would come from the north-east, on lots of only 50 hectares. Although these families might nominally "purchase" their land, for a small price over a lengthy term of years, the finance that made the scheme possible was a $40 million loan from the World Bank.

Whereas the projects of Incra and the state development companies share certain qualities—the irresponsibility and the lack of urgency of civil servants, a white-collar ignorance of problems of the soil, and an apparent orderliness which may conceal crucial human and economic difficulties—some of the purely private schemes are very different. Indeco and its driving force, Ariosto da Riva, exemplify the better private schemes. In a light plane, flying up to the Indeco property in Aripuanã from Cuiabá, he expounded his philosophy. "I believe that Brazil could be the axis of the world, because of its size, the tranquillity and industry of its people, and its ability to convert immigrants of all races into Brazilians," he remarked. Looking down at the occasional cleared patches in the forest, where other companies were developing agriculture or cattle, he expressed in decided terms his own preference for peopling Amazonia with humans rather than animals or vegetables. For him this was a passion, a hobby and a patriotic duty—not simply a commercial enterprise.

His record and approach show that this is not just idle boasting. Da Riva is now a silver-haired, distinguished-looking man in his 50s, who keeps in daily radio contact with the property in Aripuanã from an office in São Paulo, visiting it once a fortnight, and badgering banks, state and federal authorities for all the necessary support services in the meantime. His father came from northern Italy in 1910 and his mother was an Italian-Brazilian also. He became a disciple of another Italian-Brazilian, Jeremiah Lunardelli, who with his family became a leading agricultural developer and organizer of colonization schemes in Goiás and Mato Grosso. Da Riva studied earlier attempts at organized colonization in Brazil: he respects the formerly British-based Companhia dos Melhoramentos do Norte do Paraná which founded the city of Londrina, which now has over 400,000 inhabitants, in 1935. By the 1950s Da Riva was founding four towns in southern Mato Grosso as part of a controlled scheme for agricultural settlement in empty land: one of them, Naviraí, is now the fourth biggest city in the state. Hence when he put together a company to colonize a portion of Aripuanã the strength of his record made his bid attractive to a state government which still respects the fact that he is going ahead on schedule when many other developers have sat on their hands, complaining that the state will not do more for them.

Da Riva is founding five towns in Indeco's *gleba* at the rate of one a year from 1976 onwards. The first 200 families were moving into the first of these, Alta Floresta, in 1976 and he fully expected there to be 8,000–10,000 people living there by 1978, "such is the speed of growth in Brazil". Each town is surrounded by lots of 100 hectares and 302 hectares. In mid 1976 the price of these lots—on which it was claimed that almost anything from coffee to maize could be grown—was a standard 1,200 cruzeiros (about $118) per hectare. The intending purchasers varied enormously: some were São Paulo businessmen, who had been bitten by the Amazon investment bug, and who would put in a manager to clear and develop their land; one was a Japanese masseur, for example, eagerly taking soil samples from different plots for later analysis in São Paulo laboratory, who was thinking of buying on behalf of his family and friends; others were grizzled farmers from Paraná, some of whom liked pioneering new lands and then moving on, who intended to work the ground themselves. In every case Indeco flew possible purchasers up for a free inspection, putting them up overnight in clean, spartan and not entirely mosquito-proof dormitories. Alta Floresta itself, with roads laid out, one brick-built house and partly cleared urban lots, was slightly hard to imagine as a budding metropolis when I saw it. But it was being laid out firmly according to a town plan, with two hotels, a school, a hospital, an industrial area which already had a sawmill, and an ecological reserve. The construction camp itself, which might or might not remain as a shanty town, was laid out tidily with rain gauge and national flag in the centre. Da Riva had an agreement for direct flights from the airstrip to São Paulo by a commercial airline, VASP, to start in 1977 and the whole Indeco territory might well have 50,000 inhabitants by 1980.

The most striking aspect of the Indeco operation was the heavy personal involvement of Da Riva, and the intricate negotiation that was required to keep the project on schedule. Da Riva was universally known as Senhor Ariosto. He was the *patrão*, the boss, who treated both employees and visitors as part of an extended family. On the property he would give intending purchasers a little pep talk which did not disguise the fact that most Amazonian soils were poor—he just claimed that Indeco's were an exception. He promised to try to discover the wife of an employee who had lost all contact with her. He sought to reassure an elderly farmer that there would be no *pistoleiros* or bandits on the property: Indeco controlled the vital ferry across the River Telles Pires. (He did not want police on the territory until the towns were large enough to be self governing either—because he believed that police tended to create crime.) The result of Da Riva's style and experience was a purposeful but friendly atmosphere in which employees worked long hours but apparently happily, with a sense of involvement. There were few leisure pursuits apart from shooting game and playing football. Watching a football match one Sunday evening between the builders of Alta Floresta and a team from the support camp by the Telles Pires, specially strengthened by the son of Da Riva's favourite pilot, one could have imagined oneself in the Maracaná stadium in Rio de Janeiro. An exuberant commentary was being tape-recorded, to be played back at night in the dormitories; a Telles Pires supporter remarked that "the men from the interior don't have the trick" as though the Telles Pires camp itself would not be regarded as deep in the forest; and only a toddler, pushing earth over with a home-made toy bulldozer, reminded one of the purpose of both the crowd and the teams.

But behind the clearing and the building on Indeco's territory lay an exhausting process of organization and lobbying. Da Riva tried to get the Brazilian Coffee Institute (IBC) to fund coffee growing by his colonists as part of its programme for bringing more frost-free soils under coffee cultivation. He had managed to obtain two million cruzeiros ($190,470) from the federal government to put in piped drinking water for Alta Floresta, but he would have to use an electrical generator until the government built its promised hydroelectric power station on the Telles Pires. He had built an access road of 148 kilometres from the BR 163 and this would assist him to put pressure on DNER and the Mato Grosso state government to construct the BR 235, at present a rather shadowy line on the map westwards from the BR 163 which was nevertheless supposed to pass through Alta Floresta. The cost of a proposed bridge over the Telles Pires had already been agreed: the federal government would pay half through the Polamazonia programme; Da Riva and another Italian-Brazilian, Ferucci, who was trying to grow sugar on the other side of the river, would pay a quarter each. Indeco, like the neighbouring entrepreneurs who were involved in large-scale agricultural projects rather than colonization, benefited from the fact that two out of the original fifteen growth poles supported by Polamazonia were in the municipality of Aripuanã.

Nevertheless, even with the backing of the federal and state governments, there were still numerous financial pitfalls in a private colonization project like Indeco's. Although Da Riva is not the sort of man who seems likely to lose money on his undertakings his Aripuanã venture will extend over about fifteen years, always at risk from changes in the Brazilian economy and inflation and interest rates, and vulnerable to failure by official agencies which have promised to provide their services at particular times. Above all there are two problems. The first is that Indeco has to invest in quite a big way, for some four or five years, before its income from land sales and so on will balance its outgoings. Up to October 1976, when the first colonists were due to arrive, Da Riva had already spent 82 million cruzeiros (over $10 million), of which 36 million cruzeiros ($3·4 million) were spent in 1976 alone. The second problem is political, both at state and federal levels. Although all was going harmoniously at present there was always the danger of a change of personalities or strategy which could have damaging effects. The Geisel government's strategy for Amazonia was different from its predecessor's and a scheme like Indeco's, which was benefiting from Polamazonia, would be lucky to get the same kind of support from Geisel's successor. This was particularly relevant as the point at which Indeco was likely to start making profits, in 1978–9, was precisely when a new federal government was due to take over. Altogether therefore the range of possible outcomes for Indeco was very wide: it might make a lot of money, it might end up making little, and it could even founder. While Da Riva is not one of Amazonia's gamblers this uncertainty helps to explain why something more than just a commercial motivation is necessary if a private colonization project is to stand a chance of success. Da Riva himself believes that private schemes are always likely to do better than the state ones and it was clear from seeing him at work on the Indeco property—sweating, midge-bitten, poking his nose into the kitchens, worried about snorers in the communal bedroom he shared with visitors—that he took a direct personal responsibility and stamped his own personality on every aspect of the enterprise.

Da Riva was unusual in the early 1970s in having taken to heart the lessons of previous efforts at colonization. A most striking aspect of the TransAmazonica programme launched in 1970, as established by the federal government, was that it took virtually no account of previous experiments. Having decided that the PIN colonization was desirable the authorities rushed forward according to first principles which were only diluted by haste. It was only when they met disappointments, and the criticism of journalists and others, that it became respectable to remember how other attempts of this sort had fared. Yet Brazil in general, and Amazonia in particular, had already witnessed a variety of organized schemes for agricultural colonization. It is worth recalling some of the Amazonian ones for the light they could have shed on the TransAmazonica project, and as helping to explain the changing approach to colonization from about 1973 onwards.

Five different schemes can be mentioned here—two twentieth-century Japanese colonies dating from different periods, both of which were successful; the nineteenth-century colonization along the Belem–Bragança railway line which became a byword for ecological folly, but which was a failure in other respects also; and two schemes of the 1960s—one by the government of Pará at Altamira which scarcely began, and another by the government of Maranhão which originally failed but which the Polamazonia programme is hoping to resuscitate. The one common feature of nearly all previous efforts in the river basin was that they did not intend to use any of the existing people living in the locality, although they might have been expected to know something about the soils, plants and insects. Colonization in Amazonia had always been planned with the preconceptions of people living at a distance and the few who already inhabited the neighbourhood concerned were a nuisance if they were Amerindians, and were often forgotten if they were rubber tappers or *caboclo* peasants. The overwhelming lesson from the past was that several factors had to come together to guarantee success in colonization: the right soils, crops and agricultural techniques; adequate communications and markets; and sufficient support and motivation to nurse a colony through its inevitable setbacks.

The two Japanese schemes had both been carefully organized in the mother country. The first, at Tome Açu in Pará, had been founded between the wars; its fortunes started to flourish in the late 1930s as the colonists began to develop the culture of black pepper which was not grown elsewhere in Brazil. They used chicken manure to sustain the fertility of the poor soils for a crop which took several years to produce. They also grew rice, jute and vegetables and refined their techniques sufficiently so that by the 1970s, when a fungus disease threatened the black-pepper crops, their colony was rich enough and diversified enough to survive. Careful organization, a strong co-operative sentiment, and a faith in the powers of education had all been of importance. The same factors were brought to bear in a colony of 60 families, spread along the road between Manaus and Itacoatiara, which was established between 1952 and 1958 in the state of Amazonas. Both the state of Amazonas and the Japanese government offered help to these colonists: Amazonas provided free transport from Belem to the colony, health services, a school, small grants, DDT and a driver's salary so that produce could be brought to market in Manaus; the Japanese government provided transport to Belem, two lorries and a jeep, technical assistance and a building in Manaus from which the colonists could sell their produce. Even with this help, however, the colonists had a difficult start. They were only able to get two rice crops before exhausting the soil and an attempt to grow rubber, sponsored by the Brazilian government, had to be written off after six years. It was only after 1960, with a mixture of black pepper, chickens and vegetables, that the colonists managed to make a successful living.

In the Bragantina, the area along the Belem–Bragança railway, the nineteenth-century colonists never did find a way of handling the poor soils: after one or two crops much of the land was abandoned to scrub. The idea had been to develop the area as a cellar for Belem, and European colonists were encouraged to come and farm it. But many of the Europeans were quite unsuitable and drifted into the city; Belem therefore came to depend heavily on importing food by sea from the centre-south of Brazil until the late 1960s. As well as showing ecological misunderstanding, however, the Bragantina experience was a warning against relying too much on the existence of a means of communication for success. The capacity, patience and motivation of the colonists themselves would be crucial.

The Altamira and Maranhão experiences should have weighed even more strongly with the planners of the Trans-Amazonica schemes because they were even more recent, and both were trying to use north-easterners. Both emphasized the need for efficient support services if colonization was to work. In 1964 and 1965, encouraged by the state government of Pará, 125 people came to settle near Altamira in the red-earth

district. Most of them came from Ceará. But the Pará government lacked the resources to build the promised school and
township. Difficulties and costs of transport, added to marketing
failures and greedy middlemen, prevented the colonists from
increasing their capital and improving their lands. An attempt
at a co-operative failed due to the lack of solidarity among
the colonists and the manipulation of middlemen. The Maranhão scheme was launched by SUDENE after the drought of
1958. The state government set aside three million hectares
in the Mearim and Itapicuru valleys and planned to settle
12,000 families. But by the early 1970s there were fewer than
1,000 families there, in poor physical condition and practising
a poor subsistence agriculture. The message from both these
schemes, had anyone bothered to heed it, was that good
marketing, improving agricultural techniques and a spirit of
co-operation would all need to be nurtured over time if similar
ones were to succeed. For by 1970 the overriding lesson of all
previous colonization schemes in Amazonia was that they
usually failed.

Set against this background it could be argued that the
organized colonization of the 1970s had been a qualified
success, even if the TransAmazonica settlements had fallen
far short of the numbers hoped for by the Medici government
and they were not much help for the north-east. Few projects
had had to be abandoned to their fate, like the Altamira
project of the 1960s or the Xapuri scheme in Rondonia,
although there was still a fear that the ecological failure of the
nineteenth-century Bragantina could recur. The government's
objective of occupying space in Amazonia, and fixing the man
to the land, had been achieved in specific places.

But there were still a host of unanswered questions by the
mid 1970s, apart from the ecological ones. The first was
raised by the relationship between organized colonization and
spontaneous settlement. Along the TransAmazonica, for
instance, Incra had expected that there might be five spontaneous migrants for every one organized colonist. Something
of this sort happened in the event. But would the spontaneous
colonists have come at all without the existence of organized
schemes which offered a model, a magnet, and some support
services which were available to others? On the other hand the
great expansion of population along the Belem–Brasilia, which

Eliseu Resende had quoted when making his case for the Trans-Amazonica, had occurred with almost no organized colonization at all. By the mid 1970s research at the Nucleo de Altos Estudos Amazonicos in the University of Pará was comparing the spontaneous colonists along the Belem–Brasilia with the organized colonists in the Bragantina and elsewhere. According to Fatima C. Conceição, a sociologist involved in the study, it seemed that the spontaneous colonists showed more dynamism, flexibility and social mobility.[19] Apart from their value in inhibiting land squabbles, were the Incra schemes really necessary to achieve the occupation which the authorities sought?

The second area of vagueness concerned the relationship between the organized agricultural colonies and the growth of towns. Although the line of the TransAmazonica had been chosen to link existing towns their future was never planned with the attention given to the agricultural colonies. Yet would not the same drift to the towns occur in Amazonia as was happening elsewhere in Brazil? The somewhat artificial *agrovilas* were insufficiently attractive to compete with them: I met families on *agrovilas* near Altamira, for instance, where the children were refusing to join their fathers in the hard work on the lots and were looking for jobs in Altamira instead. What was the most promising relationship between agricultural settlement, urban growth and other types of industrial and economic development? Beneath an appearance of concerted planning a great deal was being left to chance.

This was particularly true of the marketing of agricultural produce, which brought the adequacy of road communications into question. Even with the 100-hectare small farmers, Incra was keen that they should sell part of their crops: as larger farms were marked out it was obvious that they would have to sell their output profitably if they were to be viable. But where were the markets in which TransAmazonica farmers could compete profitably? Even with the access roads so bad that much of the rice was never brought out, the TransAmazonica was already producing a surplus to its own requirements by 1975. Yet obviously TransAmazonica rice could not compete economically in the valuable markets of the centre-south and might even, because of the expense of transport compared with nearer suppliers, seem too dear in Belem or Santarem. The same sort of problem could arise in the colonies in Rondonia. It could only be solved as the Japanese of Tome Açu had solved it, by finding a product whose rarity and desirability offset the cost of transport. The large-scale cattle projects being set up with SUDAM incentives were planning to export their beef to North America or Europe. That option did not really exist for the colonists. While the TransAmazonica had been justified for its stimulus to agricultural settlement, communications still seemed poor and expensive when seen through the eyes of many of the colonists. The existence of a road was not sufficient to underwrite the viability of agricultural colonies. As Dr Monteiro de Castro, then director of the Amazonas highway authority, pointed out when the TransAmazonica was being prepared, there was only one agricultural colony in the whole of the much-desired 280 kilometres of the Manaus–Itacoatiara road.

But the formal colonies were only one expression of the migratory pressures which were lapping round Amazonia with increasing power by the end of the 1960s. It is worth looking at these in more detail in the next chapter.

4

ON THE MOVE

On 9 June 1976, the magazine *Veja* carried a photograph of João Luis de Souza. There was nothing special about the appearance of this 45-year-old north-easterner who was carrying a suitcase on his shoulders. Indeed he did not look prematurely aged as do so many poor rural Brazilians who have to survive on a diet of hard work and short commons. What was significant about him, however, was that he had just travelled for a fortnight on buses and lorries from his village in Pernambuco to Paranapoema in north-western Paraná. Paraná, where a wilderness had been cleared to make way for labour-intensive coffee plantations, had been an Eldorado for migrants in the 1950s. But by the time de Souza got there Paranapoema had lost much of its population. Its small coffee properties had been bought up and merged to form a mere sixteen estates in the whole municipality, nearly all devoted to cattle. Ranchers reckon that only one cowhand is necessary for every 1,000 bullocks in the extensive grazing system used in Brazil, though you might need three for the same number of cows. There is an old Brazilian saying that "where the bullock comes in, the man goes out". De Souza told a *Veja* reporter at Paranapoema, "There in the north-east everything is dry which makes it impossible to do anything. But here the only creatures to make use of this green grass are the cattle." He would have to continue with his wanderings.

It was quite possible that there were some fellow north-easterners of de Souza in a bus and a lorry which were stopped by federal police and the regional labour delegate in Rio Branco a couple of months earlier. This case, also reported in the Brazilian press,[20] was in the nature of a warning shot. The bus and lorry were bringing 63 labourers from a place called Amambaia on the frontier of Mato Grosso and Paraguay. They were being taken to work on a farm in Acre on the road between Rio Branco and Boca do Acre. Only fourteen out of the 63 possessed any documents and none had proper labour contracts. Many of the men were old, suffering from eczema, and in poor health from having done heavy manual work. Among the group there was a man of 93, accompanied by a woman who was suffering from mental illness. They had all been badly tricked and were lucky that the authorities had got wind of their situation. They had been recruited to spend 90 days on the ranch, being paid 1,000 cruzeiros (about $100) for every alquiera (2·4 hectares) cleared, and with a right to a passage home. But they had already been let down. The 1,000 cruzeiros promised in advance in Mato Grosso, to enable them to buy clothes, had never been handed over. They were supposed to have had food on the way, but all were complaining of hunger by the time they reached Rio Branco. Their costs of accommodation en route were going to be deducted from their salaries, although the recruiting agents had assured them that there would be no discounts of this sort when they persuaded them to come. The police and the labour officials let the group continue after giving official guarantees as to their hours of work and the payment of their wages. But although the case was publicized and might serve as a threat to other employers who exploited migrant labour it was the police raid rather than the process of exploitation which was unusual. The mixture of poverty and unemployment in the areas of supply, with the attraction of paid work in developing regions of Acre, was too powerful for officials to control—even if they were not frequently ignorant of or conniving with the unscrupulous employers.

Why is it that Brazil has such a mobile population? Government census estimates suggest that nearly a third of the people have moved their place of abode by a substantial distance. This is a steady phenomenon even in long-settled parts of the country: the larger number of removals may have been from the countryside to the towns and cities, but there is also a continuing migration from one rural area to another, and from one city to another. The rôle of new space that becomes practicable for occupation, as Amazonia has done in the 1960s and 1970s, is to offer a new set of destinations for these migrants. While on the one hand they offer a relief for those who are landless or unemployed by a lack of agrarian change in more settled regions, they are also an escape for persons displaced by mechanization or an adverse change in agriculture. But Amazonia does not have a substantially different function, from the point of view of those looking for work or a plot to till, than did parts of Paraná and Bahia in the 1950s, or of Mato Grosso and Goiás in the 1960s, as human penetration opened up those states. The fact that there are ecological peculiarities about Amazonia, and that it is the last unoccupied land reserve in Brazil, does not automatically change the outlook of migrants and land purchasers. When the whole history of the country has involved a gradual opening up and settlement of often difficult terrain it would be surprising if attitudes altered at some arbitrary parallel. It is worth discussing in more detail the motives which bring people to move around in Brazil and, now, into Amazonia. Here we shall distinguish between those who can only move as labourers, and those who have money with which to purchase at least some land.

For anyone with money at all the most important fact about the uncleared Amazon land is that it is cheap. The ratio obviously varies but Mauricio Dourado, a young São Paulo businessman, estimated in 1976 that the average price of one hectare of land in the states of Paraná and Rio Grande do Sul would buy 20 hectares of Indeco land in Aripuanã. This ratio varies according to the distance of a plot from the nearest main road. João Carlos Meirelles, president of the Association of Entrepreneurs of Amazonia, then quoted the price per hectare alongside the BR 158 (near Barra do Garças in Mato Grosso) as between 400 and 1,000 cruzeiros ($38–95), depending on the quality of the soil. But this price would be halved at a distance of 80 kilometres from the BR 158. For a big company this cheap land is only one of the factors that it must consider when deciding whether to invest in Amazonia rather than elsewhere: it must also assess the costs of clearing the land and putting in an infrastructure; problems of transport, warehousing and slaughterhouses; and the length of time it will take the project to become viable. But for smaller investors, and especially for families which are already small farmers in the south, the cheapness of the land is an overriding attraction. By selling up in, say, Rio Grande do Sul, a farmer may be able to buy enough land in Mato Grosso or Rondonia to provide each of his sons with a farm of his own. The uneconomic and depressing process of *minifundio*—by which farms are endlessly subdivided as the population grows, until they cease to be viable—can be avoided. This family motivation can be strong. And there is also, for all investors in land, the encouragement of inflation. Land, which is capable of yielding crops every year whatever the state of the currency, is one of the classic securities at a time of rapid monetary depreciation. It cannot be fortuitous that a country in the grip of a powerful, long-lasting, structural inflation should be pressing so persistently to occupy new lands. For the last 20 years, after all, the inflation rate in Brazil has almost never been under 15 per cent a year; for half the time it has been over 40 per cent. The incentive to put money into land is greater because, in the areas which are being newly occupied, any constructive piece of development by one owner has the effect of raising land values for his neighbours; while this some-times means that everyone is waiting for the next man to improve his property first, it can also mean that a shrewd investor can watch the value of his capital asset appreciate without doing a great deal about it himself. In 1968 and 1969 the state government of Amazonas sold 1·8 million hectares in five municipalities, giving 600 definitive titles to the purchasers: but the majority did not occupy these lands, waiting instead for roads and other support services.

If economics is one explanation for the movement into new land, agricultural change in the previously settled areas, also inspired by economics, is another. The case of north-west Paraná has already been mentioned briefly. In fact between 1970 and 1975 the population of 51 municipalities in this area fell perceptibly, although the soils there were rich and they had seen a coffee boom in the 1950s and 1960s. One reason for the reduction was that the labour-intensive coffee farms were hard hit by two consecutive frosty winters, in 1974 and 1975. But this was not the only reason. The farming techniques had caused erosion and the growing demand for meat, backed by rising world and local prices and the power of cattle interests, meant that even slightly damaged soils had a sharply rising price as pasture. Between 1975 and 1976, for instance, the price of land per hectare in this region had risen from just over 6,000 cruzeiros ($741) to over 17,000 ($1,619). Brazilian government policy also took a hand indirectly. Whereas the world market for coffee was often in a state of glut and the Brazilian Coffee Institute could only offer the sort of prices which helped the biggest and most efficient coffee farmers, government policy after 1964 tended to decontrol meat prices on the home market, and to encourage producers to export more and cash in on the world shortage.

But it would be wrong to suppose that cattle are always the stimulus for change. In Rio Grande do Sul, the traditional pampas beef producer for Brazil, the ranchers themselves have been under pressure—encouraging some of them to expand into central and northern Brazil instead. Dirceu Lopes, president of the farmers' union in Uruguaiana, Rio Grande do Sul, told the *Jornal do Brasil* in 1976 that cattle had been losing ground to crops in that area for straightforward reasons of price. "I let 87 hectares for the cultivation of rice and, taking 14 per cent of the output, I make 100,000 cruzeiros ($9,524) a year. The same land, for ranching, gives me only 8,000 cruzeiros ($761) at the most, using most modern methods. There I would put on 40 cattle and 150 chickens. And for the rice growing I'm only providing the land." In this part of the south it is rice which is challenging cattle and raising land prices; elsewhere it is soya beans and other crops.[21] With competitive pressures on the land the old-fashioned methods of stock-rearing—involving large tracts of land, little use of fertilizer, wasteful techniques of hygiene and animal husbandry and a conversion of grass into protein which would look pathetic in western Europe or New Zealand—is no longer adequate. Yet the ranchers themselves may not have the capital or scientific education to make the necessary changes. For some of the ranchers and cattlehands, therefore, just as for some of the coffee farmers and labourers, the advance into new lands is often a retreat from their old ones. Sometimes too these agricultural changes are quite ruthless: more efficient producers can bankrupt their rivals or small farmers by undercutting their prices or rigging the markets.

There is a theory, quite frequently quoted in Brazil, of a regular sequence in the agricultural development of new lands: first any timber is cleared; then pasture is prepared for cattle; finally, increasing parts of the grassland are turned over to crops. Amichay Wine, a financier in Rio de Janeiro, argued that this process had occurred in the state of São Paulo and was now being repeated in the state of Minas Gerais. Farmers in Minas Gerais, a state which is now becoming heavily

industrialized although its fortunes were founded on dairy
farming and agriculture, were now selling up and helping to
push a cattle frontier northwards up Goiás and Mato Grosso.
Yet although it is possible to speak of a cattle frontier in these
states and in southern Pará my own inquiries suggest that it is
misleading to assume that cattle-to-agriculture is the universal
sequence. The case of north-western Paraná to the contrary
was paralleled in the state of Rio de Janeiro several decades
earlier, where coffee was also replaced by cattle. Even along
the TransAmazonica, at Altamira, pre-1970 agricultural
colonists have been bought out by a rancher at one point on
the edge of the town. What seems to be the case is that to open
new land for crops rather than cattle requires more capital,
more infrastructure, better roads, a greater immediate population and some urban demand near at hand. When the crops
are sufficiently profitable, the migration is intense and public
authorities have their own reasons for providing more than
the limited services required by the cattlemen, the cattle
option is overtaken. The one joker in agricultural change is
ecological: the land may be exhausted by crops or fail as
pasture.

The pressures which cause the weaker proprietors and the
tenant farmers to migrate are even stronger for the land hungry
and the day labourers: natural disasters such as drought or
frost are exacerbated by a social structure which has taken out
no insurance against them and where the costs tend to be piled
on the shoulders of those least able to bear them. In some cases
it is the young, fit and adventurous who wander off to seek
land or employment in a city or another part of Brazil. But
quite often it is simply the most desperate. In the case of
families it is usual for one or more of the menfolk to go first, to
see whether a living can be made in a new place. If they signal
that this is possible, then their families follow later. But the
process of migration frequently disrupts families with husbands
separated from their families for months at a time, leaving their
wives and children at their former homes, or with husbands
arriving at their new place of work as "bachelors" who have
abandoned their dependants altogether. Population movement on the scale with which it has occurred in Brazil over the
last few decades can only really be explained by the poverty of
so many Brazilians: with too many mouths to feed and not

enough food or money in the family, migration can seem the
only alternative to starvation. Ironically the efforts by governments to improve the lot of rural labourers have had the
opposite effect, merely stimulating their flight to the cities and
the growth of a class of labourers who are not protected by
legislation. In 1963 the Goulart government approved the
Statute of the Rural Labourer which was designed to give the
labourer some rights of income and security versus his employer.
A recent study for the Brazilian Ministry of Labour suggests
that this attempt to extend urban labour legislation to the
countryside had disastrous results. In 1963 alone 33 per cent of
rural employees were dismissed by employers who were not
prepared to be bound by the new law: in the following two
years an estimated 20 per cent and 12 per cent of all rural
labourers moved into towns and cities. The same kind of
boomerang occurred in the early 1970s when the Medici
government sought to tighten up the Statute of the Rural
Labourer by insisting that landowners should provide schools
for the children of employees where these numbered over 50,
and simultaneously prohibiting children of less than twelve
years from working in the fields. This again provoked dismissals
by the employers while it was unpopular too among poor
families which relied on the work of their children to augment
a sparse income. Another effect of this legislation has been to
nourish the growth of the *boias-frias* (literally "cold lunches"
which is what they are provided with by employers who may
also pick them up on a lorry for work). By 1972 it was reckoned
that there were 6·8 million *boias-frias*, rural labourers with no
security of employment and outside the Statute of the Rural
Labourer. These six million men in fact represented nearly
half of the adult men living in the Brazilian countryside. Their
permanent insecurity made them ever ready to try their luck
elsewhere, or to hack out a patch of unoccupied land as a
posseiro.

Although Brazilian official opinion has been hardening
against massive migration to the cities since the 1960s, it has
only been very recently that there has been much concern about
labour migration within the rural areas. This is largely because
such migration has been seen as a good, in opening up new
lands; partly because it has been seen as inevitable, due to the
higher rural birthrate; and also because officials have often

closed their eyes to the abuses to which it can lead. There is no
real control, for example, over the activities of the *gatos* or
labour recruiters who scour the country to hire men. In 1976,
however, the territorial government of Rondonia, with Incra,
was setting up a supervisory checkpoint at Vilhena on the
BR 364 from Cuiabá to Porto Velho. This was the area where
600 families had been arriving each month, hoping for land or
work. The checkpoint would look at the people for any
contagious diseases and screen their documents. But in real
terms it would not be able to turn back migrants except on the
most serious health grounds: they would continue to scramble
for land or work, drifting to towns like Vilhena or Porto Velho
if they were frustrated in the countryside. The one semi-
official body which in some areas took a genuine interest in
helping rural workers was CONTAG (the Confederação
Nacional dos Trabalhadores Agrarios). Its membership was
usually only a small percentage of rural workers and small
farmers, and its members often saw it as merely a friendly
society, providing medical assistance and death benefits.
Nevertheless where the regional delegate for CONTAG was a
forceful personality it could sometimes intervene in areas of
social conflict, and it periodically collected critical reports on
labour conditions in Amazonia. The difficulties under which its
more vigorous officials worked were illustrated in April 1976
when João Maia da Silva Filho, its regional delegate in Acre,
sought to attend a meeting with over 100 *seringueiros*. The new
landowners had been trying to sweep out rubber tappers and
posseiros and da Silva Filho wanted to investigate the situation
to see what could be done. But a landowner, João Miranda
Vilela, the owner of a former rubber property called Bom
Destino between Rio Branco and Boca do Acre on the BR 360,
employed armed men to stop the car carrying the CONTAG
delegate on his way to the meeting. Ingeniously the landowner
claimed that he had orders from the federal police to stop the
CONTAG man going further—which in this case was not
true—and a small struggle ensued. No one was hurt, but the
regional delegate was prevented from hearing the *seringueiros*'
and *posseiros*' case at first hand. It was a classic "warning-off"
operation. In June 1976 the Deliberative Council of SUDAM,
whose discussions are covered by the press, agreed not to
discuss alleged breaches of the labour laws in public: this

followed a fruitless investigation of complaints of semi-slavery among employees of the Companhia Vale do Rio Roosevelt in Aripuanã.

The undercurrent of violence and lawlessness which accompanied the land rush in so many areas—but not along the TransAmazonica, nor yet at least in Roraima—is not only to be explained by the confusion over land titles which was worsened by fraud and speculators, nor only by the fact that the large landowners frequently hired armed vigilantes. (Over towards the Paraguayan border these strong-arm men are sometimes Paraguayans.) Both the new landowners and the new migrants quite often came from those parts of Brazil where violence and lawlessness were most prevalent, and land conflicts had always been settled most ruthlessly. This was particularly true of parts of the north-east, where even today it is normal for there to be some deaths by shooting in every electoral campaign in the state of Alagoas. It was also true of rural areas of Rio Grande do Sul, the scene of its own civil war in the 1920s and with a tradition of breeding professional soldiers which goes back to the frontier wars of the nineteenth century. It was the militia of Rio Grande do Sul which had played a big part in the military revolution of 1930. This willingness to resort to force may well have been tested afresh in a migration by stages through pioneer regions: many of those in the 1970s who were reaching Rondonia and Acre described as people from Mato Grosso had actually gone there from Rio Grande do Sul or the north-east not so many years previously.

Porto dos Gauchos on the River Arinos in central Mato Grosso is a good example of the "wild west" aspect of these migrations. It was founded by six brothers from Santa Rosa, Rio Grande do Sul, in 1955. They brought fifteen families on ten lorries and took two months to hack their way up an appalling pioneer road. This caravan was run on the lines of the ox-wagon convoys of nineteenth-century North America: every morning the initial party of 50 people would wake to the sound of a trumpet. Life at the settlement was extremely hard, for the brothers had finally ended their journey on a patch of acid soil where neither coffee nor maize, the first crops they tried, would grow on the cleared land. Many suffered from malaria. The reason that only a fifth of the first arrivals gave up was a simple matter of pride: the rest did not wish to return home admitting they had failed. The settlement, which was called Porto dos Gauchos because people from Rio Grande do Sol are known as *gauchos* (cowboys), only survived thanks to West German finance. In 1962 a West German group subsidized an experiment in rubber growing there. Although this failed the money it provided was sufficient to tide the township over the worst of its troubles. But for its first decade or so there were no police there, and there was no government-supplied doctor until 1973. Virtually every man went armed, with Winchester 24 revolvers, and any criminals were pursued by a voluntary posse. Walter Isaacenhagen, who was named as a voluntary sub-delegate of police in 1962 when the state governor said he couldn't provide a paid police official for the town, told me what this involved. "I just had to call out ten volunteers, who were all armed, and we had to solve the problem ourselves." With the road south to Cuiabá impassable from December to April justice in Porto dos Gauchos tended to be immediate and unsophisticated.

Another element in the periodic violence of the developing areas is the relative absence of women, which keeps alive the sexual myths of Amazonia. Apart from any more general effects this has on the tone of life in these districts it specifically encourages prostitution, the transmission of sexual diseases, friction over such nubile women as do live there and sometimes the molesting of Indian women. In 1974, for instance, the planning region of northern Mato Grosso was estimated to have 43,244 males to 36,376 females. But the real situation in the pioneer areas comes into sharper relief when one looks at the age distribution of the sexes. The estimated population for Aripuanã in 1974 was 1,812 males as against 1,021 females. But for those aged 20 and over there were three men to every woman—or an estimated 1,025 men to 398 women. Hence one of the best indices for the degree of "civilization" of what has recently been a pioneering area is the sex ratio among the 20-plus age group. On this basis, therefore, a municipality such as Barra do Garças in Mato Grosso was gradually acquiring the characteristics of a settled community by 1974. Although it was still estimated that there were 7,360 men over 20 as compared with 5,676 women the rate of growth among women in the most active child-bearing ages was faster than among their male contemporaries.[22] But in areas of spontaneous migration like these it may still take fifteen to twenty years to establish a sexual balance in the marriageable age groups. For this reason the planned colonization schemes of Incra and other bodies, which transfer families as a whole, have an importance for law and order and health. Although the agricultural and social distinctions between the planned and unplanned migrations may not be great, the demographic difference is significant.

Finally there is another factor which has affected the experience of migrants—the existence of a significant number of foreign landowners in the fresh lands that are being opened up. Their activities will be discussed further in the following chapter but it is sufficient here to say that the very fact that they are foreigners can add complications when conflicts over *posseiros* or labour legislation arise. An unconscious attitude of patronage on one side can evoke a spirit of xenophobia on the other. And this potential cause of friction exists whether the foreigners form part of a large multinational or are single North American farmers with relatively small estates, and whether the foreign presence is visible or absentee. An extreme case of this friction resulted in the deaths, on 3 July 1976, of two United States citizens in a hold-up in southern Pará. Two brothers, who were killed, together with their father, John Davis who was aged 55, were stopped by more than 30 armed men who had put blocks of wood across the road. The Davises too were well armed and had clearly expected trouble at some time. The two sons, John junior and Bruce, died in the shoot-out and John Davis was critically wounded. In the sequel the US consul in Belem flew down to the scene and the Brazilian authorities used both army and police to round up those who had taken part in the ambush. In Belem the initial reaction was one of horror but the local press gradually uncovered a history of conflict which at least made the murders comprehensible.

John Davis senior had heard the call of God when he was flying as a pilot in the Korean War. He had travelled to the Congo as a missionary and lived through the civil war there. In 1967 he bought more than 90,000 hectares of forest land alongside the PA 70 state road which links Marabá to the Belem–Brasilia highway. He planned to develop a stock-rearing and timber business and the following year he presented to SUDAM a scheme to raise 12,000 animals on 23,000 hectares. He wanted ten million cruzeiros (nearly $3 million) in fiscal incentives money out of the 13 million cruzeiros ($3·9 million) which the project was estimated to cost. Right from the start, however, Davis had had problems with *posseiros*. There were about 90 families living on the property when he bought it, and they rejected his offer to buy them out with a low level of compensation. After that Davis began to put pressure on them, but he was unable to control such a large area and more *posseiros* arrived. It particularly annoyed him that they extracted "his" timber. His cattle plans did not prosper: he only cleared 100 hectares for pasture and SUDAM only released 100,000 cruzeiros (under $30,000) of the ten million he had been promised. Early in 1974 there was nearly a previous shoot-out, which brought an official investigation, and more recently the problems with the *posseiros* had frustrated Davis's hopes of selling the property for 22 times the price he had paid for it. In the months before his sons' deaths he had sought to besiege the *posseiros*, cutting off their access to the PA 70 and to the only nearby pool of drinking water, and fencing them in with barbed wire. The *posseiros*, who had had no reply to their appeals for protection to the state authorities, planned the murders as a last resort. They realized that they would have to flee the area afterwards. Murders of foreign citizens are very rare in Brazil but it seemed certain that the presence of a United States owner had sharpened a not unusual confrontation in the pioneer areas.

The nomadic urge which has persuaded hundreds of thousands of Brazilians to take to the roads has had compelling causes. It has frequently led them from one set of unpleasant conditions to another which is scarcely less unpleasant. In all this they have been obeying social and economic forces over which Brazilian governments have had only an uncertain and erratic influence. It is worth turning to the situation of the receiving states in Amazonia to see what sort of resources they have available to meet this influx.

Put simply the position of the receiving states is that they have responsibility for all the basic services—health, education, local roads, water supply and the like—which have to take the strain when the migrants flood in. But both their funds and their administrative capacity have to run fast in order to catch up.

They have to rely extensively on what they can squeeze from *ad hoc* federal funds to cover their investment in new services—although the federal funds are biased in favour of the dramatic agricultural and industrial schemes which create the demand for less glamorous services. As a result, a territory like Rondonia always seems to be lagging behind the needs created by rapid population growth while Roraima, protected from migrants by poor communications and the long delay in completing the BR 174, is able to build up its infrastructure in advance. Above all, perhaps, the process of migration is a cheap option for the federal government for none of the states or territories in Amazonia is sufficiently populous to make a vocal bid for resources. The problems of Rondonia may seem stark enough when seen from its capital of Porto Velho, but they disappear into insignificance in Brasilia when set against the clamant, bursting poverty of the north-east, or the demands of the wealthy centre-south which is providing an economic base for the whole country. Although they depend on federal largesse to make a success of their process of development the Amazon states are supplicants with a relatively low priority.

The Costa e Silva government tipped the financial balance further towards the central government, and against the states and municipalities, when it reduced their proportion of federal revenue from 20 per cent to 12 per cent. Now therefore a state like Amazonas raises 52 per cent of its budget requirement from its own tax resources: 48 per cent is supplied by the federal government. Yet the sum it raises itself is swallowed up in administering existing services, which means that the federal government can largely dictate where new investment goes. In the territories the governments are totally dependent on federal funds. Rondonia, which got a share of 133 million cruzeiros ($12·6 million) in 1976, had to reckon on the money being paid over late, and on probably not getting this agreed amount because the federal fund concerned is always liable to be raided for immediate crises in other territories and municipalities. For an area whose population is growing at the rate of Rondonia's this is highly unsatisfactory. While Roraima was able to spend nearly two-thirds of its budget on new improvements in infrastructure in 1975 the bulk of Rondonia's had to go in propping up its overstretched administration. In the circumstances therefore it was not surprising that Dr Jacob, Rondonia's health secretary, confessed in 1976 that his services were being defeated in the battle against serious diseases: there had been a big increase in malaria and leishmaniasis and he was pinning his hopes on receiving a special allocation from the federal Ministry of Health for SUCAM, the federal organ which combats malaria. The contrast in situation between Rondonia and Roraima also appears in the educational field. Whereas the influx of migrants and lack of funds means that a significant number of children in Rondonia are not in school, and the turnover of primary teachers is high, Roraima has an above average rate of literacy for Brazil. Sr Aldo da Costa, Roraima's secretary for education, told me that almost all children aged seven to fourteen are in school. Whereas an estimated 40 per cent of the Brazilian population is illiterate the comparable figures were 23 per cent for Roraima as a whole, and only 9 per cent for its capital of Boa Vista.

Federal funds in Amazonia, although always described as conforming to priorities laid down in the national and regional development plans, frequently appear arbitrary and disjointed in the states concerned. Different federal funds seem to compete against each other. Although more than half of Rondonia is covered by a growth pole under the Polamazonia strategy, for instance, Governor Humberto da Silva Guedes told me in 1976 that up to that point his territory had received no assistance at all from SUDAM's fiscal incentives.[23] The huge state of Amazonas is benefiting from only one of Polamazonia's poles, which cover an area of timber resources between the Jurua and Solimões rivers. The state government itself has adopted a scheme for sixteen growth points—four of which fell within the Polamazonia pole—for the 1975 to 1979 period. Its own plan had been announced after a sophisticated exercise organized by its United States-educated planning secretary, Roberto dos Santos Vieira. This had included Delphi forecasting and elaborate surveys in all parts of the state. But at the end of the day, with the state depending entirely on the federal government to transform the paper plan into reality, there was a question as to how much of it would actually happen. This was all the more relevant as the federal government appeared unwilling to pay out in support of the "north-east pole"—covering the populous but decayed Bragantina district—which it incorporated late into the Polamazonia programme in response to lobbying by the government of Pará. Pará wanted to do something about unemployment in this zone and proposed that Polamazonia resources should be pumped into the growth of service industries, including hospitals and educational institutions. But the presidential office in Brasilia itself seemed sceptical. Two years after the Polamazonia strategy was announced no money at all had been disbursed for the northeast pole.

If the finances and basic services of most of the Amazon states are not well equipped to cope with the shock of a sharp increase in immigration it goes without saying that there are serious administrative weaknesses also. Although many of the state officials are highly capable they are fighting against the relative poverty of their own authorities, the problems of a thin and dispersed population, and the poor physical and educational levels of so many in the rural areas. The feeling that distances alone were preventing state officials in capitals like Manaus and Belem from properly administering all parts of Amazonas and Pará helped to foster a campaign in Brasilia to redivide Amazonia and create more states there.[24] Congressional hearings were being held on this proposal in 1976. But size was not the only difficulty. Another was that the zone alongside the Brazilian border and the length of the Trans-Amazonica were both national-security areas. This meant that certain administrative decisions could not be made on the spot but had to be referred to the military authorities, and if necessary to the National Security Council, for approval. Governors and mayors in the territories, like mayors along the Trans-Amazonica, were appointed by the federal government directly. This could lead to friction with their elected councils, especially if a majority supported the opposition party. On the other hand Governor Guedes of Rondonia argues that it is better for a territory to acquire an effective administrative structure before it acquires the greater autonomy and elective governors and mayors of statehood. In his view the neighbouring state of Acre had suffered from being granted statehood before it had the administrative capacity to exercise it successfully. There are also risks that appointed officials may misunderstand the territory they have to administer; while there is no evidence that this has been the result in Roraima, Governor Fernando

Ramos Pereira chose several people who were not inhabitants of the territory to join his cabinet in 1974–5.

At a local level the unit of government in Brazil is the municipality. As areas become more populous and developed existing municipalities are subdivided to create new ones. This procedure is logical enough. But in practice, in the districts of rapid population growth, this can mean that either the municipality is trying to cover too big an area for its resources; or that its personnel are involved in all the uncertainty and lobbying that goes with local government surgery; or that possibly inexperienced new municipal bodies are being brought to birth in the middle of a population explosion. The rate of municipal growth can be fast. On 21 May 1976 the number of municipalities in Acre almost doubled, from seven to twelve. At that time Rondonia, whose area was divided between only two municipalities based on Porto Velho and Vilhena, was still thought to have its administrative structure spread too wide. It was actively planning to make three new municipalities in the south of the territory.

Finally, in discussing the situation which awaits migrants in Amazonia, it is worth paying some attention to the great exception: Roraima. In 1976 its population was only 55,000 of whom Boa Vista, its capital, had around 35,000. But everything about it seemed as neatly planned in reality as only the planning documents elsewhere would suggest. Boa Vista was laid out around a large central square with a sculpture of the *garimpeiro*, its heroic pioneering miner, in the middle. There were no beggars to pester the visitor and even the red-light district was organized a few kilometres from the capital—ten brothels set apart with their own street lamps, police post and taxi rank. Three new colonization projects are being started in the period of the 1975–9 plan (although there had been a small misunderstanding when both Incra and the territorial government had been planning different projects in the same neighbourhood). Incra has settled land titles in three-eighths of the territory within three years. The basic services seem ready to cope with an influx of migrants; they have already managed quite well when the population rose by over 44 per cent in the 1960s with migrants from Maranhão and Rio Grande do Sul to the fore. But this air of efficiency was bred of isolation. Until the mid 1960s the territory had been largely supplied with

goods by air from Guyana—which accounts for such quirks as
the fact that Boa Vista, where a third of the adults possess a
motor cycle, is the motor-cycling capital of Brazil. Communications with the rest of Brazil still depend heavily on planes and
some Roraima officials admit that, if the Manaus–Caracaraí
(BR 174) road had been completed on schedule by the early
1970s—it was delayed by technical difficulties and conflicts
with Indians—it could have destroyed their orderly image by
opening the territory to a mass immigration. Roraima, like
Mato Grosso or Goiás, contains a mixture of climatic and
geographical zones. Its southern third is forested. Its central
portion, where Boa Vista is situated, is savannah grassland. Its
northern frontier with Venezuela is mountainous. This
configuration makes settlement and development somewhat
easier than in states like Amazonas which are almost universally
covered in jungle. But the lesson from Roraima, which must be
encouraging for all the less penetrated areas north of the main
river Amazon, is that a local administration can prepare
effectively for migrants and development so long as it is not
rushed off its feet. There is no need for the haste that surrounded
the TransAmazonica, or the disappointments and land struggles
that have occurred round the south-western fringe of the
Amazon basin.

Within Brazil as a whole, as in other developing countries,
the main trend of migration has been from countryside to town.
The Medici government's drive to occupy Amazonia was a
conscious attempt to divert it. But Amazonia too presents
examples of the general phenomenon, particularly in the
growth of its great regional capitals of Belem and Manaus.
After the departure of President Medici, both federal and state
governments seem to have given more thought to the rôle of
the towns in the development of Amazonia: there are now a
number of projects for the redevelopment and resiting of
Amazon towns, of which the most ambitious is to build a new
city of Marabá on higher ground beyond the risk of floods, to
house 200,000 people by 1980. But of all the Amazon cities
none is more interesting than Manaus. Its population doubled
between 1966 and 1976 to approximately half a million—
sucking in river dwellers from Amazon tributaries on a scale
that went far to undo the policy of extending human occupation
in the basin. Its main tool of economic development, the

customs-free zone, was quite different in its effects from
SUDAM's fiscal incentives or the federal government's road-
related penetration. And, although it obtained a road link to
Porto Velho, its main transport links remained the air and the
rivers.

In less than a decade the centre of Manaus has been transformed from a somnolent entrepôt, conscious of its history and
dominated by its river trade, to an aggressive, huckstering
version of Hong Kong. Its shops are stuffed with cameras,
pocket calculators and airconditioning units, most of them
made in the Far East and selling at duty-free prices. Its old
tiled buildings are being rapidly replaced by 20- and 30-floor
office blocks. Its advanced international airport, built by
Camargo Corrêa and formally opened early in 1976, was the
third biggest air-freight centre in Brazil. A new industrial
estate, built on the east side of the city, has competed with the
shops to secure new labour. Economists at SUFRAMA (the
superintending agency for the customs-free zone) estimate that
in 1967 Manaus only had 22 industrial establishments. Between
1967 and February 1976 the city attracted a further 100
industrial firms, providing direct employment for 20,000
people. The momentum was such that a further 40 firms,
employing an extra 6,000, were set up in the second quarter of
1976 alone—before President Geisel curbed the import quota
for the free-trade zone to $280 million in 1976, because of
Brazil's balance of payments difficulties. And what sort of
goods have these factories been making? Just as in the shops it
has been the consumer-goods firms which have been quickest
to establish themselves in the industrial district: 60 per cent of
Brazil's colour TV sets are now made in Manaus, and Honda
and Suzuki are both making light motor cycles there.
SUFRAMA insists on a steadily increasing proportion of
Brazilian content on the assembly lines, but other fiscal advantages mean that the free-zone products will still have a price
advantage elsewhere in Brazil even when all the components
are local.

But what has been a commercial and industrial success has
come near to being a social disaster. By the mid 1970s the
annual population growth of Manaus was still 8·1 per cent
a year. New *favelas*—shanty towns formed by squatters—
developed quickly, some of the worst being in Coroada, where

land had been allocated to the new University of Amazonas for its expansion, Alvorada and Japiimlandia. Sometimes this caused friction with the landowners and police tried to move the squatters: more usually the squatters established their right to stay even though they lacked electricity, sewage or piped water and their shacks might be washed away in the annual floods. In one week, for example, 3,000 *favelados* moved in on land whose ownership was unknown which adjoined the Ajuricaba housing estate. They merely climbed over a fence and started marking out house plots. Police and municipal representatives came to look, but did not try to clear them away. Their view was that if nobody declared ownership within 48 hours they would "liberate" the land for the *favela*. Health problems inevitably arose as these insanitary dwellings, often taking their water from stagnant pools cut off from the River Negro except during its flood, blossomed suddenly around the city. Children were sometimes abandoned. A lively subterranean world of gangsters provided endless copy for the police pages of the Manaus press.

Two features of this rapid expansion were especially disturbing. The first is that, as has happened in less isolated Brazilian cities, it has attracted migrants to Manaus without being able to provide them all with work. The second is that it has worsened the city's incapacity to feed itself from sources nearby. Just as the TransAmazonica settlements looked like Eldorado when seen from the north-east so the free-trade zone of Manaus seemed paved with gold when viewed by the backland *caboclos* upriver. The unemployment realities were harsher. The new jobs in the shops, which were stimulated by the growing sales to other Brazilians who flew into Manaus to take advantage of the low duty-free prices and the foreign goods, were mainly jobs for young women. The industrial sector grew later—although here too many of the jobs were in light assembly work. The jobs for unskilled men in the city were hardly growing and nor were the training facilities which could equip them for skilled work. In fact a number of better educated people from the south were to be found in the "modern" office sector—in planning, computing and market research. One achievement of the state government of Amazonas was to keep pace in the provision of schools with the growth of the population of Manaus from the mid 1960s on, but it would not be until the 1980s that the problem of the illiterate, unskilled adult worker could be expected to diminish.

Manaus has long had a food-supply problem. The rapid growth of the city in the last few years has merely worsened it. At the end of 1969 it was decided to set up an agricultural and cattle district under the aegis of SUFRAMA on the northern side of the city. This would enjoy all the customs exemptions of the industrial zone, fiscal incentives and technical help. Almost 590,000 hectares were set aside for this project alongside the BR 174 towards Caracaraí: the plan provided for a balanced use with horticulture, dairy farming, cattle and pig raising, fruit crops, cocoa, rubber and forestry. But little happened until around 1975, and when I drove along a stretch of the BR 174 in mid 1976 there was little to suggest that a vigorous agricultural area was being set up. There were a few small farms, with up to 50 head of cattle, but no signs of activity on a scale that would make Manaus self-sufficient within the medium term. Although SUFRAMA was seeking to put more effort into the project in the mid 1970s it was clear that it had received much lower priority than the commercial and industrial activities in the early years of the free-trade zone. Dorival Kniphoff, a leading Amazon entrepreneur interested in timber growing, says that he became thoroughly disillusioned with SUFRAMA bureaucracy when he negotiated to set up an agricultural and forestry project within this agricultural district. After two years of bargaining, in which SUFRAMA required him to undertake some expensive research and then asked him to alter his plans drastically, he decided to write off his hopes there and buy land elsewhere in the basin. The failure so far to develop an agricultural hinterland means that food still has to be transported long distances to Manaus and is consequently expensive on arrival. Meat is almost unavailable at times.

The real criticism of the customs-free zone so far, however, is that it has done little to propel economic development outwards into western Amazonia. This was the ostensible case for the SUFRAMA zone: that it would act as a super growth pole for a very wide region, causing investment in related projects at some distance from the metropolis. Although the rules of SUFRAMA provide for a gradual increase in the indigenous content of goods made in the industrial district, and although the city's growth had created a demand for some products like

a & b Outside and interior of traditional home of sorva collecting family

c Engine of the defunct Madeira-Mamoré railway, outside the army barracks, Porto Velho, Rondonia

d President Medici, who authorized the TransAmazonica

e Aerial photo of TransAmazonica in the early construction phase

a   Camargo Corrĕa
workers at Prainha

b   Camp followers: the girls who kept the
road builders company

c   An Incra colonist near Itaituba. Manuel
Arruda, originally from Ceará, left home at
fifteen and went to Acre, Bolivia and
Santarem before claiming his 100-hectare
plot

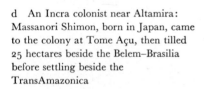

b

d   An Incra colonist near Altamira:
Massanori Shimon, born in Japan, came
to the colony at Tome Açu, then tilled
25 hectares beside the Belem–Brasilia
before settling beside the
TransAmazonica

d

c

a   Typical Incra agrovila
beside the TransAmazonica

b   Ariosto da Riva, entrepreneur

c   Simple brickworks at the Indeco base by the
Telles Pires

b

c

a A squatter's family near Cachoeira Porteira,
a construction base for Andrade Gutierrez north
of the River Amazon

b João de Souza, the disappointed migrant who
arrived in northern Paraná to find no work

c The high street of Amaporã, Paraná: one
source of settlers for Amazonia

a Humaita: DNER housing for lower grade highway employees adjoining the TransAmazonica in a new part of the town

b Iron shaft at the Serra dos Carajas, June 1976, still undeveloped nine years after discovery of reserves claimed to be the world's biggest

c Daniel Ludwig in Belem. A rare picture of the US citizen said to be the world's richest

d Zebu cattle belonging to colonists, being herded along the TransAmazonica near Marabá

a   A DNER ferry in Amazonia

b   Typical dirt highway—a well preserved section of the BR 174 north of Manaus

c   Poolside of prestige hotel at Ruropolis President Medici—closed and deserted 17 June 1976

d   Traditional river transport: a paddle ferry across the River Itacaiunas, Marabá

a Housing in the science compound at Aripuanã-Humboldt, now under-used

b Memento of an earlier assault on the jungle—the turn of the century bandstand at Bragança

c & d Lucrative but illegal assault on the wildlife—dead jaguar and skinned crocodile

a Assimilated
Indians. Macuxi
village school,
Maloca de Contão,
northern Roraima

b Non-assimilated
Indians. A family of
Ahairabu Indians in
the upper Rio Negro
liable to be affected
by the Perimetral
Norte. Father holds
the child to suck
while mother picks
lice from his hair

c Yanomama girl with full facial
decoration

timber and cement, this effect has not yet occurred generally. It is possible that it may yet do more, in concert with other developments elsewhere in Amazonia, but this is more likely to come about in reaction to the initial disruption that the burgeoning of Manaus has caused. For the denuding of the tributaries and the social stresses of rapid expansion in the city itself have now forced the government of Amazonas into an active town development policy at a distance from Manaus. The hope is that this will staunch the human flow into the state capital. And in spite of the efforts to create an industrial base in Manaus the city's prosperity is still firmly import based. In 1974, for example, the value of imports through the customs-free zone was $203·5 million (27·6 per cent from western Europe, 27 per cent from Japan and 24·8 per cent from the United States). Yet the value of exports in the same year amounted to only $26·4 million. While the 30-year life of the customs-free zone recognized that balanced development would take a while to establish, its early impact was decidedly eccentric. A quarter of a million extra people had congregated in a city whose main motive seemed to be buying foreign goods to the loss of the Brazilian treasury. The extraordinary luxury of the new Hotel Tropical, built in a colonial style on the out-skirts of the city and opened by Varig airline in early 1976 with an eye on the growth of tourism and the conference market, seemed to epitomize the exotic quality of this function. In spite of the duty-free goods the actual cost of living in Manaus is relatively high for Brazil.

One reason for the migratory rush to Manaus hitherto has been the very limited attractiveness of so many of the smaller towns in the river basin. Unless they happen to be on a new main road, or adjoining some new mine or agricultural development, they are probably still little changed from 30 years ago. People of the river valley call such towns "aban-doned". It means that there is little work to be had there; few shops; the town is dominated by a few buildings like the town hall and the main church or cathedral; that the better houses and shops overlook the river, but "the port" is inactive. Although life may be pleasant enough for the established families who control such towns it offers no sense of urban excitement to others—no up-and-coming football team, no cinema, no choice of bars and restaurants, no feeling of bustle

E

or people making money. Brazilians have a word, *movimento*, to describe this sense of urban activity. Its absence has been quite as important as the lack of economic vitality in small towns along the tributaries. Now the state of Amazonas—and the state of Pará in the case of New Marabá—is seeking to redevelop a handful of towns like Boca do Acre and Tefe. The objects are twofold: to make the new towns capable of growing in their own right, and to put them above the floodline of their rivers. These objects are more closely allied than might appear, however, for every recent flood in its region has tended to send a new wave of migrants to Manaus. Like the highways these removals away from the river's edge tend to break the "river mentality" of Amazonia.

The plan for New Marabá, which is supported by Pará and SUDAM, is different in scale. By 1980 it is expected that there will be 200,000 people on the new site, a few kilometres away from the Tocantins and Itacaiunas rivers, while the old site which was flooded in 1974 and 1975 will have another 100,000. In all therefore the municipality expects the town's population to multiply its 1976 population of 55,000 more than five times in a period of only four years. In other countries such a rapid expansion would seem daunting. One of the strengths of Brazil is that officials can cheerfully plan for such projects, in part because they know that most of the new citizens can be expected to build their own houses and in general look after themselves. The arguments for New Marabá are three: that it will put paid to the flood risk; that it can service the growth of the Serra dos Carajas iron mines (although there is also a company town of 30,000 being marked out at the Serra itself); and that it can mop up population overspill from Maranhão and the rest of the north-east. In intention, at any rate, it demonstrates the superiority of the integrated planning of Polamazonia over the simple priority for roads under the PIN programme. For New Marabá will be loosely related to Serra dos Carajas and will get hydro power from the new Tucuruí dam project (though that may not arrive in large quantities until the mid 1980s); it will be fed from the agricultural schemes along the TransAmazonica and from the cattle ranches to its south; and it will be close enough to the north-east to recruit all the labour it needs. The deliberate use of a new-town concept on this scale as a way of funnelling migrants into economic development is something

new in Amazonia. Its weakest element seemed to lie in the plans
for employment: it rather looked as though the people would
arrive before there were jobs for them.

When I visited the site of New Marabá the roads had already
been laid out in the forest and a water supply, with stand-pipes
at intervals, had been installed. A few houses had been built in
an organized fashion. Certain plots had been partly burnt off.
A few families were sleeping under sacking as they made
standard Amazon dwellings, using palm leaves and trees on the
spot for walls and thatch. (The simplest Amazon shacks can be
built in a day where the materials are readily available and
there are several helpers.) Eduardo Rodrigues dos Santos was
at work on a solid wooden house of two storeys. He wanted to
open the first restaurant in New Marabá. An elderly man, who
had first come from Maranhão to Marabá in 1939, he clearly
did not mind having to build himself another house. He
reckoned that the wood and materials for it would cost 5,000
cruzeiros ($476) and that he might have to pay another 4,000
cruzeiros ($381) for the price of the plot. Elsewhere on the site
of the new city a family of ten from Goiás, whose father worked
at the town hall, were camping out on their plot and a tiled
house stood out among the straw huts. One old pensioner of 71
said he had built himself a new home in order to get out of the
house of his relatives. For those who could afford bricks there
was an ample supply from the many small brickworks and
claypits beside the River Itacaiunas.

What are the general social effects of mass migration as it
has occurred within Brazil over recent decades? These differ
according to whether the perspective is that of the families
involved, or that of the wider society. For the families the
opportunity to move somewhere else provides a second chance
and an escape valve. For some of the individuals concerned it
also permits an escape from family responsibilities, as well as
an adverse situation of land tenure or eroded soils. But it is
perhaps a mistake to generalize too rashly about the motivations
and status of the rural families involved in this exodus.
Research among city *favelados* by Janice Perlman[25] and others
has shown that, in spite of their poverty, those who have gone
to the towns have been more highly motivated and socially
aspiring than the families they left behind. This may well be
true also of those who are migrating from one rural area to

another. Indeed wherever crude selection procedures apply—
whether by Incra or the labour recruiters for private employers
—they tend to exclude the most poor because they are the most
sickly and unfit.

Knowledge of the existence of potential places for emigration
means that, even if families do not want to move at once, the
possibility always exists. Indeed, while it is only a possibility,
they may be more tolerant of their existing condition and they
certainly benefit from the departure of their fellows. The point
about the availability of fresh lands in Amazonia after 1970 is
that it maintained a rural option for families who actually
wished to move. There is little doubt that, if they could be sure
of obtaining their own plot, many rural families would always
prefer to stay in the countryside rather than go to the city. But
in spite of Brazil's vast size the firm structure of landownership
in settled areas and the steady occupation of non Amazonian
lands meant that the supply of land elsewhere for small farming
was drying up. This was occurring at a time when the general
squeeze on working-class incomes in urban areas for most of the
1960s may have made the cities seem slightly less attractive,
while the supply of would-be migrants from the north-east and
parts of the south showed no sign of drying up. It was hardly
surprising if rural families equated the rhetoric of national
development in Amazonia with the possibility of their own
advancement.

At a structural level the rôle of migration and the existence
of fresh lands to occupy has some similarities with the rôle of
the western frontier in the United States in the nineteenth
century. It weakens the demand for agrarian reform, or
the opposition to farm mechanization, in the countryside.
Indirectly too the constant migration to the cities keeps labour
cheap and inhibits the growth of unions. In the minds
of Delfim Netto and others round President Medici when
he launched the TransAmazonica programme there were
probably other thoughts. While the programme might uncover
new resources and would impress outside investors it would
also help to mop up the excess of labour over jobs in the
Brazilian economy. For one effect of the western capitalist
model adopted after 1964 was that it had encouraged the
growth of "advanced" capital-intensive industries which were
making little contribution to employment. This was a particular

criticism of the rôle of SUDENE in the north-east. On the other hand the planners for the military régimes were emphatic that they did not wish to dabble in Maoist or African socialist policies to mobilize the human resources of the peasantry: they were heavily committed to building up the most advanced economy in Brazil that was possible. Amazonia in practice, and the idea of Amazonia for those who only thought about moving there, could help to fill the employment gap in Brazil's economic model.

But the essential thing about migration is that, while it tends to even out demand and supply in the labour market, it is the migrants who carry all the costs of the process. It is a socially conservative process, for it diverts those who might challenge the property rights and power of landowners in settled areas. Yet in spite of the violence at times in Brazil's newly-occupied lands the migrants who arrive there will probably also find themselves in a dependent situation, as they do if they come to a city. The policy of Incra—although it is now showing some interest in agricultural co-operatives—has on the whole been to re-create a diversified and unequal structure of private ownership in the new lands. This also appears to have happened spontaneously in those parts of Amazonia where Incra has merely had to document the state of landownership. Padre Jorge Marskell, the local apostolic administrator, recently examined the distribution of land in the municipality of Itacoatiara, Amazonas. Using Incra data up to 29 March 1976 he found 76 proprietors owning over 500 hectares and averaging 3,323 hectares each; 225 middle-sized owners with between 100 and 499 hectares and averaging 215 hectares each; and 2,006 small proprietors with average holdings of 21·4 hectares. The situation was familiar: 3·3 per cent of the proprietors owned 71·5 per cent of the ground at one extreme while, with the smallest holdings, 86·9 per cent of the proprietors owned only 14·8 per cent of the land between them.[26]

Migration as it has taken place in Brazil is often an inefficient process. As with João Luis de Souza, whose plight was quoted at the start of this chapter, there are plenty of people who move on the basis of out-of-date or inaccurate information. Even when they are not actively misled they are only too willing to imagine a glowing contrast between their destination and their present situation. Disappointment at the other end encourages some to move on again, helping to make the migratory process self-sustaining. North-easterners from the drought areas too are legendary for their homing instinct: even when they have gone elsewhere in search of food and work there are always some who return to the north-east after the backlands there have received rain. Nor is it very easy for government action to canalize the flow of migrants. As will be discussed further in chapter 6, describing the situation of the Amazon highways now, it is doubtful whether the TransAmazonica carried an exceptional weight of migrants from the north-east in 1976 although that was another year of serious drought in the region.

Is migratory pressure in Brazil likely to diminish in future? The fact that a majority of Brazilians are now living in urban areas, and that the birth rate there is falling, suggests that there may be a gradual reduction in migration within rural areas towards the end of this century. This is likely to be more rapid if the towns are allowed to continue importing labour from the countryside, or if standards of living in the rural areas rise sufficiently to make it unnecessary to have large families as a means of insurance. But as of now there is still a large potential demand for migration in areas like the north-east and Rio Grande do Sul and it is for this reason that official agencies anticipate a continuing flux into Amazonia. Even if land pressures should subside in the already settled areas Brazil is likely to witness a continuingly high level of general migration. As with the United States, which also has a highly mobile population, a culture of movement established in the pioneer days is likely to continue even when all land available for settlement has been taken. By then a nomadic national life-style, supported by better communications, has its own momentum.

Finally it should not be forgotten that there is a sort of triangular equation involved in migration to incorporate new lands. This includes the Brazilian government, which has national economic and strategic interests in the occupation of fresh territory; the migrants themselves, who seek to better their situation; and the large companies who seek to exploit the agricultural and mineral resources of the unpopulated areas, and to establish new markets for their bases in the centre-south. It is an alliance of big capital with cheap labour which needs the leadership of the government to provide an infrastructure of penetration and to reduce the risks of the other parties. The strength of this pressure to occupy new lands is only likely to change significantly when the government is satisfied that its strategic and economic ends are served; there are fewer poor peasants; and the companies with the resources to invest in Amazonia no longer feel the need to. In the next chapter we look at Amazonia from the point of view of the companies.

5

MINERALS, RANCHING AND
MULTINATIONALS

THE SITE OF what is claimed to be the world's biggest reserve of iron ore must also be one of the most beautiful settings for a mining operation in the world. Flying south-west from Marabá after an hour and a half the vistas of forest suddenly give way to the hills of the Serra dos Carajas, where there are bald patches of scrubby bushes and spindly grass where the ironstone is close to the surface. The plane lands at the first mining camp on top of an escarpment. From there, and especially from the company guesthouse at the edge of the cliff which could easily become a tourist resort long after the iron is all extracted, there are breath-taking views of the forest. As light falls you can pick out among the bird song a faro, the small white bird with a long loud warning cry. The scenery of the *clareiras*, as the bald patches are called, is no less interesting. On the surface you can see lumps of rusty iron ore just lying around. It occurs to the visitor that the discovery of the deposit in 1967—by North American geologists of the Companhia Meridional, a subsidiary of US Steel, who were actually looking for manganese at the time—must have been one of the easiest things in the history of mining. And on the ferrous earth grow white orchids of great beauty. This variety is not known elsewhere in Brazil and it has only been possible to transplant individual specimens from the serra when accompanied by a liberal quantity of their native metallic soil.

Serra dos Carajas, named after an Indian tribe whose nearest representatives now live hundreds of kilometres away on the Ilha do Bananal, is the centre of an amazingly rich geological area. The company charged with developing it, Amazonia Mineração SA, has proved 18,000 million tons of iron and, at conservative estimates, 40 million tons of manganese, 46 million tons of nickel and 67 million tons of bauxite (aluminium). The average iron-ore content in the deposits is high: 66·7 per cent.

At present AMZA has 170,000 hectares in its concession but it has been trying to buy 400,000 from the state of Pará. One reason for this is that geologists believe that the discoveries so far by no means exhaust the possibilities of the area. Other companies including Meridional and International Nickel Corp. have also been prospecting in the neighbourhood of AMZA, 51 per cent of whose shares are now owned by the Brazilian state-controlled iron company, Companhia Vale do Rio Doce. In 1976, for instance, a team of Canadian geophysical fliers based in Marabá were scanning the whole region under an aid agreement between Canada and the government of Brazil. This territory, lying between the Araguaia and Xingu rivers, is geologically the most interesting in the Amazon basin. Copper and tin have also been discovered and zinc is suspected.

But the story of what is believed to be the world's biggest iron-ore reserve is one of delay, complexity, and of enormous financial requirements. Although the deposit was discovered in 1967 and fully proven by the early 1970s the most optimistic forecast date for production is not until 1981 and that could slip back. In Amazonia, it seems, mineral resources have to be of unheard-of magnitude to be worth developing at all, and then the process is costly and long-drawn-out. It is worth looking at the factors which are holding back the Serra dos Carajas because they help to put into perspective the widespread concern over the rate at which major projects are being introduced in Amazonia. These factors involve finance, politics, transport, energy and labour. For the opencast iron mining operation is possibly the simplest and cheapest part of what has to be done in order to realize these deposits. A special electrified railway, covering at least 940 kilometres and expected to take four years to build, must be constructed from Serra dos Carajas to the port of Itaqui in Maranhão. There too new port works must be constructed. Power for the railway depends on completion of the 7,000 kw Tucuruí hydro dam on the Tocantins, which will also provide energy for processing of the large bauxite deposits of the River Trombetas at a plant near Belem. There are also infrastructure costs for Carajas, including the building of an approach road, a township on the site, and the new city of Marabá. To get an idea of some of the costs involved one needs only to quote two of the 1976 estimates: that AMZA itself would need to raise $2,700 million for its direct investment, while the railway alone would cost $3,000 million. In the circumstances it is scarcely surprising that Brazil must depend almost entirely on foreign finance to carry out this project, and that nearly all the iron ore is scheduled to be exported. In this Carajas is representative of other big industrial and agricultural schemes in Amazonia: huge development costs in areas lacking population and support services are beyond Brazil's own financial resources, and require foreign investment; as a result, and also because Amazonia is the part of Brazil which is nearest to Europe and North America, such projects are frequently export-oriented and their rate of introduction and profitability depends on world market conditions.

In the case of Carajas the world recession of 1973–6, particularly in the steel industry, had a serious delaying effect on all aspects of the financing. For much of this period AMZA itself had been trying to alter its capital structure in order to obtain a new injection of outside finance and, perhaps more importantly, secure long-term sales for the ore with partners abroad. The Medici government had insisted that Brazil should have 51 per cent of AMZA's shares on traditional nationalist economic grounds. This left US Steel with 49 per cent and, in its own interest and also to bring in other ore purchasers, it was anxious to run its own share down to 24 per cent. In the middle of 1976 it was being suggested that the new pattern might include the French Usinor group, the British Steel Corporation and the Spanish Altos Hornos group with 5 per cent each, and a Japanese consortium might take another 10 per cent. In May 1977, in the continuing world steel recession, US Steel sold its whole stake to the Brazilian state-controlled CURD for only around $50 million. But the problems for AMZA itself were simultaneously affecting the Tucuruí dam. Although Brazil seemed to be more willing to press ahead with the dam works, almost irrespective of the negotiations to pay for them, a loan for Tucuruí was one of the major practical points raised when President Geisel visited France and Britain in early 1976. Tucuruí was obviously more crucial than Carajas, because more projects depended on its electricity: its energy impact would be felt for hundreds of kilometres from Belem south to the ranches of the Araguaia valley and, as the first big dam in Amazonia, it was critical for the economic development of Pará. But the financing difficulties of the early seventies—which meant that all real work at Carajas apart from the building of an approach road was stopped for five years—illustrated how vulnerable any inter-related project was to delay in any connecting part.

The politics involved for Carajas were not only the international politics of trade and finance. There was also a lively battle between the states of Pará and Maranhão to make money out of the transport of the iron ore. Pará, backed by planners based in Belem, wanted the metal taken down the River Tocantins to Belem and there trans-shipped for export. AMZA, however, regarded this route as slower and less satisfactory than a railway to the port of Itaqui—a view in which it was, of course, supported by the state of Maranhão. Although navigation above Tucuruí would improve with completion of the dam, there are rapids on the Tocantins and, if that route had been preferred, the company would still have had the problem of getting the ore to the river. A main argument against the river route was that it would not have the capacity to carry 50 million tons of ore a year, but the mine would not be profitable at less. Although the railway to Itaqui would need six major bridges and would be difficult to build it would still, in the company's view, provide a simpler, self-contained method of transport.

For several years the battle between Pará on one side and Maranhão and AMZA on the other was fought at the level of paper studies and politicking among the federal agencies and government. It was only settled in May 1976 when President Geisel himself decreed that there should be a railway. But a significant pointer to the way in which the Geisel government was likely to arbitrate had been given two years earlier, when the Polamazonia strategy had been framed to embrace Maranhão. The battle between the two states was for a substantial sum of money, which was even more valuable to the poorer state, Maranhão. In mid 1976 the *Estado de São Paulo* estimated that Pará could expect 204 million cruzeiros ($19·4 million) a year from its state minerals tax, of which 40 million ($3·8 million) would go to the municipality of Marabá which contained the reserve. Further, the state could expect an annual benefit of 74 million cruzeiros ($7 million) from the salaries paid by the project. For Maranhão the equivalent benefit would be at least 221 million cruzeiros ($21 million), apart from any gains from railway traffic between Carajas and Itaqui. But President Geisel's decision did not settle all the local political conflicts around Carajas by any means. The same report in the *Estado de São Paulo* (21 June 1976) added that AMZA had reached an impasse with the government of Pará over paying for the long road-and-rail bridge across the Tocantins. This dispute, which involved SUDAM and DNER also, arose because AMZA was refusing to pay when it discovered that the bridge was going to cost 86 million cruzeiros ($8·2 million) more than the 140 million ($13·3 million) originally agreed.

The political and financial delays, and the sheer complexity of Carajas, are creating their own ripples and eddies. Two particular effects of the delays are that the projects which depend on Carajas are also being postponed, and that land occupation and speculation could burgeon in the meantime. The indirect economic and employment benefits of Carajas are probably a great deal more important than those of the mine and railways. (One unofficial estimate is that, when fully developed, the Carajas mines will employ 150,000; the indirect employment in the region would then be 750,000.) For example a firm named Prometal SA is wanting to build a metal alloy factory at Itaqui. This was designed to produce 100 million tons a year of ferro-manganese and ferro-silico-manganese on its opening in 1978. To do so it would rely on manganese from the ICOMI (Bethlehem Steel) reserves in Amapá, and iron from Carajas. It was planning to invest 436 million cruzeiros ($41·5 million) by 1980 and would create 600 jobs directly and 3,000 indirectly. This was just one of the consequential projects which could obviously not achieve its initial target because Carajas itself was behind. Similarly the build-up of New Marabá, mentioned in the previous chapter, risked being a build-up of unemployment.

Property speculation and squatting by *posseiros* is of course a perennial risk where any major investment is being undertaken. AMZA officials were still surprised when 42 men turned up, totally without authorization, and started demarcating lots for sale in the area where the company wanted to build its mining town. AMZA had checkpoints on the road running between the potential mining sites, but it was not too hard for others to set up their shacks and start clearing land on the main access road built by Camargo Corrêa from Marabá. Incra and ITERPA (the state body, Instituto de Terras do Estado do Pará) were keen to create an agricultural support area for Carajas, but they wished to do so in an orderly fashion. Hence ITERPA planted notices, warning against the invasion of state lands, at intervals along the access road. But when I drove along it in mid 1976 there were scores of people who were squatting there all the same. The Belem press reported that ITERPA officials were going to investigate the situation. Shortly after, I heard from a trustworthy source that AMZA had requested the army to make a sweep along the access road, and about 100 *posseiros* fled. Although the delay to the mining project could give the authorities time to organize land title and agricultural development, this experience suggested that it could stimulate conflicts also.

One school of thought in Brazil, to which Roberto Campos belongs, has it that minerals extraction ought to be the top priority in the development of Amazonia. The argument is that where a deposit is large and valuable enough it can most certainly justify the transport and energy investments that any serious project in the river basin is bound to require. Agricultural projects, by contrast, involve greater risks in raising the crops or cattle, in affecting the local ecology, and in regard to the state of the world market by the time they come to fruition. This approach, which is opposed to any widespread occupation of Amazonia, has had considerable influence on the policy of the Geisel government: six of its original fifteen Polamazonia poles were built round mineral resources, and the Ministry of Mines and Energy has published an estimate that, in the three years from 1975–7, a third of all Brazil's mining and metal processing investments will be in the north region. The attraction of this logic was greater because Brazil was in any case seeking to expand its export trade in minerals and the world was becoming more conscious that sources were limited. Between 1970 and 1974, for example, Brazil's proportion of world iron output rose from 4·69 per cent to 10·18 per cent: this was entirely based on reserves in the centre-south, where there were still some 12,000 million tons of iron to extract. However, the very accessibility of these other reserves, for which a new railway line is now being built to link the steel town of Volta Redonda to Belo Horizonte and São Paulo, tends to give Carajas a lower priority. Just as Carajas' importance to US Steel varied with the state of its battle with Venezuela over nationalization of its nearer iron interests there, so even an export logic for Amazonian iron cannot guarantee that the Brazilian government will give it overriding support.

Manganese and tin, however, provide clear existing examples of Amazonia's potential. Between 1973 and 1974 the value of tin exports, originating from Rondonia and Amazonas, rose from $5·6 million to $21·6 million; the value of manganese exports from Amapá jumped from $18·8 million to $49·6 million. Brazilian manganese accounted for 11 per cent of world output in 1974. The story of the manganese operation in Amapá is worth telling in more detail because of the light it casts on the minerals business in Amazonia. The deposit in the Serra do Navio was found in 1945. According to one widely accepted belief it was found when someone asked a fisherman, who was using a lump of manganese to anchor his boat, precisely where he had obtained it. According to Marcos Arruda, Herbet de Souza and Carlos Afonso (*Multinationals and Brazil*) the original discoverer was a poor miner named Mario Cruz who was effectively relieved of his find. In any event control rapidly passed to A. T. A. Antunes, one of Brazil's biggest industrialists, whose mining firm CAEMI took a 51 per cent share in a special subsidiary named ICOMI, with the remaining 49 per cent in the hands of Bethlehem Steel. ICOMI built a special railway line from the serra to the port of Macapá and the mining operation itself, with high wages and good conditions for the workers, is widely regarded as a model. However, even this commercial success story has its lessons. J. S. Marinho Nunes, vice president of CAEMI, explains that the manganese enterprise was only really able to get established in the 1950s through two strokes of luck on the world market. First the project was able to get 100 per cent financing from the Export-Import Bank of the United States for strategic reasons, because the Soviet Union was threatening to cut off manganese supplies to the West during the Cold War. Secondly, the closure of the Suez Canal in 1956 suddenly raised the world price: this was because manganese for North America and Western Europe was being shipped from India. "Anything in Amazonia has to be much bigger than in the centre-south in order to obtain bank financing," Marinho Nunes remarks. "A manganese mine to extract one million tons in the south would be justified, but ICOMI had to prove at least ten million tons in Amapá in order to obtain support." This emphasis on the need for big reserves and an encouraging situation in the world market is underscored by the fact that CAEMI/ICOMI is currently spending $10 million a year on searching for minerals in Amazonia—without so far having discovered any significant new reserves.

But there are also two other lessons from ICOMI. The first is that minerals extraction can indeed provide a trigger for other types of development in Amazonia. Apart from its wages and investments in the territory, the company is paying over $2 million a year to the Amapá government in royalties: when shortly its income-tax waiver runs out, it will have to pay a 30 per cent tax on its profits also. Not later than 1980 the royalty payments will be transferred to the territory's electricity utility. Hence Amapá has obtained from the manganese a quite useful resource for the general betterment of the territory, even if some might argue that it could have struck an even more advantageous bargain. Secondly ICOMI and its associated companies have developed a broader commitment to investing in Amapá. This "Amazon idealism" is a quite specific phenomenon among some individuals and companies who have become involved in the river basin: it is a more than commercial motivation which lures them into schemes beyond their original type of undertaking, in spite of considerable difficulties. ICOMI is now looking for other projects to support in Amapá and is planning to develop pine growing in the territory's savannah region for pulp, in a partnership with Scott Inc. of the United States. It had already become involved in a pulp operation with another partner, Bruynzeel NV of the Netherlands, for non-commercial reasons. Bruynzeel, which was then active in the Dutch colony of Surinam, was anxious to pull out of its Amapá scheme in 1962–3 when the political and economic situation in Brazil seemed highly uncertain. ICOMI representatives flew to Holland to try to persuade Bruynzeel to stay, largely because of the adverse effect on Amapá that Bruynzeel's departure could have. In the upshot ICOMI ended up by taking almost total control of this pulp business for a while, although Bruynzeel has now exercised its right to resume roughly 50 per cent of the shares. Obviously this widening interest of ICOMI suits the Amapá government which wants to diversify the territory's economy. Although the extraction of minerals may induce a wider growth the minerals themselves have only a limited lifespan. Amapá's manganese, first exported in 1957, is likely to run out by 1986.

Amazonia has proven reserves of uranium, China clay and rock salt, apart from the more common minerals. Although oil prospecting is now being actively pursued in Acre, where there is an oil field across the Peruvian border, and in the central Amazon basin, where foreign companies are taking risk contracts for exploration and small quantities of oil have been discovered in the past, no major finds have yet been recorded.

But before summing up the situation for minerals it is worth mentioning bauxite, the raw material for aluminium. Brazil is an importer of aluminium, so the major Amazonian discoveries of bauxite have an even greater balance of payments significance than others whose potential is solely in export. The biggest bauxite reserve is near Oriximina, on the River Trombetas; other important ones are near Almeirim, on the northern bank of the Amazon, and near Paragominas, near the Belem–Brasilia road in the state of Pará. Estimated reserves at Trombetas and Paragominas together add up to some 1,800 million tons, but the bauxite projects have suffered from delays in financing and development in a way which is reminiscent of Carajas. The reserves at Oriximina, which are being worked by a company named Mineração do Rio Norte, were totally owned by Alcoa. Then, after the world aluminium price had fallen in 1972–3 and Alcoa had come under pressure from the Medici government to permit Brazilian participation, its structure was re-formed: CVRD obtained 41 per cent, Alcoa's share fell to nineteen per cent, and about half a dozen other companies held smaller proportions. The plan was for the ore to be transported by ship to a smelter to be built near Belem at a place called Abaetetuba. (The possibility of a new railway from Paragominas to this centre is also under study.) This meant that paying for the smelter at Abaetetuba came to take on a strategic importance for the whole future of Amazon bauxite. Apart from Alcoa other companies involved in the different bauxite reserves included Alcan, Rio Tinto Zinc and

Daniel Ludwig—all of which had other world-wide interests to consider. It may have been for this reason that the Brazilian government was by 1976 pinning its faith on Japanese finance for the smelter, but even with the Japanese negotiations were proving far from simple. By 1976 it was already clear that output from Oriximina was at least two years behind the target laid down in the Polamazonia strategy: the first shipment would not be until 1979 at the earliest, rather than 1977, and it was possible that output would begin sooner from the reserves at Almeirim where CVRD was in control.

How important then are mining and minerals in the contemporary penetration of Amazonia? It is obvious from the instances quoted that a distinction has to be made between the process of exploration and discovery, which had scored notable hits like Carajas before the Medici government came to power and was given a big fillip by the RADAM survey, and the process of exploitation. To exploit the various reserves requires markets, finance, energy and transport. International companies, which have been given every encouragement by the military governments since 1964, are keen to get their hands on proven reserves but do not always share Brazil's urgency to exploit them. Often the costs seem daunting. Amichay Wine, for instance, says that he found it impossible to justify the extraction of a known potassium reserve in Amazonia simply because of the high freight costs. Nevertheless, even if optimistic government targets are going to continue to be missed, it seems reasonable to assume that some of the biggest discoveries—such as Carajas and Trombetas—will be actively exploited by the mid 1980s. And when this happens the economy of specific parts of Amazonia—particularly the Belem area and southern Pará—will be massively transformed. Furthermore the big operations will help to make smaller deposits economic. Industrialization round Belem and Marabá would undoubtedly involve further forest clearing but, compared with agricultural colonization, it could be argued that minerals extraction involves a more limited impact on the environment. Bulk movements are cheapest by river, where the river is navigable and direct; the second best method of transport is by railway, which has a less automatic impact on the territory through which it passes than a road.

But simply because the mining operations are so costly this is the aspect of modern penetration of Amazonia which is most dependent on foreign finance. Brazilian government policy here seems to be split between two ambitions: the first is to generate exports to improve the balance of payments; the second is to provide raw materials for the further development of industry in the centre-south. The utilization of Amazonia's raw materials in Amazonia, to improve employment prospects and the standard of living in the river valley, comes a poor third in the colonialist perspective of Brasilia or São Paulo. And because the investments are large and Brazil needs them more than the international companies—at least until resource shortages become more acute—there is always a danger of Brazil giving more than it gets in tax revenue and permanent betterment after a mine is exhausted. Any mining project in Amazonia now could hope to get 75 per cent of its investment paid for by the government through SUDAM's fiscal incentives money. And it is significant that ICOMI, in Amapá, was only paying the full tax rate in the last third of the life of its manganese mine.

Colonel Costa Cavalcanti, when he was Minister of the Interior in the Medici government, once remarked, "The spectre of hunger throughout the world will tend to diminish before the potential of Amazonian cattle." On the other hand the cattle manager of a major international firm with an experimental ranch in Pará said to me, "When it comes to Amazonia we're all looking over each other's fences to see how the other fellow is doing." Nevertheless cattle are perhaps the most formidable agents of change in Amazonia, advancing up through the cerrado savannah lands on the southern rim of the forest, then causing the trees themselves to be cleared and replaced by pasture. They have already had a powerful impact on the landscape in the Araguaia valley and southern Pará; you can see the first ranches cut out of the forest as you fly across northern Mato Grosso; and in Acre their progress from 1973–6 has converted a state which was having to import meat from Bolivia into one which is now self-sufficient and capable of exporting to other regions.

The theory of cattle raising in Amazonia varies in sophistication according to the type of rancher. For some of those concerned the overriding facts are that the land is cheap and, if a project can get the blessing of SUDAM, fiscal incentives money will pay for most of the investment. But for the bigger, more hard-headed firms, and for the federal government, the promise is more ambitious. Their eyes are concentrated on two aspects: the first is that in the tropics cattle should be able to put on weight all the year round, without the expense and wasted time of winter feeding; the second is that, with world meat demand shooting up for the foreseeable future, Amazonia's convenience for the markets of Europe and North America should guarantee a profitable export business. There may also be an element of commercial politics in the involvement of the more unexpected international concerns, such as Volkswagen do Brasil and the Italian firm Liquigas, in ranching in Amazonia. It has been suggested that the goodwill they obtain by providing a new export income for Brazil and collaborating in the federal government's desire to open up the interior may be used to justify a high level of profits remission from their principal activities like cars and gas. By 1976 multinationals were under strong pressure to contribute to the improvement of the balance of payments: a government study of 115 multinationals in Brazil showed that in 1974 they imported $2,100 million more products than they exported.[27]

It is worth looking first at some of the bigger cattle operations, and then discussing more broadly the future of ranching in Amazonia. The fact that the three particular examples chosen—Liquigas, Volkswagen and Swift-Armour—are international firms should not mislead one into thinking that international companies have the lion's share of the ranching operations in Amazonia. Although some of the foreign-owned schemes are big the overwhelming majority, both by hectares and number of projects, are being promoted by Brazilians. One critic of foreign investment (Marcos Arruda in *Multinationals and Brazil*) estimated in 1974 that the total proportion of the state of Goiás in foreign ownership was 3·5 per cent. While this proportion may well be higher elsewhere in Amazonia, Goiás has been a rapidly expanding cattle state since the mid 1950s. Equally it should be remembered that not all the foreign companies which have long been active in the Brazilian cattle business have risked getting involved in Amazonia. One notable example here are the British Vestey companies.

The Liquigas property, the Fazenda Suia Missu, covers a surface area of 566,000 hectares in the municipality of Barra

do Garças, Mato Grosso. The company, which is said to have
the Vatican as a principal shareholder, bought the property
from the Ometto sugar family in 1971 and set up a special
subsidiary, Liquifarm do Brasil, to manage it. By 1976 the
company had cleared 70,000 hectares of the forested land and
was rearing 70,000 cattle: some of these cattle were the humpbacked zebu, originally from India and now adapted over
several generations to the tropical areas of Brazil; others were
the result of cross-breeding the zebu with Marchigiana and
Chianina bulls from Italy, a programme of stock improvement
by which Liquigas set great store. The investment in Suia
Missu was considerable: 150 million cruzeiros between 1971
and 1976 (say $25 million), with a further 680 million
cruzeiros (say $64 million) being spent between 1975 and 1985.
By the time the second phase of the project is due to be complete, in 1985, there should be a quarter of a million cattle on
20 farms of 10,000 hectares each, complete with a special town
of over 7,000 inhabitants to be known as Liquilandia. The first
pasture on the site was laid down by the Ometto family in
1963. Liquigas, like other proprietors in Amazonia and its
fringes, has been sowing the burnt or cleared land from the
air.

But as with other ambitious projects in Amazonia it is far
from clear exactly when the scheme becomes profitable. David
Marcovitch, the marketing controller for Liquifarm, was
unable to forecast a date for me when I met him in São Paulo
in 1976.[28] But it would seem unlikely for the scheme to be
commercially viable before 1977–8. In 1977 the project is due
to have its own slaughterhouse, processing 15,000 tons of meat
a year in its first phase. But the company will then also need to
be served by all-weather roads, which means that genuine
viability may depend on how quickly DNER can asphalt the
BR 158 and BR 80 roads. In any event there are some indica-
tions that Liquigas has had setbacks in its cattle enterprise. The
Italian bulls are said to have been unwilling to do their
biological duty by the zebu cows. Other cattle experts observed
that, in one year, Liquigas got caught out by a mixture of
price movements and the poor state of the roads. Apparently
the company held off selling its beef cattle when the price of
meat fell, then found the state of the roads so poor due to the
rainy season that it could not get them out at all. The result was

that it ended up by having some 14,000 head more on its property than it had planned. Overstocking on the light Amazon soils—where the norm is often as little as one beast per hectare—appears to be one of the most common mistakes that ranchers make. Finally a slight loss of confidence may be detected in the fact that, instead of seeking to develop the whole property for itself, Liquigas is now leasing a part of it to someone else for agriculture.

The Liquigas scheme was launched with a fair amount of optimism and money. The firm has a jolly publicity film to explain its plans, has a high-flown "scientific philosophy" about becoming a group involved in all sorts of proteins, animal, vegetable and mineral, and created some amusement among other cattlemen with its talk of airfreighting filet mignon to the Italian cities. But its operation would seem to be quite serious, with a good chance of success by the 1980s.

Volkswagen do Brasil, whose European owners always seem a by-word for their commitment to the car industry, is perhaps one of the most surprising investors in Amazonia. In mid 1974 the company started to go ahead with a ranching and industrial scheme beside the PA 70 state road which links Marabá to the Belem–Brasilia. The idea was to produce meat, wood, cellulose and paper with a total investment of 1,000 million cruzeiros ($146·7 million). The president of the firm, Wolfgang Sauer, told the Minister of the Interior, Rangel Reis, that the company wanted to do this "in view of the need to diversify the activities of the business, and because of the incentives which the federal organs are offering". In fact the company seemed to get involved for a mixture of reasons, of which the availability of the fiscal incentives and the personal enthusiasm of senior figures in the firm—two of whom were subsequently killed in a plane crash when visiting the property—were probably crucial. The Brazilian subsidiary had been so successful in dominating a fast-growing car market that it was providing top management for the main group and in 1973 its profits were sufficient to cover losses on production in Germany. It was thus freer to develop a purely commercial orientation, making money wherever this might be possible: indeed the Brazilian subsidiary achieved a useful profits bonus in 1975 thanks to purely financial operations in the money markets. By 1976 the project in southern Pará was spending one million cruzeiros (over

$95,200) a year on pasture seeds and was busy importing German agricultural machinery.

However, the Vokswagen project illustrates how multi-national ranching schemes are always liable to suspicion in Amazonia. In the course of 1976 the company faced a sudden demand for 63·8 million cruzeiros ($6·1 million) from IBDF, the official forestry agency, as a fine for illegal clearing of trees. The circumstances were that the United States Skylab satellite had produced photographs of an area of apparently one million hectares on fire in southern Pará, in the neighbourhood of the Volkswagen ranch, where the company had only had IBDF approval to clear just over 9,000 hectares. The space pictures had been passed to Brazil's space agency which had then alerted the IBDF—although the actual fires might have been several months before. A public polemic developed in the press with IBDF demanding its fine and Volkswagen resting on the some-what inadequate defence that, because SUDAM had approved the project and would not release the fiscal incentives money until half the ground was cleared, Volkswagen had had no reason to seek further approval from the IBDF. The IBDF eventually sent some of its small staff of officials to inspect what precisely had occurred. In fact ranchers of all sorts, Brazilians and others, have at times resorted to lighting fires as an inexpensive way of clearing trees in spite of increasing criticism from ecologists that such fires can easily get out of control. The fact that Volkswagen was accused drew more publicity and, apparently, a harder line from the IBDF.

If Liquigas and Volkswagen represent two of the more exotic investors in the Amazon cattle business it should also be mentioned that one of the world's biggest meat firms—the US-owned complex of Deltec International, Swift-Armour and King Ranch—has an apparently successful Amazon operation under way near Paragominas. This conglomerate tends to be reticent about its activities but it owns 70,000 hectares, possibly going up to 110,000, which it is treating as an opportunity to experiment. In 1976 its subsidiary running the Paragominas ranch, Companhia Agro Pecuaria do Pará, had only 7,000 head of cattle on 16,000 hectares of new pasture in a deliberate attempt to avoid overstocking. So far the project appears to be going well: in particular the theory that young cattle can put on weight continuously in the tropics seems to have been borne out with bullocks weighing 6 cwt, or half their sale weight, at only eight months. But the firm is applying considerable care and resources to the ranch. It is not only experimenting with different varieties of cattle but with different grasses—some of which have been attacked by a spit beetle. It is spending a lot of money on fertilizer, something that may be crucial in sustaining the nutrients in grasslands established in the place of forest, but which is beyond the means of many Brazilian ranchers. This large-scale programme aims to cover 10,000 hectares a year at a cost of $400,000—of which about $200,000 is the price of the material and the rest is the price of the aerial spraying.

The firm is also creating its new pasture more tenderly than some do. It has 800 men clearing the trees by hand, to avoid losing the precious topsoil by pounding the ground up with tractors. The dry season at Paragominas is reckoned to start around 1 June and between May and September this force of peons will have cleared 5,000 hectares. At the end of October the scrub and unwanted timber is burnt: the land then lies fallow until the last two weeks of January when it is sown with grass seeds by air. Cattle are already grazing on the newly-formed pasture by the end of May. The basic cycle of clearing the woodland thus takes twelve months altogether but Companhia Agro Pecuaria do Pará again varies from some of its competitors in being slower to build the carrying capacity of the new pasture. In its second year, for example, the men try to clean out weeds from the new pasture, and improve its quality. Not until after three years is the land carrying its full quota of cattle. But other ranchers cannot afford to wait so long. Hence what is significant about this Paragominas ranch, managed by a firm which has extensive cattle interests in the centre-south and elsewhere in the world, is that it can spend a lot of money, carry out genuine experiments to see what mixture of cattle and grasses is effective, and afford to be patient. It is also quite ingenious: the manager of the Paragominas ranch is toying with the use of balloons to lift logs off the property.

Making specific mention of three of the foreign-owned ranching operations should not divert attention from the fact that the great majority of these are owned by Brazilian individuals and firms of the most varied types. Earlier it was mentioned that Sebastião Camargo of the construction firm has a model farm in Mato Grosso with feed and water delivered automatically to his prize bulls which are kept in luxurious stalls. But there are also older ranching families, like Moacir and Miranda in Marabá and firms that have no previous knowledge of the business, like Aços Villares, a steel firm, or Zela, a salad-oil manufacturer which now has 12,000 head of cattle on a ranch in the Nambiquara valley, Mato Grosso. Banks like Bradesco, Brazil's largest private bank, and Bamerindus have joined in the craze. Inevitably such a galaxy of owners have frequently run into trouble, misunderstanding the men, the soils or the cattle in what can be a tricky business even in the centre-south. Around Paragominas, for example, there are ranches which have already failed and where the land is reverting to scrub. Techniques of management which work fine on large *fazendas* in the state of São Paulo simply fail, and the land becomes burnt out. One notorious failure was on a project belonging to the Mappin family, descendants of the British family which started Mappin & Webb and who came out to Brazil to run stores in São Paulo and Rio de Janeiro. SUDAM which was pumping money into so many of the ranching projects did little to ensure their success: it was rare for a farm to be looked at by their officials more than once in three years. Although there was a rumour in cattle circles in Belem in 1976 that SUDAM was no longer going to back ranches, because it had decided that pasture in the Amazon needed fertilizer and Brazil could not afford to import more, an official denied this to me. In fact of course cattle remain a major priority within Polamazonia. Ranchers also vary in the way in which they treat their *vaqueiros* (cowboys) and some of their own successes and failures are explained by this: whereas some of the ranchers pay only the minimum salary, deducting the price of the greasy meat and beans which they provide even though the managers may be enjoying French wines and the best cuts, a firm like Companhia Agro Pecuaria do Pará is paying 150 per cent of the minimum salary. The same *fazenda* also runs a blanket insurance scheme for all workers and the first malaria control programme for employees in the region.

Ranching may be the main way in which modern Brazil is trying to exploit the forest lands of Amazonia but there are also some large-scale agricultural and forestry projects. I shall consider two here in particular: D. K. Ludwig's extraordinarily ambitious agricultural, forestry and minerals project on at least 1·2 million hectares of land by the River Jari in Amapá; and Dorival Kniphoff's basically timber enterprise on one million hectares between the Rivers Juruá and Bió on the south side of the Amazon.

D. K. Ludwig is an unimpressive figure, a short man with baggy trousers, who since the death of Paul Getty in 1976 is reckoned to be the richest man in the world. A US citizen of Austrian descent, born in 1897, he was already estimated to be the fifth richest individual in 1957 by *Fortune* magazine. He has simply gone on getting richer. His fortune, like other shipping men's, was founded during and just prior to the Second World War when he discovered a way of making a 100 per cent profit on building cargo boats and tankers. Basically he would obtain a charter for the ship's use before it was built, and then get a bank loan to cover the cost of its construction. Even though the ships were chartered, he retained ownership and during the Second World War he received encouragement from the US government on grounds of the national interest. His controlling company is called National Bulk Carriers but since the Second World War he has extended his business into many other areas—from hotels and gambling in the Bahamas to the Cromarty Petroleum Co. whose plans for a refinery at Nigg Bay have been hard fought by local people in Scotland. Much of his shipping business is now said to be run by bright young men in London. He is now an old man himself, with no children, who has told friends that he is planning to leave most of his fortune for cancer research. He has set up a cancer research foundation in Switzerland. He is extremely reticent about his activities but he first started obtaining land on the River Jari in 1964. The actual quantity of land he now controls there is in some doubt—estimates range from 1·2 million to four million hectares. Nor is it absolutely certain on what basis he has this land. While he is usually described as "owning" this property Arthur Ferreira Reis, the former governor of Amazonas, told the author that he believes Ludwig merely has a lease for some 90 years.[29] Mysteries of this sort help to explain why the Jari project is by far the most controversial international enterprise in Amazonia.

What precisely is Ludwig trying to do with his territory? There are three main strands—rice and cattle, timber and pulp, and minerals. The special issue of *Realidade* in 1971 reported that Ludwig was getting at least eight tons of rice per hectare off the flooded *varzea* land, with two crops a year. What it did not say was that this crop rate, which it rightly pointed out was one of the best in the world, was coming off a mere ten hectares—and this was the size of the experimental plot at least until 1976. According to Ernest Bolton, the North American manager of the Jari project in Belem, there would be 5,000 acres under rice by the end of 1976. This area would then be extended until the target area of 35,000 acres was under cultivation by the end of 1982. But why was the project so slow to get started? Delays in getting combine harvesters and other mechanical equipment to the site—which seems not unconnected with certain quarrels with SUDAM over releasing finance for Jari—plus technical problems seem to have delayed this scheme by at least five years. The cattle business, by contrast, seems to have got going faster. By 1971 he already had 12,400 head.

The timber now seems further advanced. Ludwig is growing a mix of gmelina, a fast-growing tree from India, and pine—in the ratio two-thirds to one-third. The gmelina takes eight to ten years to mature. By 1978, 250,000 hectares are due to be covered with this mixed woodland and in that year a floating pulp mill—now under construction by IHI of Japan for Ludwig at a cost of some $280 million—will be anchored in the Jari and begin output. The quantities involved here are very large: later the area of timber is to be extended to 500,000 hectares, involving a second factory barge, and cellulose and paper will also be produced. The use of a floating pulp mill has not gone unremarked: if Ludwig's concern had a row with the local authorities or Brazil had a change of attitude towards foreign investors it would be possible for the factory ships just to sail away. Ecologists like Warwick Kerr of INPA have strongly criticized the replacement of heterogeneous Amazon forest with merely two types of tree. The gmelina in fact suffered a bad fungus epidemic in 1971—the sort of danger ecologists had anticipated for a newly introduced species—but it was overcome. However, the forestry project also demonstrates Ludwig's autocratic obstinacy. Although he was keen to use the gmelina he is believed to have sacked as many as fourteen forestry managers—including Donald Cole, one of the best US

foresters, who subsequently became FAO expert in Brazil—
because he was slow to accept that a mixture of gmelina and
pine would be best for the soil and pulp operation intended. One
of his few trusted men, his citrus-fruit expert in Panama, had
advised him that this approach would be impossible. His
single-mindedness also drove off Kimberly Clark, a US wood
firm, which was keen to collaborate with him: this was because
he insisted on using an untried floating mill, and would not
allow the pulpers any say in the kind of forestry he undertook.

Ludwig's two main minerals interests are in bauxite—
adjoining the competing Alcan and Alcoa concessions in
Trombetas—and in kaolin (china clay) which is mined up the
Jari. The progress here has been markedly different. In the
case of the bauxite, where the Brazilian government has been
trying to bring the rival producers together, Ludwig was
threatened with the loss of his concession in mid 1976 for
failing to start output within six months of getting approval for
his project from the Department of Mines. He was appealing
for further delays. Precisely why he seemed to be dragging his
heels is uncertain, but one may guess that it had to do with the
complicated financial, energy and inter-company equations
which surrounded the Trombetas developments. The kaolin,
however, which is used for china and fine paper, was more
straightforward. In 1972 Jari was already exporting 5,000 tons
and the target for 1980 was 110,000 tons.

All this suggests that the various Jari enterprises are not an
unalloyed success, although the timber and rice ought to start
proving their potential by 1980. Total costs by mid 1976 had
reached $203 million and over $800 million more would be
invested by 1983. However, the size of the schemes, in an area
which is at least a third the size of Holland, have led to antag-
onism in Amazonia. While they require their own company
towns and hydro developments, journalists are only allowed in
on rare occasions, as when President Medici visited the property
in 1973. Goodwill has not been increased by the fact that the
holding company for the Jari enterprises, Universe Tankships,
has it registered headquarters in Liberia. Opposition to Jari
was fomented by Brazilian newspaper accounts of poor
labour conditions there and came to a head in an extraordinary debate in the Deliberative Council of SUDAM on
24 March 1976, which stalled a decision on tax exemptions for

the rice and forestry projects. Journalists and Medici himself noted complaints of poor pay, food and housing from peons working at Jari. As a result Medici sent his Ministers of Labour and the Interior to check on whether the labour legislation was being observed: the Ludwig officials blamed *gateiros* and middlemen for any shortcomings, but the government then introduced a provisional labour permit for peons and an office was set up in Monte Dourado, the centre of Ludwig's empire, to try to supervise relations between Jari and its workforce. However, when a *Jornal do Brasil* reporter got admission to Monte Dourado by a trick in 1974—he claimed that his plane had a defect and had to land—he found that conditions for some 5,000 peons paid only eight cruzeiros (under $1·20) a day had scarcely improved at all. (There are also, it should be added, nine groups of Apalai Indians who traditionally dwelt on the lands Ludwig controls: little is known about their state now.)

The SUDAM council meeting in March 1976 heard two sharp attacks on Jari. Warwick Kerr asked, "How can we justify tax exemption for a firm which doesn't have its head-quarters in Brazil?" Arthur Henning, the governor of Amapá, made it clear that he hadn't more than the faintest idea as to what the company was up to on his territory. Although the territory was contributing financially to help, its representatives could not at present get onto the property. He was therefore unable to say whether or not the development of such a large business was helping the region or not. He did hint, however, that if Jari was to allow some Brazilian financial participation "it would not meet any problem". Significantly two who spoke up for Ludwig were the regional director of the Bank of Brazil, Vanildo Torres, and the director of natural resources for SUDAM, Clara Pandolfo, who has been criticized by some ecologists for too willingly allowing SUDAM to approve projects with possibly dangerous effects. The SUDAM council postponed any decision, but only after a representative of President Geisel's planning secretariat had made it clear that SUDAM would have to endorse a conclusion reached "at other levels". He said, "The owner of Jari has personally handed President Geisel a study claiming the right to the imports he needs, pressing for the exemptions."

In fact Ludwig has nearly always enjoyed support at presidential level. This does not mean that he can get away with anything, as Medici's attempt to get the labour laws enforced indicates. Military presidents may be particularly embarrassed by the suggestion that Brazilian sovereignty has been set at nought, which is why the naval governor of Amapá, Arthur Henning, must have felt badly snubbed to speak out as he did. There is a rumour that Medici told Ludwig that he could only keep his autonomy on condition that he did not then ask the Brazilian government for special financial favours. On the other hand, in spite of Jari's non-existent public relations and bad press, the military governments are rather stuck with Ludwig. His is a paradigm of the grand project which they have been trying to instigate since the foundation of SUDAM. If it failed, not only would the federal government probably have to step in with a costly rescue, but it would have a devastating effect on the willingness of other private investors to tackle Amazonia. It would be like Henry Ford's fiasco at Belterra, only much more so.

What benefit to Brazil or Amazonia is likely to come from the Jari enterprises? Some money, if not much, is distributed in wages—mostly to peons from Maranhão who work on six-month contracts at Jari, but who are unable to save much by the end of them. The various firms will pay some taxes, even though they may not start for a while and then pay less than is usual in developed countries. Amapá is acquiring some agricultural and industrial infrastructure that the territory would not otherwise have. But the Jari enterprises are almost totally export-oriented; the minerals are of course non-renewable; even the pulp mill could sail away. It is hard to resist the conclusion that the benefits to Brazil or Amazonia may be relatively slight for many years compared with those for Jari—even allowing for Ludwig's considerable investment and the risks he must overcome. It is a stark case of an old-fashioned entrepreneur dictating most of the terms in the least developed part of a country with a capitalist bias which is hooked on the idea of development. The outcome is the more uncertain because Jari is so much the ambition of one man, Daniel Ludwig, who is elderly and without obvious heirs.

Dorival Kniphoff, however, is a much more likeable figure. He is trying to get a timber, agricultural and rubber project going on one million hectares by the River Juruá. He only bought the land in 1974, from various individual proprietors, on behalf of APLUB, an insurance firm with 75,000 associates, which is the second largest investor in Varig airline, a major shareholder in CVRD, and the owner of its own bank, Multi-banco. Of Russian descent and from Rio Grande do Sul, where he was involved in timber and cattle, he once made a slightly boastful remark on a Manaus radio station. He said that only *gauchos*, backed with money, could make a success of Amazonia. He was promptly challenged by the then Minister of Agriculture to justify this claim, left his interests in the south and, after the breakdown of his attempt to establish something in the SUFRAMA agricultural zone, got going further south. He is unusual in that he is seeking to make use of the mixed forest that already exists, and to assist the *caboclos* living in the region now, rather than to transform the environment and swamp it with outsiders. One of his first moves was to provide the scattered rubber collectors with an acid which coagulates the latex and cuts out the time-consuming and physically dangerous smoking process. Whereas in 1975 a stem of bananas in Carauari, the existing river town on the Juruá which is his centre, was worth nothing, a year later, thanks to his powers of organization and the general confidence he had given the population, they were worth seven cruzeiros (nearly 70 cents) each and being shipped down to Manaus. It was typical that when he found 80 members of the Katahiro tribe living on his property, addicted to *cachaça* and with no FUNAI post within reach, he should have made it his business to find someone to help them. While he too is keen to "fix the man to the land" and has a scheme for *agrovilas* and growing crops ranging from pineapples to coffee his main interest is in forestry. With help from Kimberly Clark and INPA in Manaus he is planning to use the heterogeneous forest for pulp, cutting it selectively in swathes which allow for natural renewal. He is also having another try at creating natural rubber plantations: he was putting in 250,000 saplings in 1976. His approach could not afford a greater contrast with Ludwig's. "I adore the forest and working with the land," he told me. "I find it easy to talk and work with the *caboclos*."

What is the breakdown between foreign and Brazilian commercial interests in Amazonia? As a rough generalization the foreign element seems strongest in minerals, but relatively weak in ranching and other fields. But such generalizations ignore two important factors: the overwhelming dominance of multinationals and foreign firms in Brazil as a whole, and that, irrespective of ultimate ownership, it is nearly always Brazilians themselves who are doing the developing in Amazonia. The dominance of foreign companies in Brazilian commerce is very marked and has strengthened with the growth of new capital-intensive industries and favourable government policies since 1964. In August 1973 *Visão* examined the ten biggest firms in each of six major sectors. It found that 31 were foreign-owned, fifteen were Brazilian private enterprises, and fourteen belonged to the state; in the same year it was estimated that the country had only 27 companies with annual sales over $100 million a year, of which fourteen were foreign-owned, eight were state-owned, and each of the remaining five which were privately owned in Brazil had an important foreign partner.

This certainly makes it possible for foreigners to take strategic decisions for Amazonia, as for other parts of the Brazilian economy. For example in 1972 a meeting took place at a São Paulo farm belonging to Ambassador Salles Oliveira which was attended by A. T. A. Antunes, Daniel Ludwig and the heads of Coca-Cola and the First National Bank of Chicago: this concentrated largely on investment possibilities in Amazonia. In late May 1976, there was a highly suggestive meeting of representatives of international capital in Rio de Janeiro. Gathered in the form of the Consultative Council of the Chase Manhattan Bank, which is chaired by David Rockefeller whose family has long-standing and widely diversified interests in Brazil, this included: I. K. Pao the shipping magnate, Giovanni Agnelli the head of Fiat, Guillaume Guindey of the Compagnie Internationale des Wagons-Lits, Sir Reay Geddes of Dunlop, Pehr Gyllenhammar of Volvo, William Verity junior of Amco Steel Corp., P. E. Hagerty of Texas Instruments, Alberto Bailleres of the Grupo Cremi in Mexico, Carl Gerstaker of Dow Chemical, Chugiro Funjino of Mitsubishi, and Antonio Calloti the president of Brascan. Although such visitors might have passed uncommented in New York, Paris or Frankfurt the Brazilian press treated them with awe and they saw President Geisel as well as the finance minister, Mario Henrique Simonsen. These were men who were felt to have enormous power over the Brazilian economy.

Within Amazonia itself, with its historic tension between international and national concern, there is continuing worry as to whether SUDAM and the federal government have really got the foreign enterprises under control. Significantly Congress set up a parliamentary inquiry commission (CPI) in 1967, before the new impulse of the TransAmazonica, to investigate the sale of Amazon lands to foreigners. This followed a major scandal in which a US swindler, Stanley Amos Sellig, went into partnership with a Brazilian from Goiás, João Inacio, to sell some 20 million hectares of land which they did not own in central Brazil. They forged titles and gave North Americans "an invitation to meet at the foot of the rainbow to divide the pot of gold". The racket did Brazil no good—Sellig was shot dead in his Indianapolis office by an angry investor—and although the inquiry was promoted by an opposition deputy who subsequently lost his political rights, the government was forced to take some action. On 30 January 1969 the Costa e Silva government passed an act (AC-45) under which rural property could only be acquired by Brazilians or foreigners resident in the country. Two months later this was followed by a decree law making it clear that the government was anxious to know exactly where foreigners owned land and that it was against the establishment of large foreign enclaves: article 8 made it illegal for non-Brazilians to own more than 120,000 hectares which would have struck a deadly blow not only at Jari or timber concerns like Georgia Pacific but also at foreign ranchers. However, in the interval between Costa e Silva's paralysis and Medici's presidency the temporary junta effectively undid this measure in October 1969 with a new decree which excluded from the March decree "acquisitions of rural areas necessary to the execution of industrial projects which are considered of interest to the national economy". This really opened the floodgates again. Volkswagen and Liquigas, for example, purchased their properties under that clause. Further measures by the Medici and Geisel governments (law 5709 of October 1971 and decree 74,965 of November 1974) prevented foreigners resident in Brazil, or subsidiaries of foreign firms, from buying more than 25 per cent of the land in any municipality. This was the maximum to be held by all foreigners together and, within that quarter, no individual foreigner or foreign firms could hold more than 40 per cent. However, firstly this was too late to have much impact on the problem posed by foreign purchases and, secondly, the large size of some municipalities in Amazonia meant that even a quarter could amount to as much as 3·5 million hectares. (The London *Daily Express* reported in August 1974, for instance, that Harry Kershaw, the son of the Conservative MP, Anthony Kershaw, was raising some $2 million to buy some 55,000 hectares of jungle in Rondonia: he was planning to raise cattle and grow rubber and Brazil nuts.) Though it might cause some foreign firms to resist the subdivision of municipalities this legislation was unlikely to have much effect while SUDAM was prepared to declare large projects as being "of interest to the national economy".

The foreign ownership issue gets periodically aired in the Brazilian press and the fact that the Congressional inquiry had spotlighted it in the late 1960s may well have encouraged President Medici's TransAmazonica programme: he wanted to be sure that at least a central swathe south of the Amazon was properly colonized by Brazilians. But the whole debate has diverted attention from two other factors: that mere ownership was not the same as successful exploitation, however grandiose the projects of the foreign firms might appear; and that, with the exception of Jari and the minerals firms, there was little to distinguish the projects of the foreign-owned firms from those of the Brazilian-owned ones. Both sorts were usually conceived by people living outside Amazonia, whose primary aim was not to benefit the inhabitants of Amazonia. Both sorts were normally executed by Brazilians from the centre-south and the sensitivity of a Dorival Kniphoff, both as to the environment and the traditional river-dwellers, could not be counted on. Sr Francisco Vanderlei Dantas, the young governor of Acre, was saying more than he realized when he told the *Jornal do Brasil* in 1973, "The southern press exaggerates when they say that Amazonia is being bought up by foreign groups. It isn't true. In Acre, for example, much land is being sold to southern businessmen and they all promise to observe the legal requirements." The question was whether the state and federal governments could police the law adequately in such a vast

F

area under such considerable pressure, and whether the laws and government policies were in any case appropriate for the most sensible use of the land space involved.

How far have all these industrial and ranching projects really got in terms of penetrating and transforming Amazonia? It is instructive to use SUDAM project approvals as a guide here. Figures given in 1974 showed that SUDAM by then had approved 321 ranching and agricultural projects (for which the owners were putting up 893 million cruzeiros ($131·3 million) and receiving 2,662 million ($391·4 million) in fiscal incentives money from the government) and 170 industrial projects (for which the owners were putting up 1,352 million cruzeiros ($198·8 million) and receiving 2,982 million ($438·5 million) in fiscal incentives). As has been suggested earlier, however, not all these schemes were proceeding equally fast, if at all. In the early years there had been some notorious cases of firms putting up paper projects merely to get SUDAM's fiscal incentives money—a blatant tax dodge. A few others, particularly round Belem, failed almost as soon as they opened. With the PIN programme, of which many businessmen approved if only because it tended to raise the value of any investments they had in Amazonia, there was a diversion of fiscal incentives money from business projects into roads and colonization. With the world recession and the arrival of the Geisel government the emphasis on infrastructure was maintained: only some 20,500 million cruzeiros ($2,531 million), out of a total SUDAM budget of 48,800 million cruzeiros for 1975-9 ($6,024 million) was scheduled for agriculture, industry and mineral development. Expenditures on energy and transport alone were budgeted at 17,000 million cruzeiros ($2,098 million). At the same time the Geisel government tightened up considerably on the application of fiscal incentives money. SUDAM rather than individual companies in the centre-south became responsible for selecting the destination of their fiscal incentives money within Amazonia, and only President Geisel himself would be able to authorize total exemption from import tax. In 1975, as Brazil's financial and balance of payments difficulties increased, SUDAM only authorized half the projects which it had in 1974; in the first four months of 1976 there was an almost total standstill. Clearly the recession was not only putting a brake on new projects, but it was halting or holding back some which had already begun.

It would be a mistake to assume that the SUDAM approvals are coextensive with *all* projects in Amazonia—indeed Rondonia, with its growing cattle and tin operations, was not due to receive any fiscal incentives money until 1977—but they probably include most of the bigger ones. Great though the activity is that they have stimulated when compared with the past, it is not really so much when compared with the extent of Amazonia. In terms of impact on the environment it would probably be safe to estimate that by the end of 1976 over 90 per cent of Amazonia was still in its primeval state, whatever the state of ownership or the plans drawn up for the rest. (Dr Bento de Souza Porto, secretary of planning for Mato Grosso, says that only 1 per cent of his state was cultivated in 1976.[30]) And the velocity of expansion into the area had been, at least temporarily, reduced by external economic forces. However, SUDAM figures do bring out one point. The direct financial impact of public agencies in the region is a lot more important than that of private firms. To that extent government policy from Medici onwards has been successful in keeping a grip on developments in Amazonia—and is correspondingly more to blame than the private firms if these turn out to be unwise. And it should not be forgotten that many Brazilian companies, including banks, are extremely wary of involvement in Amazonia.

The interlocking nature of so many of the schemes for Amazonia—depending on roads, energy and so on—makes them peculiarly vulnerable to delay. SUDAM and official bureaucracies have sometimes compounded the delay with red tape. At the same time even the relatively simple and inexpensive ranching operations require some infrastructure. Among the most critical items for them are slaughterhouses, freezer plants and meat-packing facilities. Their construction marks a point of consolidation in any newly-developed cattle region. It is therefore significant that certain obviously expanding regions, such as north-east Mato Grosso and the Araguaia valley south of Marabá, are only just becoming important enough to make such projects viable. Cuiabá in Mato Grosso got its first Sadia freezing plant in July 1976, while Sudanesa, a firm from Rio Grande do Sul, is opening another at Barra do Garças in the course of 1977. The Swift-Armour-Deltec-King Ranch alliance is actively considering building a $270 million meat plant in Marabá to serve that district.

To conclude, therefore, the ambitions of private enterprise are obviously a significant element in contemporary pressure on Amazonia but the actual achievements of many of the firms have been too easily inferred from their prospectuses. More important is that they work in symbiosis with the federal government and other public agencies—stimulating them to act, working for them, and benefiting from general improvements in infrastructure and services. They may vary in their effectiveness at overcoming the technical problems of Amazonia but they have one option always open to them. They can do nothing at all or go slow with their plans. Quite a number have acted in this way. Federal policy may not always help them: while completion of the BR 319 caused prices of land alongside to rise from 500 cruzeiros ($61) to 3,500–5,000 cruzeiros ($333–476) per hectare, and Mato Grosso is regarding the Cuiabá–Santarem road as a development pole, the Trans-Amazonica itself has so far proved crucial to no major private investment. By its nature private enterprise prefers to operate in areas where the risks are known and limited, and the profits certain. Brazilian companies, whether national or foreign owned, are no exceptions. It is for this reason that such elaborate inducements have been developed to encourage them to invest in Amazonia, and why their response is still short of overwhelming. Where firms have taken the plunge the personality and enthusiasm of senior managers have often been more important than the attraction of fiscal incentives. At present, although the boundaries of the forest are being chipped away, most businessmen and ranchers who are trying to set up in Amazonia regard themselves as pioneers.

6

THE ROADS NOW

WHAT DO THE roads look like now? There is not much traffic, so that a sloth, for example, crawling painfully slowly across the TransAmazonica, still has a pretty good chance of reaching the other side. In the dry season it is incredibly dusty on the dirt roads: even if all the car windows are closed when a lorry is in front of you somehow the dirt, reddish along parts of the Trans-Amazonica, will find a way into your lungs, getting through on to your hands and clothing. If a driver is behind another vehicle he is wise to keep his lights on. When it rains, traffic on the dirt roads tends to slow considerably and, in the rainy season, there is always a risk that a dirt road may no longer be passable. Cars need to load up with extra jerricans of petrol because the distance between petrol stations—even on quite long-established roads like the BR 364 between Rio Branco and Porto Velho—is too great to travel without a refill.

The scene along the roads depends on whether the colonization is continuous or not. Crossing north into the state of Amazonas from Rondonia, driving up the BR 319 from Porto Velho to Humaita, there was a sudden absence of neat little Incra dwellings as one crossed the state boundary. I stopped and talked to a family who lived by collecting *sorva*, a poorer quality natural rubber used in making bicycle tyres, when driving along this road. Their home was a traditional Amazon house on stilts, cooled at night by its openness to any breeze that was going. They had recently moved from the River Madeira to live by the road, and were an example of that spontaneous transfer which the authorities wish to see. They told me that they collected about 3,000 kilos of *sorva* in the season, for which they were paid three cruzeiros ($0·28) a kilo, and they found it much more satisfactory to sell to a lorry travelling along the road than it had been to trade with one of the boat merchants. In general, the boat merchants would charge double the price paid for goods in the cities whereas the lorry men charged them much less. The pre-highway style of life is perhaps most vivid on the northernmost section of the BR 319, where the road travels on built-up land between water and canoes, fishermen and houseboats go about their traditional business within sight of the road. A couple of times travelling the roads in 1976 I came across people who had shot fish in the water with arrows, using the old Amerindian technique.

Along the TransAmazonica itself one notes the cows, the rice and manioc crops, and the neat bags of rice awaiting collection by the roadside just like milk churns in an English country lane. At intervals there are Incra-built schools and, particularly along one central section of the TransAmazonica, Baptist chapels. (Roman Catholic churches do not yet appear outside the established towns.) It may be evangelical religion or merely the optimism of the colonists which has made some of them call their homes names like "New Canaan" or simply "Hope". Along the TransAmazonica too one may see horses and donkeys being ridden, and people walking beside the road carrying heavy burdens. Sometimes the burdened families will try to hitch a lift, but employees of federal agencies are not supposed to give lifts, and a high proportion of the cars and vans on some stretches still belong to DNER, Incra and the like.

A driver is still conscious of the nearness of the forest on most of the new highways. Even where the land has been cleared beside the road the trees are usually visible, often only a kilometre away. Sometimes the woods are right alongside the road, either because colonization has not yet begun or the way in which settlers are observing SUDAM's rule that only 50 per cent of forest cover can be removed on any forest property means that they are clearing backwards from their homes, rather than laterally along the roads. Along parts of the TransAmazonica, particularly between Itaituba and Altamira, trees already seem to have encroached on the cleared strip adjoining the carriageway so that it feels as if the road itself has narrowed. And the presence of the forest, sometimes the Somme-like silver dead trees in stagnant waters, but usually the luxuriant green of the tall trees, looking particularly impenetrable because of the dense secondary growth that has grown where the road builders cleared, means the presence of wildlife. Sometimes the wildlife is apparently ordinary—the occasional snake, and the endless urubu birds, the large black Amazon vultures, looking vaguely sinister and as big as chickens. But even the most ordinary creatures can be breathtakingly beautiful, as when clouds of yellow, blue, green and black butterflies wheel and turn beside the numerous pools and small streams. Periodically one sees a colonist walking along with a sporting gun, as a reminder that there is game to be had in the woods, although quite often colonists who are grateful for the meat will tell you sadly that their own neighbourhood is "hunted out".

At the same time the pace of change obviously accelerates near the towns. A notice outside Marabá, "Drive with care—pioneer road in the jungle" already has a dated look as what was forest has been turned over to crops and pasture. Nearer the towns too there seem to be more schools, more traffic, more people walking along by the roads. When one sees the forest line in the distance there it may be an illusion: settlement of some kind may continue for up to 20 kilometres down access roads so that what looks like the forest line may just be an uncleared patch between cultivated lots. The Incra administrative headquarters are sometimes established just outside towns, as at Marabá and Itaituba, and the DNER encampment outside Altamira is also a few kilometres away. These places—and the same is true of the Incra *agropolises*—look like the uneasy compromises they are: company townships dominated by one administrative activity, and just a little neater than any spontaneous town.

The sociable points along the roads are few and treasured: the cafés selling large meals relatively cheap because their proprietors have an elaborate barter trade with the lorry drivers; the occasional petrol station (one of them has grotesque polystyrene igloos nearby for overnight stops); and the ferry points where everybody tends to get out and talk because there is a bar on either side and even if the river is narrow you may have to wait for 20 minutes for the ferryman to come back if he's just left. The ferries are always called *balsas* (rafts) and, though all are run by DNER, many of them still justify their name, with the vehicles loaded on to a platform which is tugged and nosed from shore to shore by not very powerful motor boats. The most common cause of delay at a *balsa* is that either a lorry driver or the ferry pilot has miscued the landing so that a lorry gets stuck in the mud or partially falls in the water. Water, indeed, is inescapable in Amazonia, though the roads try to ignore it with little plank bridges and numerous galvanized metal culverts to let the streams through. Just sometimes one wonders whether the culverts are sufficient to let through all the water during the flood seasons, especially when you are driving on top of an earth embankment along the side of a hill.

But for the traveller along these highways, at least in mid 1976, there are two overwhelming impressions. The first is that to the naked eye everything seems peaceful and orderly. If there are any social tensions—and there are along the BR 364 if not along the BR 319 or TransAmazonica—they are rarely apparent. The second is that it is far from easy to assess the pace of economic change, and the substitution of forest land, along the strips beside the roads. This is the more true when one meets obvious oddities like a large expanse of natural savannah along the BR 319 near Humaita which is totally unoccupied by cattle—although one is assured that a Paraná group which has bought a sawmill in the town is just about to put a herd on it. Trusting to his eyes alone a visitor's judgement could oscillate wildly, seeing the major highways as the vanguard of a process which must inevitably clear the trees from most of Amazonia within, say, 40 years; or, on the contrary, being impressed rather by the sensation that these are narrow funnels through wide tracts of largely untouched forest, and that it is inconceivable that such a huge area could be transformed within the foreseeable future.

The roads now, even with their limited traffic, are playing a significant social rôle. There is, for example, a whole sub-culture of lorry drivers, quite different in outlook from the more leisurely but more grasping ways of the steamer captains, which has been unloosed on Amazonia as a result of the roads. A tough but modern breed, driving big lorries just within the weight limits permitted by DNER's highway police and the scales they operate outside each town, they carry with them the attitudes of the small entrepreneurs or labour aristocrats of the centre-south. They give lifts for money. They trade in meat and other foodstuffs. They patronize and support the cafés, and the motels and their prostitutes, along the roads or just outside the towns. They are the nomads who help to keep

the VD strains alive and threatening in Amazonia, and
whose support of brightly dressed, free-spending prostitutes
causes a ripple of envy and imitation among the teenage
girls. Some of the drivers take their girl friends with them
in their cabs, with children if necessary. The lorries provide
contacts and transport for scattered settlers in the absence of
regular or sufficiently cheap buses. In mid 1976, for instance,
although buses were travelling from Marabá to Itaituba
along the TransAmazonica, the authorities had only just
requested tenders for services from Humaita to Manaus on the
BR 319, a road which had been open for four years.

A quite different effect of the roads is to give the traditional
riverside occupants a choice: they can, as many officials want,
go inland along the road and farm; or they can stay put with
their fishing, their good crops on the flooded *varzea* lands, and
the old towns with which they are familiar. A few seem to be
moving—though if they find that they are not able to get
consistently good crops off unfertilized land they move back
again—but the majority seem to be staying put. As Judge
Hosannah Florencio de Menezes of Humaita puts it, "There is
a difference of mentality between the man of the river and the
man at the side of the road. There is a big resistance to the idea
of going inland." The result is that there is a partial separation
between the new and the old communities of Amazonia, which
relates not only to dependence on different transport systems,
but to different attitudes to the land and to making a living.
Although the original riverside people may benefit from better
shopping, school and health services based in the expanding
towns, in many other ways the roads-related economic development may simply pass them by. To quote Judge Hosannah
again, "The traditional population of Amazonia is not getting
any benefit from the wave of development except by moving to
the little cities."[31] This is a consequence of the colonialist
approach to the contemporary occupation of Amazonia: the
higher ground away from the rivers must be settled by outsiders from the north-east or centre-south and for their benefit,
and the best thing the riverdwellers can do is to move themselves and their way of life to join them. Their own society is
challenged almost as directly as the ecology of Indians, trees and
animals which used to exist on the higher ground where the
roads now run.

Ironically, but as some Amazonian experts and officials fully realize, the economy of these unfashionable riverside families may be much more viable in the long run than all but the richest and biggest operators along the roads—apart from the fact that they are almost no threat to the natural environment. They are using some of the best lands in the basin, which are regularly fertilized free. They have regular access to fish protein, whereas meat is unobtainable for many in the *agrovilas* and along the roads. Their rivers provide transport for anyone who can paddle a canoe, while the cost of buying and running an outboard motor is much less than it is for a road vehicle. The recent history of Manaus shows that the riverdwellers are not immune from the attractions of urban living, but where the choice is between the river banks and the sides of the roads it is rather more than mere conservatism that is keeping the majority where they are.

But if some of the most isolated riverdwellers risk becoming the forgotten lowest stratum in the new social structure of Amazonia one of the most striking results of the new roads is to plant a new middle class in the region. This is supplied largely by the salaried officials of the federal agencies—DNER, Incra, Funrural (the old-age pension for rural people), Operation Rondon (whose students also have an honorary middle-class status whilst they are in Amazonia), IBDF, SESP, army officers and so on. Such people share close ties of friendship—playing football and volleyball together, eating at the same few restaurants, competing to take out the same local girls, supporting Altamira's only genuine nightclub (they may also, like others, support the brothels), and gathering round the DNER engineer's pool. Their conversation is not always rarefied: I once spent an hour in such company at a restaurant in Altamira, listening to a hundred jokes told non-stop and watching demonstrations of safety matches converted into rockets. But the same people who may act in a childish and humorous way when relaxing have enormous power and may, as a DNER engineer or Incra official, be responsible for the employment or destinies of hundreds of people. They are usually graduates, male and unmarried (though one of the attractions of the Rondon students is that at least half tend to be female). They are usually in their early 20s to early 30s— but look older, because they are overworked and carry heavy responsibilities. They come from many parts of Brazil, are idealistic about what they are doing, and have been trained to use modern planning techniques. For the places they are living in they are relatively well paid—thanks to the bonuses paid to public officials along the TransAmazonica—and they like to escape at intervals for a holiday in a big city or the centre-south. Most are birds of passage, liable to be moved by their agency or, in the case of doctors or dentists, perhaps feeling that they should migrate to avoid professional stagnation. Promotion for them can be quicker than in the centre-south and their agencies tend to treat them generously on the grounds that they are living in a *fim do mundo* (at the end of the world).

Their nature and generally high capacity would be recognizable to any historian of the British colonial civil service: although they work for different bodies they are the leaders of a process of compulsory modernization, consciously exercising power and influence, even if the more democratic and easy-going tone of Amazon towns prevents them from appearing as a caste apart. Their significance, however, goes beyond just what they are doing in Amazonia and their rôle in spearheading a modern class system in the service towns, which is just as important as the social stratification which Incra and land sales are promoting in the countryside. They are also a paradigm of what the 1964 revolution has sought to create: a remodelled, more technocratic, better-educated and more enterprising Brazilian middle class, more aware of the realities of life in a vast country. There is a possible parallel here between Amazonia as Medici saw it for the north-eastern settlers—an officially sponsored escape route from poverty—and Amazonia for the young professionals—an officially sponsored proving ground for the agents and ideas of a more modern Brazil. In both cases needs which had been created in the more settled parts of the country were being displaced into the emptier north without, at least initially, putting at risk the *status quo* elsewhere. Development is made a substitute for reform. But although Amazonia can be a playground and inspiration for the younger and better educated, the TransAmazonica at least is sharply distinguished from most of the frontier zones in North or South America's past by the strong presence of government agencies.

This is underlined by the presence of the army. Each town along the TransAmazonica has its barracks for jungle infantry; in Altamira, for instance, this is a large, spacious and aesthetic set of buildings, which might well pass as the campus for some new university. Further west, in Acre and Rondonia, one is more aware of the presence of the BECs, the construction-engineering battalions diverted to Amazonia from Rio Grande do Sul and the north-east. The BECs build and maintain roads, sometimes using civilian labour to help, but they do other construction jobs besides. As Lt.-Col. Xavier Pinto of the fifth BEC in Porto Velho explains, his battalion has also provided Rondonia's capital with its water supply and electricity and a military hospital which is open to civilians because it is operational for 24 hours a day. (In return, it should be added, the battalion's barracks in Porto Velho was effectively paid for by the Ministry of Transport.)

Residents in Amazonia are quite aware of the military, even if at a time of supposed tension with Guyana there were not many troops to be seen in the border area of Roraima. From their TransAmazonica barracks, however, the jungle infantry march off for weeks at a time on exercises in the forest. They perform on ceremonial occasions—as when Governor Henock Reis of Amazonas paid a state visit to Humaita in June 1976, although the troops lined up for review withdrew at nightfall when he had failed to arrive in time to inspect them by daylight. They conduct periodic "blitzes" on the road itself, setting up machine guns beside the TransAmazonica and checking everyone's papers. Maps of the Cuiabá–Santarem road show a segment in the middle as being set aside for military purposes only and the fact that the TransAmazonica itself has been declared a national-security area—as is the band along Brazil's frontier with her Amazonian neighbours—is not an empty gesture. Not only are the *prefeitos* (mayors) in the Trans-Amazonica towns therefore appointed by the federal government rather than elected, but army authorities have some say in all kinds of activities in the district. At a strictly military level the army has removed whatever threat there was from the guerrillas near Marabá. When President Medici visited the TransAmazonica he did so in a heavily-armed helicopter and there were great security precautions. But by the middle of 1976 the army in Marabá was relatively unobtrusive. The real significance of the troops stationed along the TransAmazonica is that they provide a psychological support for law and order and the federal agencies. As Judge Hosannah of Humaita puts it, "The existence of the jungle infantry discourages the growth of land friction and title frauds." For the troops Amazonia is obviously important for the army's ethic of nation-building, but how do other people react to their presence? The officers form part of the professional fraternity described above, but there is some evidence that anti-army feeling—perhaps due to anti-government feeling as much as to hostility to the local conscripts—is a factor in the barracks towns. By mid 1976, for instance, army football teams were no longer willing to play other local teams in Humaita because the town crowds always supported their opponents.

If the roads are patently playing several social rôles, what is their economic importance now? It should be remembered of course that their advocates, like Eliseu Resende, always argued that they would need a decade or so to justify the investment in them. Nevertheless any analysis of the trends involved should start with the traffic that the roads currently bear. This does not always seem very much. On 28 May 1976, for instance, in 7½ hours' driving between Rio Branco and Porto Velho I met only 63 vehicles—thirteen cars, 46 lorries and four buses. In early June the BV 8, the international road from Boa Vista to Caracas which had been open for seven years, was averaging eight lorries and four private cars daily. This total, counted at the border, included movements in both directions: the main freight was Brazilian wood for export, a trade of some environmental significance as Venezuela has tighter rules on the extraction of timber than Brazil. Again, in the month of May 1976 the total traffic at the TransAmazonica ferry at Humaita averaged only fifteen vehicles a day—a total for the month of 258 lorries, 188 cars and thirteen buses. Obviously there are seasonal variations in these traffic levels but they underline the point that the mere existence of a road in a region like Amazonia does not automatically generate traffic, or anything like an equal utilization of different sections.

Long-distance traffic may be specially slow in coming. For in the same month that these low figures were reported on the TransAmazonica ferry at Humaita—a town conceived by transport planners as a major junction in western Amazonia because the TransAmazonica meets the BR 319 at right angles —the DNER at Altamira was reporting traffic levels which were twelve times higher between Altimira and Itaituba, and four times higher between Altamira and Marabá. The exact totals in both directions were 1,169 between Altamira and Marabá (as counted at the Altamira checkpoint) and 6,308 between Altamira and Itaituba. An important reason for the much greater flow on the Itaituba side of Altamira rather than on the Marabá side, which might have seemed surprising as the road link to the north-east and centre-south lay via Marabá, was that the Incra colonies west of Altamira were creating a lot of traffic. By Marabá itself the local traffic was getting heavier still. The May total of traffic passing the Marabá checkpoint was 12,995 vehicles on the Altamira road. DNER officials were speculating that their normal requirement for paving a road— a daily level of 500 vehicles—would be met on the Trans-Amazonica east of Marabá by about 1978. Significantly too, the Altamira sections of the TransAmazonica showed a traffic gain of nearly 40 per cent between May 1975 and May 1976— a rise in the number of vehicles passing through the town in those two months from 5,371 to 7,477.[32] To that extent therefore the hopes of Eliseu Resende, though they might seem rebuffed in some parts of the river basin, may well be justified along the TransAmazonica with time.

But what sort of traffic is this and how important is it economically? Obviously the answers will vary, but I obtained a full breakdown from DNER for traffic on the BR 319 between Porto Velho and Manaus, with figures obtained for April 1976, from vehicles crossing the Madeira ferry. Their interest lies in the big claims that DNER and the Ministry of Transport have made for the BR 319 as a valuable link for Manaus and the fact that the road had then been open for a few years with an all-weather asphalted surface for a few months. Yet in the whole of April the total in both directions was only 3,130 vehicles, of which 1,078 were lorries, 1,809 were cars and 243 were buses. Two-thirds of the private cars (1,245) were just travelling to or from Humaita, the one town between Porto Velho and Manaus. The pattern of lorry traffic was more varied. Out of the total of 1,078: 172 were from Manaus passing through Porto Velho bound for the centre-south—and 226 were doing the same in the opposite direction; 141 were travelling from Manaus to Porto Velho itself—and 154 were doing the reverse; 172 were going just from Porto Velho to Humaita—with 149 in the opposite direction; and a mere 34 lorries were coming to Porto Velho from the TransAmazonica—with 37 doing the reverse. These figures tend to suggest that, in pure transport terms, the BR 319 is unimportant as yet for either Manaus or Porto Velho. Porto Velho, where the governor of Rondonia told me that asphalting the BR 364 was a great deal more crucial for his territory than the construction of the BR 319 in the first place, was never expected to benefit rapidly from the link with Manaus. But for Manaus, where it had been trumpeted by transport officials as an escape from dependence on river and air transport, an average of only just over 23 lorries a day in both directions did not seem a major contribution to a city of half a million inhabitants.

This impression is confirmed by a closer look at the loads which were carried. Although half the loads from the centre and south for Manaus consisted of perishables, 60 per cent of the loads from Porto Velho were of bananas which would mostly be trans-shipped from Manaus: in other words it is hard to argue, in terms of the number of lorries involved, that the BR 319 is really rescuing the regional capital from its known problems of meat and food supply. Nor, though any additional outlet has a value, could it be said that this road is providing Manaus with a major export outlet for its growing industrial activity: half of its loads for Porto Velho were of fish, and a further 30 per cent of wooden goods, while for the centre-south 40 per cent of the lorries contained wooden products and another 20 per cent carried natural fibres like jute and *malva*. The one manufactured product from Manaus which was being taken south via Porto Velho was bicycles—at a rate of just over one lorry load per day.

The BR 319 figures are suggestive precisely because there is so little intermediate settlement between Porto Velho and Manaus. Although the TransAmazonica data indicate that the roads can justify themselves where they form part of a planned or spontaneous process of settlement (the Belem–Brasilia settlement which gave Resende his tactical arguments was largely spontaneous) the BR 319 underlines that, as long-distance trunk routes, such roads are much slower to gather importance.

They are, even in this perspective, able to make some contribution. Two examples I came across in Humaita show how entrepreneurs have exploited the BR 319. In the first case the most successful and cheapest supermarket in the town is run by a Japanese-Brazilian who also has a store in Porto Velho; the secret of his success—which unhappily does not include control of the dogs and other creatures running freely in his shop—is bulk purchase for stores in two towns and his lorry supplies up the BR 319 to Humaita. The second was more ambitious. Fernando Goncalves de Sousa, whom I met on his "mother ship" on the River Madeira, used to be a salesman for the Matarazzo combine in São Paulo. He then built this large boat, complete with a refrigerated hold, in his garden at São Paulo as well as a number of small canoes to be powered by outboard motors. Then he moved to Humaita which he uses as a centre for a completely road-based fishing enterprise— catching the delicious fish of Amazonia, like pacu and tucunaré, and then transporting them via Porto Velho and Cuiabá to the São Paulo market. He and his brother who helps him have periodic rows with the DNER which complains that their lorry is breaking the weight limits. But the basic costings are attractive to de Sousa. As he told me, the fish sell for four cruzeiros ($0·38) a kilo in Humaita, six cruzeiros ($0·55) a kilo in Porto Velho and 20 cruzeiros ($1·90) a kilo in São Paulo; the cost of transport to São Paulo works out at only two cruzeiros ($0·19) a kilo. These two instances also show how the roads can help to introduce an entrepreneurial and cash-economy approach to the basin—and that it is those who are in some sense outsiders who may be best placed to take advantage of them.

Although the Medici government pinned such hopes on roads it was developing them in a region already relatively well served by air and river traffic. Assuming that planes could carry small, high-value articles and wealthier people for whom time was expensive, and that the rivers could carry bulk, low-value goods and poorer persons for whom time was less important, the roads had to provide not only a new network of destinations but a kind of freight midway between the two other systems. In some respects the roads and rivers can complement each other naturally. During the rainy season, when the rivers are highest and most easily navigable, a dirt road is at its most doubtful:

similarly in the dry season, when the water is low and more rapids are exposed in a river, a dirt road is at its most useful. But in general the roads have to fight for their custom, partly because the existing distribution of towns in the valley follows the rivers. A senior employee in I.B. Sabba of Manaus—the river-based Shell oil distributor in the valley and a general trader—estimated that 90 per cent of goods were still going to and from the city by boat. Similarly the owner of a fleet of barges plying between Manaus and Belem, who served the centre-south via Belem and the Belem–Brasilia road, said that not only was the new asphalted BR 319 not providing any real competition, but that it would be years before that road established itself. Leaving the plans for settlement on one side, therefore, there is some risk that the new roads may merely duplicate each other and compete for the same traffic from Amazonia to the centre-south. When the Cuiabá–Santarem (BR 163) road is established as a carrier there will be three north–south links in parallel—the Belem–Brasilia, the BR 163 and the BR 319. Some people in the valley consider that the arrival of the much delayed BR 163 could have a devastating effect on the prospects of the BR 319 because the BR 163 will provide a more direct connection with the centre-south from the north and west of Amazonia. At the same time Santarem may challenge Manaus as a regional centre as it is nearer the mouth of the main river.

The high noon of road transport investment in Amazonia was registered in the integrated transport plan for the region (1971) which called for nearly twelve times the investment in roads between 1971 and 1985 (9,421 million cruzeiros, $1,777·5 million) than in ports, rivers and airports together. But the actual experience of the new roads in the region, the rise in petrol prices, and the recognition that roads were not going to be able to contribute in more than a subsidiary way to making projects like Trombetas bauxite or Carajas iron ore economically viable, had caused a sharp change by 1974 when the Geisel government came to power. SUDAM's financial programme for 1975–9 forecast that only one-sixth of SUDAM expenditure would go on transport and within that sector more would be spent on railways (3,125 million cruzeiros, or $385·8 million) than on roads (2,703 million cruzeiros or $333 million). The comeback by railways,[33] part of a national revaluation following the Yom Kippur war, is particularly ironic in Amazonia where a couple of lines had just been closed in the 1970s due to falling traffic—the Estrada de Ferro Tocantins, built in 1910 on the left bank of the river between Tucuruí and Jatobal, and the notorious Madeira–Mamoré line from the Bolivian border to Porto Velho. The Tocantins line, where one of the steam trains had once been attacked by Indians and arrived at its destination with arrows dug into its wooden carriages, had been replaced by a spur road from the Trans-Amazonica. The Madeira–Mamoré, whose closure required the approval of the Bolivian government under the Treaty of Petropolis, 1903, had seen its station and rolling stock consigned to museum status in Porto Velho although its old metal bridges were far too useful for a similar fate; at least five have been incorporated into the BR 364 between Abuna and Porto Velho.

Unofficially in the Ministry of Transport in Brasilia I was told that, after the long love affair with roads which culminated in the TransAmazonica programme and the new enthusiasm for railways which involves 85,000 million cruzeiros ($12,500 million) of investment and some 2,500 kilometres of new track between 1974 and 1979, it was almost inevitable that Brazil would turn once more to the potential of navigation by water. Amazonia could be a prime beneficiary of such a policy switch. It is, for example, technically feasible to join the Amazon and River Plate systems by canals to provide navigable links for barge traffic from Belem to Buenos Aires via central Brazil; as the economic growth of Mato Grosso and Goiás continues this might become attractive. More immediately a port-modernization programme for Manaus is long overdue. While cargo movements almost doubled between 1968 and 1972, and a glamorous new airport was opened in 1976 to handle the growing air freight, the ancient British-built port is still debouching lorries into the centre of down-town Manaus in an inefficient and congesting way. The DNER, to give credit to the planners of the TransAmazonica, always saw part of the benefit of the new road in terms of its linkage with the navigable rivers it crossed. But when I travelled along the TransAmazonica there was little evidence of a growth in the transfer function between road and river, nor really of any expansion of river traffic to the junction towns; the hopes for new ports on the Xingu and Tocantins seemed to have got delayed, while at

Itaituba there were no facilities as such—unloading was by
hand from moorings beside the town. As with other aspects of
the TransAmazonica it seemed as if the political will and the
available funds had not stretched as far beyond the building of
the road itself as the planners had initially hoped. It was the
same syndrome that had afflicted Incra's neat paper schemes
for *agrovilas, agropolises* and *ruropolises*. On the other hand a
combination of spontaneous growth in shipping, plus a switch
in policy in Brasilia or Amazonia, could in future cast a new
spotlight on river facilities as funds became available. The
Trombetas aluminium project, for instance, will require new
port services both there and at the projected site for the smelter,
Abaetetuba.

In any case, how good are the roads as roads? Sceptics at the
time the TransAmazonica programme was announced had
doubted whether it would be possible to maintain such an
expanded network in Amazonia against the threat of heavy
rain, flooding, heat and humidity. As a generalization, however, one can say that it is perfectly possible to sustain the
traffic-bearing capacity of the Amazon roads and that this is
being done although the maintenance costs can be heavy. I
travelled on three. The TransAmazonica itself had a good dirt
surface; but it was cut both in 1974 and 1975 only 20 kilometres
west of the ferry point at Humaita for a month or so each time
in the rainy season. A lake filled by the River Madeira during
the wet season came up and covered the road and, although I
was assured by DNER in Manaus that this would not recur,
there was no sign on the spot of embankment works which
would assuredly prevent it. (This interruption on the Trans-
Amazonica caused jokes throughout Brazil and was deeply
embarrassing to the highway authorities.) The BR 364, which
I travelled between Rio Branco and Porto Velho, is a dirt road
which was not in such good condition—rutted and broken up
in places, requiring a driver to pick his route carefully across
the carriageway. My original hope in mid 1976 had been to
drive along the BR 317 from Boca do Acre to Rio Branco but
this road, which had sometimes appeared as an extension of the
TransAmazonica in its early days, was frankly described by
DNER as "precarious"; one look down it at the point where it
joined the BR 364 east of Rio Branco suggested that it was too
rutted to be carrying much traffic at all. The BR 364 between

Porto Velho and Cuiabá has been troublesome to maintain in the past but Lt.-Col. Xavier Pinto of the fifth BEC told me in Porto Velho that it was now passable all the year round although, during nearly six months of the rainy season, the army imposed a weight restriction on lorries and gave priority to food and petrol cargoes. The BR 319, the recently asphalted road which I travelled all the way from Porto Velho to Manaus, was in good condition although repair works were already necessary on one stretch where the thinness of the tarmac cover was only too apparent. As a generalization too the condition of the wooden bridges, made out of the strongest and most durable timber, was good; however, in nearly all cases these are only of one vehicle width and lorries periodically collide with and damage them.

But what is the price of maintaining this network? The integrated transport plan for Amazonia in 1971 had estimated that the cost of maintenance between 1971 and 1985 would be nearly 20 per cent of the total investment in the region for that period; in practice the construction programme has been delayed and maintenance work, like road-building itself, has become more costly because of the rise in petrol prices. The DNER's second federal district, which is responsible for nearly all the TransAmazonica between Marabá and Humaita, has a fleet of 366 vehicles ranging from bulldozers to lorries to conserve that road. In 1976 I was authoritatively given a price of 12,000 cruzeiros ($1,143) per kilometre for the cost of maintaining the BR 319, and of 7,000 cruzeiros ($667) per kilometre for the TransAmazonica: if these figures were correct they would have made the annual maintenance cost between Porto Velho and Manaus 10·4 million cruzeiros (nearly $1 million), and of the TransAmazonica between Estreito and Humaita 16·25 million cruzeiros (over $1·5 million). However, these tariffs were surprising in that the cost of maintenance of dirt roads is normally higher than for tarmac roads—this is one of the main justifications for asphalting a road. Although it is possible that some of the cost of asphalting the BR 319 had been included in this price it is also possible that DNER was willing to allow Andrade Gutierrez, the contractor retained to maintain the BR 319, more generous cost limits than it was for its own teams along the TransAmazonica. (It was standard practice for DNER to get the contractors to maintain a new road for one or two years after they had completed it: the contractors on the whole did not like this function because it was neither technically interesting nor financially rewarding and could only too easily confront them with their mistakes.) Local engineers employed by DNER along the Trans-Amazonica were certainly being warned in 1976 that funds were scarce and that they would have to use all their ingenuity to make them stretch as far as possible.

The condition of the Amazon roads has been of continuing interest to their critics. In June 1974 the *Estado de São Paulo* had a tart editorial comment:

No one knows exactly how much the federal government has spent up to today to cut through the TransAmazonica and other roads of the same type, like for instance the Brasilia–Porto Velho, nor even is it known how many days per year these routes can be used. They deteriorate rapidly as a consequence of the torrential rains peculiar to Amazonia, or of the bad quality of the materials employed in their construction. The impracticability of these roads has reached such a point that, little by little, the old river navigation is being re-established which used to bring such advantages to the up-country settlements, but which was abandoned with the prospect of the opening of the road network.

By 1976 this seemed an unfair description of the state of the main federal roads—though not necessarily of the local access and state roads in Amazonia—but it was clear that there had been a maintenance crisis on the TransAmazonica in 1974–5. In 1975 the DNER quadrupled the number of employees concerned with maintaining the road to 1,200; bought new equipment worth 30 million cruzeiros ($3·7 million) and spent a further 30 million cruzeiros on conserving it; and made one of the construction firms, Rabelo, remodel the 394 kilometre section between Itaituba and Jacareacanga which had never been effectively open.

The relative simplicity of the Amazon roads allows for steady improvements as traffic grows and money becomes available: the dirt roads can be realigned and asphalted; the wooden bridges can be replaced with concrete ones; the rivers which have to be crossed by ferry can always be bridged. (It would, even now, be possible to bridge the Amazon itself at Manaus—though fabulously expensive.) But all this process of improvement can be frozen in a financial blizzard, even though it may disappoint public expectations. Perhaps the best example during the cutbacks of 1976 was the decision to allow the fifth BEC only sufficient money to asphalt 20 kilometres of the BR 364 between Porto Velho and Cuiabá. The official excuse was that these army engineers had never had to asphalt a road before. In practice it was obvious that the DNER did not have a sufficient budget to go ahead on a proper scale. But this incident underscores the fact that, even in transport terms, the PIN programme had had a distorting effect which outlasted the actual construction of the TransAmazonica and BR 319. On any economic calculation unaffected by the symbolism of the PIN programme the asphalting of the BR 364 deserved a higher priority than the asphalting of the BR 319.

But here even the critics of the roads in Amazonia can find themselves assisting their original targets: for the kind of scepticism expressed by the *Estado de São Paulo* in June 1974 justified spending more money on maintaining the prestige roads, at the expense of more worthwhile road projects. The plan to tarmac the 1,480 kilometres from Cuiabá to Porto Velho is a particularly relevant case because DNER and the state of Mato Grosso are taking the opportunity to completely change the line of the road: the new asphalted BR 364 will swing west out of Cuiabá to serve the active agricultural zone round Pontes e Lacerda along the line of the present BR 174, and abandon the more northerly existing BR 364 which was drawn on a map in the early 1960s but which has markedly failed to instigate economic development on its northern side. This stretch of the BR 364 has been treated as a boundary to agricultural growth rather than as a stimulus on either side, and the experience should caution one against assuming that roads in Amazonia must always promote economic growth, or that official policy will continue to support them where they fail to do so.

Meanwhile, how about the international aspect of the Amazon roads network? One objective of the Medici highways programme, duly explained at Panamerican transport conferences, was to provide Brazil with more links with her neighbours in Amazonia. But these depended not only on Brazil completing her own roads—and, as we have seen, both the Perimetral Norte and the roads in Acre and western Amazonas have been delayed—but on the other states spending the necessary money to build the connections on their side of the frontier. So far the progress in developing these international links has been slow and where they do exist, as with the BV 8 between Boa Vista and Caracas, the traffic growth has sometimes been disappointing. (It remains to be seen whether there is a rise in vehicles on this route when the BR 174 between Boa Vista and Manaus is finally used.) Although most of Brazil's neighbours are making some effort to develop their bits of Amazonia the linking roads are nearly always more important to Brazil than to them. Thanks to these roads Brazil will obtain access to the north-west coastline of South America, as well as to the markets of countries which will often be unable to compete with Brazilian products: the scoop-shaped boundary of Brazil in Amazonia will have acquired a new geo-economic value. However, what seems good for Brazil may seem bad for the surrounding states and a traditional suspicion of Brazil amongst them has been strengthened with the growing economic power of the military régimes since 1964. Hence there are political as well as resources reasons why the other states are not hastening to take roads to the Brazilian border. By the end of 1976 the picture of Brazil's overland connections was as follows: no link with Surinam; a road to the frontier with Guyana (BR 401) which, because of the hostility with Forbes Burnham's socialist republic, is unlikely to be continued in the foreseeable future; a link with Venezuela which exists but carries little traffic; no link at all with Colombia because the Perimetral Norte hit quicksands west of São Gabriel de Cachoeira; a link with the Peruvian border at Assis Brasil in Acre which is frustrated because 180 kilometres on the Peruvian side has not been built; and several links with the Bolivian system in Rondonia and Mato Grosso of which Guajara-Mirim and Corumba are perhaps the most important. The most harmful of these delays to Brazil is the absence of a good road between Acre and Peru. When the link from Assis Brasil is completed it will mean that a lorry from there need take only two days to reach the Pacific port of Callao. This would not only produce a new export route to Pacific destinations like Japan for goods from the centre-south: it could also open a new market for the beef, rice and tin of Acre and Rondonia, and give Rio Branco a wholly new importance as an entrepôt centre rather than a town on the periphery. The most economically valuable road for Acre is the one that is not being built on the Peruvian side of the frontier.

One of the main fears officially admitted when the Trans-Amazonica programme began was that it could endanger the health of those involved. Brazil's good scientific record in the identification of tropical diseases, the ghastly experience of building the Madeira–Mamoré railway, and the precedent of the SESP health service established during the rubber-collection campaign in the Second World War all encouraged an approach of vaccinations, vigilance and research. Rocha Lagoa, the Minister of Health in 1970, said that he was putting in hand studies to avoid "a repetition of Madeira–Mamoré". This was in marked contrast to the official attitude to soil and agricultural surveys or to the economic and social effects of the roads where the government acted first and only belatedly evaluated what was happening.

As might have been expected, therefore, the health situation generally along the TransAmazonica is now quite creditable. In important respects it is probably better than the average for Amazonia and setting standards for the rest of the region. Although there are still considerable problems—most children still suffer from worms, for instance—there is less malnutrition than in the north-east and malaria is under control. Fortunately for Brazil the anopheline mosquito species which carry malaria in that country are ones which have not yet developed resistance to DDT. Throughout Amazonia SUCAM, the special agency charged with controlling the disease, carries out a regular spraying programme, marking the houses as it goes. Along the TransAmazonica, in spite of the initial chaos in the colonization programme, this process has steadily become more effective. A team based on the Instituto Evandro Chagas in Belem and led by Dr Francisco Pinheiro, which took a large number of samples from people along the TransAmazonica between 1971 and 1974, found that the percentage of positive slides rose from 12·25 per cent in 1971 to a peak of 15·35 per cent in 1973 and then dropped slightly to 14·3 per cent in 1974. Although the incidence of malaria is usually worse during the dry season and varies somewhat from year to year there are grounds for believing that the tide turned in 1973. Dr José Rocha Conceição in Marabá, for example, told me that the rate had been steadily dropping since 1973 while Dr Kenneth Dixon of the Walter Reed Army Institute of Research involved in a collaborative programme with Evandro Chagas told me that in the first half of 1976 there had not been a "good outbreak" of malaria anywhere along the TransAmazonica.[34]

What were the main disease worries when the PIN programme was launched, apart from worms and malaria? Among those which evoked concern were leishmaniasis, which causes mutilating skin ulcers; schistosomiasis (bilharzia), a sometimes fatal disease which is carried by water snails; Chagas disease which hits the heart cells and is carried by a bug in household belongings and the leaves, mud and thatch of dwellings; more familiar diseases ranging from TB and VD to whooping cough and tetanus; and more unusual or localized diseases, such as the black fever of Labrea, whose appearance could not be forecast but which might arise forcefully when settlers without the local immunities were rapidly introduced into new areas. Leishmaniasis, carried by sandflies and a particular threat during any timber felling phase in Amazonia, is, in the view of Dr Heitor Dourado, head of the Hospital for Tropical Diseases, Manaus, on the increase throughout the region. The Wellcome Parasitology Unit's skin-test surveys suggest that at least 50 per cent of the adult, rural population in the region eventually acquire the infection. However, along the TransAmazonica, now that the initial burst of settlement and clearing is over, it may well be that its rate of growth diminishes. Schistosomiasis is currently found in only a few places in Amazonia—in Fordlandia, Belem and eastern Pará; between 1971 and 1974 Dr Pinheiro's team diagnosed 310 imported cases in Altamira and Marabá, all of which were treated with hycanthone, and there has been no sign of the disease spreading.

Chagas disease, which is estimated to affect some four million Brazilians altogether, seems to have made no advances along the TransAmazonica as yet although it is common in one area that produced settlers for the Incra colonies, the interior of the state of Bahia. Given the ease with which the relevant bug can hide in clothes or belongings, and the decade that may pass before the incubating disease actually damages someone's heart muscles, it would be premature to say that the Trans-Amazonica has escaped entirely. Preventative vaccinations have had an undoubted success in controlling yellow fever: although in parts of Amazonia as many as 45 per cent of monkeys have yellow fever antibodies and it is quite impossible to break the yellow-fever cycle in the forest Dr Pinheiro's team did not observe a single case among TransAmazonica colonists up to the end of 1974.

In some respects the more universal diseases, like TB, VD or whooping cough were more of a threat along the Trans-Amazonica. VD, although it was obviously at its height during the road-building phase, was still causing some health concern as late as 1974. Whooping cough was a killer during the initial period of settlement although by mid 1976 Dr José Rocha Conceição could tell me that, along with tetanus and diph-theria, it was almost completely extirpated from urban Marabá. TB, on the other hand, was still producing plenty of hospital cases there, although a programme of infant inoculation was under way.

If the fears of a mass transfer of diseases along the Trans-Amazonica have not been realized—and they had always left out of account the normality of large-scale migration within Brazil and other movements within Amazonia—neither too have numerous new tropical scourges emerged from the jungle. The one known local disease, the black fever of Labrea which can be fatal to children, is believed not to be exportable by Dr Heitor Dourado: he told me that it is bound up with a type of vegetable matter which only grows in the vicinity of the town. In fact, because the extension of the TransAmazonica westward from Humaita to Labrea has been so delayed the risk of this disease spreading has hardly been tested yet. The one new disease to have been diagnosed among Trans-Amazonica colonists, though it probably existed in the neigh-bourhood of Altamira before, was discovered by Dr Pinheiro's team and reported in *The Lancet* in 1974. Christened the Haemorrhagic Syndrome of Altamira (HSA) this involves skin bleeding and is transferred by the bites of black-flies: 163 cases were noted between 1972 and 1974, of which three resulted in death, and as nearly all the sufferers were settlers it is assumed that this is a disease against which older inhabitants have built up an immunity.

But a bald account of the disease situation along the Trans-Amazonica does not fully bring out the superiority in health of colonists there when compared either with the north-east from which the bulk of early arrivals came, or with the average for Amazonia. While health services down the access roads to the more remote *agrovilas* could be extremely irregular for the colonists their dietary intake was generally better than it had been in the north-east. Similarly the weight of government effort along the TransAmazonica, involving several agencies in the health and prevention field, meant that the communities there were almost certainly better treated than parts of Rondonia or Manaus. (In Manaus, for example, there was an increase in TB cases between 1974 and 1975 in spite of an immunization campaign, and the authorities decided that from 1977 fathers who do not present health cards proving family vaccinations against polio, diphtheria, tetanus and whooping cough will not get their family allowances; in Rondonia, Dr Jacob, the health secretary, told me in 1976 that cases of leishmaniasis and malaria were increasing and that the territory was losing the battle against serious disease.)

Along the TransAmazonica—and traditional inhabitants within its influence benefited with the new settlers—the federal government had made a health commitment which tended to be strengthened as deficiencies were brought to light. After making a visit in August 1972, during which he came across 40 north-easterners with schistosomiasis, Machado de Lemos, then Minister of Health, ordered stricter health controls on potential colonists. They would have to be checked in their place of origin and given a health card; this would then be inspected by Incra before they could receive a plot beside the highway. This did not stop an elderly doctor from Rio Grande do Sul resigning as head of Incra's medical services in Altamira only six months later: he did so in protest at SESP's lack of equipment and medicines, the amount of bureaucracy, and the fact that colonists were being asked to pay money for treatment which they did not possess. It would be wrong to imagine that health services were marvellous along the TransAmazonica. One estimate I was given in mid 1976 was that there were 23 doctors in Marabá, but only four in Itaituba. The immunization programmes, in which the Project Rondon also took part, did not reach all the settlers and *caboclos* within range of

the highway and it was hard to persuade someone who felt fit
to spend the time and money necessary on a trip of perhaps
300 kilometres for an injection. Nevertheless both hospital and
other medical services along the TransAmazonica seem to be
better than in most of the region. The explanation for what so
far must be regarded as a success story lies in the fact that the
government recognized potential health hazards from the start
and that tackling them in no way conflicted with the essential
political commitment to the highway programme. It was
significant of the favoured and controlled status of the Trans-
Amazonica settlements that Incra was able to impose health
requirements among intending colonists in a way which the
territory of Rondonia, for example, could not among its
incoming migrants. It is doubtful whether the health operation
along the TransAmazonica was bought at the expense of
improving standards elsewhere in Amazonia. What it did
underline, however, was that it was perfectly possible to
achieve more in states with some of the poorest health in
Brazil when public authorities had a strong political incentive.

No one who visits the towns along the TransAmazonica will
fail to be informed of the great change that has come over them
since it was built. As a barman in Marabá put it to me, "In
1968 this town only had three cars—and all of them were old."
The figures for population growth are remarkable, even in
Brazil. Numbers in Humaita rose from about 1,400 in 1970 to
about 8,000 in 1976; in Itaituba they went up from just over
2,100 in 1973 to about 12,000 in 1976; in Altamira they jumped
from about 2,800 in 1970 to some 18,500 in 1976. The municipality of which Altamira is the centre had seen the number of
schools providing any secondary-level teaching go up from one
to five between 1970 and 1975, while registered commercial
establishments of all sorts had multiplied from 68 to 415.

But figures of this sort can only give a partial account of the
transformation that has occurred. New building in places like
Humaita and Marabá has changed the whole axis and shopping
patterns of towns—in Marabá this was true even before the
New Marabá project got under way. Individuals, like the
Italian nicknamed Jimmy in Altamira who runs a sawmill,
have greatly enriched themselves. Judge Hosannah Florencio
de Menezes of Humaita quoted a second hospital, better
secondary schooling, electricity 24 hours a day and a new

football stadium as among the benefits for his town. More candidates wanted to run for elective office. But the same judge also felt that the rapid increase in population had thrown up several problems—especially the lack of recreations for teen-agers among whom crime had increased. The short-lived boom in prostitution during the building of the Trans-Amazonica—the number of brothels in Humaita had risen from one to four, but by 1976 had fallen to one again—had left a continuing sense of disturbance among teenage girls who had glimpsed a quick way to make money. On the other hand the "modernizing" impulse behind the TransAmazonica, and the arrival of better-educated people in these towns from elsewhere in Brazil, has also had a positive effect. Young people, and those in their 20s who take courses at night school, display a hunger for learning that is more typical of the centre-south than of small towns in Amazonia or the north-east. More effort seems to be put into the administration of the TransAmazonica towns than is usual; the *prefeito* of Altamira, a man with a go-ahead reputation, was selected to go on a management course in West Germany in 1976 in competition with public officials throughout Brazil.

But shop prices are still relatively high in the Trans-Amazonica towns because of freight costs, the fact that the buying power of the farmers is concentrated in the months of July to December, and because inefficient traders with small stocks rely on a high mark-up to survive. Much of the money earned by people working in the region is still being remitted to families elsewhere and lucrative activities which one might expect in the towns have not yet developed. Itaituba, whose goldfields a few hours' flight away have diverted a number of potential settlers into the hazardous life of a gold panner, exports around 500,000 grams a month to São Paulo. But there is only one goldsmith in the town itself. In Altamira, in spite of the traffic build-up, a lawyer working for Funrural told me that it was impossible to find a garage that could maintain his particular make of car. Senhor Khaled, a Lebanese who opened a dress shop in Altamira in 1970 when it was important to keep the store open on Sundays because that was the day that the road-builders had off, gave me a frank analysis of the commercial scene in his line of business. "The shopkeepers who come here are adventurers. Many of them are refugees from

places in Ceará and the north-east which have more competition. Some settle here. Others move on. The businessmen who
were here before the TransAmazonica complained at the arrival
of the others but the truth is that they were complacent and
gave little attention to their customers. Two things are necessary
before the retail trade really develops here: better incomes for
the agricultural settlers and a bigger population for the town.
It is difficult for shops selling household electrical goods, like
refrigerators, to persuade people to buy on hire purchase."

Entertainment of all sorts is limited. Itaituba—whose
cinema was showing *Tarzan King of the Jungle* when I was there
(Tarzan films are popular in Amazonia)—is not well equipped
with restaurants. Altamira, which has a discotheque, was still
beyond the reach of TV transmitters in 1976. The celebrated
hotel at the Ruropolis President Medici—criticized by journalists for irrelevant luxury during the construction of the road—
was completely shut up, with its swimming pool empty, when
I looked at it on 17 June 1976. Limitations like these, plus the
existence of the TransAmazonica as a perennially beckoning
route for escape, give rise to feelings of dependence and aspira-
tion which are not dissimilar from those felt in the colonies in
the days of the British empire. Middle-class people along the
TransAmazonica revel in their ability to make occasional visits
to Belem or Manaus; secretaries yearn for bigger towns with
more activity. It may have been chance, but I was more aware
of these undercurrents in Altamira and Marabá at the east of
the TransAmazonica than in the more isolated towns of
Humaita and Itaituba to the west. Although the much-
expanded towns are standard bearers in a nationally-publicized
process of pioneering, the attitudes of at least some of their
citizens betray a lack of confidence in such a mission.

Finally no consideration of the Amazon highways now would
be complete without commenting on two other questions:
whether their use in general has become much more expensive
as a result of rising petrol prices; and whether the Trans-
Amazonica in particular is still providing a refuge for north-
easterners in times of drought. Firstly, it is plain enough that
everything to do with the roads—their construction and maintenance has become more costly since 1973, and that Brazilian
policy is now seeking alternatives to road transport and a
development approach to Amazonia which is less fixed on road

communications. But as far as the roads which now exist in
Amazonia are concerned it is hard to tell whether traffic
growth would have been very much faster if oil prices had not
gone up so steeply. There is nothing to suggest that traffic
growth in Amazonia has been much different from Brazil's as
a whole. Although water-borne transport has become relatively
cheaper, shipping, like planes is still oil-dependent, if to
differing extents from road transport. In my own inquiries I
did not come across specific cases of potentially road-borne
freight being kept off the roads because of cost increases:
nevertheless one would expect the growth of long-distance hauls
to be reined in where there is an alternative source of supply
by river, and for the economic justification of Amazon roads
to turn increasingly on the development of their hinterland
rather than on long-distance links. But the reason why it is
impossible to be more certain of what is happening is because
no detailed socio-economic analysis of traffic along the PIN
roads has yet been done. Trafecon, a private consultancy firm
contracted by DNER's institute for roads research (IPR), has
produced reports on the socio-economic impact of the Belem–
Brasilia road and in mid 1976 was hoping to be commissioned
to do a similar study of the TransAmazonica. It is extraordinary that such work was never put in hand by the Medici
government when PIN was launched. One may speculate,
however, that one result of the adverse pricing change for road
transport will be to freeze a sharp economic distinction between
the more developed eastern end of the TransAmazonica, from
Altamira to Marabá, and the thinly populated western end
from Itaituba to Humaita.

This lack of any reliable monitoring, which might well not
have confirmed the assumptions of the authors of the PIN
programme, also makes it hard to give a definite answer to the
second question. However, I myself was travelling eastwards
along the TransAmazonica at a time in 1976 when over 100,000
men were working on labour fronts in the north-east and the
drought there was sufficiently serious to set President Geisel on
a tour of inspection which reminded journalists of President
Medici's in 1970. (He did not, incidentally, announce any
dramatic relief measures.) I did not see large numbers of north-
easterners heading westwards in the way that the theory behind
the PIN programme might have led one to expect. Although

there is no doubt that the Tucuruí dam project and the new city at Marabá were attracting north-easterners I am sceptical as to whether the TransAmazonica is, compared with other possible escape routes, a significant relief system as yet in a drought emergency. If the various industrial projects between Serra dos Carajas and Belem materialize in the 1980s then the TransAmazonica might begin to perform in this way. In the meantime it is not doing much to stop the sort of tragic exploitation reported from Piauí by *Veja* on 26 May 1976. "Thousands of persons are leaving the south-east of the state and are coming to pay up to 40 cruzeiros ($3·80) to lorry owners to take them anywhere, since even the water for individual consumption is running out. And in Bocaina, 370 kilometres from Teresina, the exodus in recent days reached its most dramatic point: 30 men were sold for 200 cruzeiros ($19) each to landowners from Goiás." Reading of incidents like this it is hard not to conclude that the TransAmazonica, with all the expenditure and risks it has entailed, was sold to Brazil on a misleading prospectus.

7

THE ENVIRONMENT—
EFFECTS AND ARGUMENTS

THE EXPERIENCE OF the scientific nucleus at Aripuanã in northern Mato Grosso, formerly known as Humboldt in honour of the German scientist, Alexander von Humboldt, is a parable of environmental intentions which misfired. It was launched grandiosely as a "science city" as a direct response to the UN Environment Conference in Stockholm of 1972, and also as some answer to the murmurings of all those who were worried about the ecological risks of the new push into Amazonia. In July 1972, a month after Stockholm, preparatory work on Humboldt began. It was inaugurated on 13 September 1973. A Dutch architect, Johann van Lengenn, won a competition to lay out the city and designed a network of simple wooden dwellings on stilts, prefabricated in São Paulo and flown to the site. Yet when I visited it at the end of May 1976, there was only one scientist to be seen—Carlos Roberto Bueno, a young agronomist, who is in permanent charge of what is now just a field station for INPA in Manaus. What is Aripuanã/Humboldt like now, and what went wrong with the environmental project?

When I visited the site, in company with a Japanese-Brazilian electricity engineer who had come to maintain the generator, Aripuanã was not yet linked by road with the rest of Mato Grosso and the mayor, who was doing all he could to stimulate development of his huge municipality, was working from an office in Cuiabá, the state capital. On the way in from the airstrip at Aripuanã there was an ironic sign stuck to a tree, "Welcome to the Dardanelles, 1917". The wooden housing capable of taking 100 researchers in nine blocks, was exactly as described in a 1975 pamphlet of the Brazilian Embassy in London which had also set out a most ambitious research programme. The well-built scientists' housing, empty apart from Bueno himself, was in sharp contrast to the poor

G

Amazonian huts of employees of the enterprise, or early Aripuanã settlers, which were separated by a barbed-wire fence from the science compound. The compound itself was only a few metres from a beautiful, 130-metres high waterfall on the River Aripuanã which, if the district is able to develop its tourist potential in future, could well become one attraction. Spindrift spray from the falls periodically blows across the science compound. The name Humboldt is no longer used for the science project on the orders of Dr Warwick Kerr of INPA: it will in future be used for one of the streets in the new city of Aripuanã. It was dropped partly because Kerr is a nationalist, and partly because he wanted to make a clean break. Forest clearing is proceeding in a gingerly fashion on the INPA estate as Dr Kerr is extremely hostile to unnecessary felling.

But although this is not the large, permanent jungle campus originally proposed in the development plan for Humboldt, Dr Bueno explained that a number of botanical and other experiments are taking place. He himself has an interest in the poor germination of the Brazil nut tree, whose protein-rich products are one of the most valuable resources collected in the forest; he is also trying to cross a sweet-tasting papaya tree which grows tall with a more ordinary variety whose fruits can be picked from the ground. The field station, which is visited by parties of a dozen scientists at a time for periods of a fortnight, is also growing ten different varieties of manioc, and sugar, sorghum, coffee and maize. The station is experimenting with animal husbandry—rabbits, chickens and pigs. The arrival of eighteen cows in Buffalo aircraft shortly after my departure was apparently the social occasion of the year: all 620 surrounding inhabitants, apart from three who were ill, turned out to welcome the arrival of a fresh milk supply for the settlement, and the aircraft had to make several dummy approaches before it could clear the airstrip of people and land. Soil samples are being sent to an institute at São Paulo, with whom INPA has an agreement; wood samples are being analysed in INPA's own facilities at Manaus.

But what had gone wrong with the original scheme? This had been under the management of the Federal University of Mato Grosso and the research objectives set out in the government's development plan were extraordinarily diverse. They ranged from architectural and engineering experiment in the construction of cities in the tropics to "ichthyological engineering"—the improvement of the ornamental fish industry; from research into links between eating habits and environmental diseases to the construction of self-propelled river barges; from behavioural studies into the possibility of night work to avoid the heat of the day to the design of a light electric railway to be used in areas subject to flooding in the rainy season. All of this had been abandoned by the time I visited the place: half of the studies listed by the embassy in London as "research under way" had left no trace, while the agricultural and botanical work was proceeding in the more modest way appropriate to a field station. For some Brazilian scientists the original scheme had always been too grandiose to justify—the cost of building adequate library and laboratory facilities in the middle of the forest could only be high and at the expense of establishments elsewhere. João Carlos Meirelles, president of the Association of Amazonian Entrepreneurs who had agricultural interests elsewhere in the Aripuanã region, dismissed the project as "science fiction". But although its plan acknowledged that it was a response to the UN Environment Conference and would mark "the beginning of measures to protect the environment from man" the bias was towards an applied science centre for the more profitable exploitation of Amazonia. Its research intentions lay within the Medici government's policy for the region and did not overtly examine whether certain processes —such as the tree-felling, or the attempt to convert forest land to pasture or crops—might be harmful for the environment and self-defeating for the humans engaged on it. It was not going to check on the fear that forest destruction could affect the oxygen cycle, nor on the efficacy of the law enforced by SUDAM and the IBDF that 50 per cent of all properties should be maintained with their forest cover.

According to Dr Kerr, the main reason why the initial Humboldt failed was due to bad management of scientists. An engineer had been put in to run it and, while he was efficient at getting the housing built, he had poor judgement in choosing research projects and in handling scientists. In spite of the splendid array in the development plan the experiments were slow to get going and the scientists began to quarrel with the administrators; then the scientists started to leave. By 1974-5 the crisis came to a head and management was transferred from Mato Grosso University to INPA: according to one scientist elsewhere eight million cruzeiros (nearly $1 million) were lopped off the budgets of other establishments in 1975 to rescue the Aripuanã outpost. Dr Kerr does not rule out the possibility that in future, when the town of Aripuanã itself has developed some infrastructure, it may be possible to reinstate the concept of the science city. But this is unlikely to be for some years yet. In the meantime Aripuanã/Humboldt offers a further example of the international-national dialectic referred to in chapter 1, with the concerns expressed at Stockholm and elsewhere somewhat transposed to serve the interests of the Medici government; of the existence of some environmental consciousness and responsibility in Brazil; of the "symbology" of the TransAmazonica-related advance into Amazonia—for Humboldt in its way was just as sensational and propagandist as the highways; and of the wide distance which can separate paper plans in Amazonia from actuality.

Yet precisely what were and are the fears of scientists and naturalists which have been raised by the TransAmazonica programme? In the abstract, of course, when most of the world's population lives in a man-made environment, and much of that continues in a sustainable equilibrium, why should anyone be particularly alarmed if man attempts to alter the inherited balance of nature in another corner of the planet? For Europeans and North Americans in particular, whose fields and towns often look so established that it is easy to forget that they once replaced forests, marshes and natural grassland, usually without ill effect, ought not the very success of their modern land-use encourage other countries to make similar changes?

Behind the controversy over changes in the use of land in Amazonia, on which a tropical forest has flourished for millennia, it is important to realize that a radical change in world sensibility is working itself out. A new scientific realization of the inter-relatedness of man, habitat and natural species, supported by the modern world-communications system, is struggling to alter the old view that man can transform the natural situation without risk to himself, and should if it offers any chance of bettering his condition. The ecological approach is challenging not just individuals' ancestral desire for material self-improvement—a main drive of the human race—but is also wanting all modern states, with their plans for economic development, to reconsider and redirect their aims and methods. The fact that the main impetus for this revolution in world thought is coming from the richer countries, whose sophisticated educational and planning processes have been erected on the basis of a definitive human occupation of long ago, is an unfortunate coincidence. People in poorer countries, even where instinctively or intellectually they can see the force of this argument, are understandably unwilling to buy the idea of conservation at the price of continuing in poverty. Just as the idea of preserving the countryside in western industrial countries has only made progress with the support of towns-people, so in third-world countries the ecological approach can look like neo-imperialism if it is merely seen as the latest propaganda from the rich states, but it can also become one of prudent self-interest if adopted by their own emerging urban majorities with regard to their territory as a whole.

Amazonia in all this is a focus area. On the world scale the tropical forests, which were difficult to penetrate and affect before our contemporary technological civilization had developed, have been depleted at an increasing rate since the Second World War. This is true in Malaysia, Indonesia and south-east Asia; in Zaire and Africa; and in forested parts of central America and non-Brazilian Amazonia as well as in Brazilian Amazonia. The rate is such that Robert Allen argued in the *New Scientist* (24 April 1975) that "if current attitudes and practices persist, all the world's tropical rain forest, apart from a few scientific mementoes, will be destroyed within 20 to 30 years". For Brazil itself the social context is finely balanced. On the one hand it now has an urban majority and falling population growth rate and, in spite of its unequal wealth distribution, perhaps 10 per cent of its people—more than the population of Sweden—enjoys a European standard of living. On the other, its pattern of human occupation is still as thin and scattered relatively as England's was in Anglo-Saxon times and, in so far as it is necessary to draw on all the country's resources in order to bring the standard of living of the whole population up to a European level, there is pressure to exploit Amazonia rather than to conserve at all costs.

Most of the environmental fears for Amazonia relate to the

destruction of the forest, although pollution in the rivers and loss of fish and other river-based species such as turtles and crocodiles also give rise to some concern. The worries about the tree-felling, and the attempts to replace jungle by agriculture, pasture or even more uniform artificial tree plantations of the Jari type, have been touched on earlier. To summarize, however, the main ones are as follows: that tropical forest plays a major rôle in converting carbon dioxide into oxygen because photosynthesis continues all the year round, and that felling in Amazonia therefore increases the danger of atmospheric pollution; that felling on the present scale affects the water cycle and degrades the generally poor Amazon soils—speeding the run-off rate and therefore increasing the flood risk, leaching away what humus and nutrients there are in the soil and thereby creating "deserts", and eventually reducing rainfall in the region because the forest is more effective in generating rainfall; that whereas a forest which is cut in a rational manner is self-renewing the attempt to replace it by crops or pasture is not only fruitless within around three years unless fertilizer is applied on a massive scale, but it leaves the soil in a permanently damaged state which cannot easily be restored either for trees or agriculture; that the Amazon forest is one of such complexity and diversity, with many plant and animal species distributed on such a local basis, that any major felling programme is bound to result in the loss of some species for all time, and that some of those would be of scientific or commercial interest if they were known about. The related worry over the survival of the Amerindians, which is threatened because of the transformation of their forest environment, deserves special consideration in the next chapter. But, taking these environmental anxieties together, how justified are they? How much damage has been done already and what sort of momentum or graph of future forest-felling seems likely? What controls exist to safeguard the resources of Amazonia and how effective are they?

In all these areas it is important to recognize that there is still considerable ignorance—ignorance of the theoretical effects at a scientific level, ignorance of the likely effects among those practically responsible for altering parts of Amazonia, and ignorance still of the contents and nature of the forest mass which they are tampering with. That said, it is possible to give some current estimate of the reality of the main fears which have been expressed. The first, which was given popular currency in the special issue of *Realidade* (October 1971) suggested that "Amazonia must be responsible for 50 per cent of the oxygen produced on the earth" as a result of its biological action. However, this claim appears to have been based on misunderstanding of work by a West German scientist, Harald Sioli, and Goodland and Irwin, strong critics of the present push into Amazonia, commented, "Amazonia may well contribute 50 per cent of the world's oxygen production, but this annual production is minuscule when compared to the total amount of oxygen in the atmosphere." Nevertheless Goodland and Irwin do accept that extensive burning of the forest, plus the reduction of its magnitude, could contribute to an increase in gaseous carbon in the atmosphere and there are still good scientists who believe that there may be something in the oxygen issue. While alarmism therefore is uncalled-for, there are still questions that can only be answered by fundamental scientific research.

The second fear, regarding the water cycle and soils, can already receive a more definite response. The leaf and root systems of the forest retain substantial quantities of water themselves, slowing the run-off rate and protecting the soils from the heavy and continuous tropical downpours. Indeed the biomass of the forest itself provides a closed ecological system in which the nutrients never move far, but circulate between the tops of the trees and their often shallow roots: this is the secret which can create an apparently luxuriant forest on poor soils. But once clear, the trees and leaching and erosion proceed at a formidable rate. Figures from Adiopodoume in the Ivory Coast in 1956 (quoted by the Brazilian ecologist Antonio da Rocha Penteado in the *Revista Brasileira de Cultura* number 16, 1973) leave no doubt of what happens. Between 15 May and 17 July 1,434·5 millimetres of rain fell on an experimental area: this removed 78,017 kilos of topsoil per hectare from bare soil on a gradient of 7–8 per cent, but only 1,947 kilos from soil which was covered by forest on a steeper gradient of 12–15 per cent. An area which was cultivated but where the plants had just been put in lost 46,851 kilos per hectare. However, in the second half of the year, from 28 September to 20 January 1957, when only 665 millimetres fell the bare soil lost 50,094 kilos per hectare, the steeper forested area lost 464 kilos, and the cultivated land—where the plants were by now fully grown—lost only 351. The ecological department of INPA has produced comparable figures from parts of Amazonia, which also stress the much faster run-off rate of water from pasture land, as well as the higher rate of erosion: Dr Warwick Kerr in 1976 blamed tree-felling to make new pasture in upper Amazonia for the excessive flooding at Manaus and elsewhere. Professor L. C. B. Molion of Brazil's space research institute (Instituto de Pesquisas Espaçiais) also believes that widespread forest clearing may affect the climate as well as the water circulation on the ground—reducing rainfall in Amazonia and thereby altering the climatic balance further afield also. As Kerr put it to me, "If the rainfall doesn't come to Amazonia, it must go somewhere else."[35] There is also a detectable rise in temperature where the trees have been cut: INPA has found that even in urban areas the presence of trees between houses can reduce the maximum temperature by as much as 4 degrees centigrade. These consequences are not in doubt, although there is room for argument about the amount of clearing in particular localities or in Amazonia as a whole which would have the adverse effects described. It also seems likely that where the crops being grown instead of the forest approximate to tree crops— such as bananas, cocoa and natural rubber—many of these objections could be met.

How about the fear of reducing soil fertility and making "deserts"? Here too the evidence that short-cycle crops— such as rice, manioc and beans—can impoverish the poor soils seems overwhelming, although there is little likelihood that Amazonia could ever be turned into a dust bowl. Experience of numerous agricultural attempts in the region prior to 1970—of which the colonization of Bragantina was only one— had underlined the high risk of a loss of soil fertility after two or three years. This was why IBGE, the Brazilian geographical and statistical institute, warned against the TransAmazonica colonization schemes when they were announced and suggested that "a disaster of enormous proportions" was impending. IPEAN, an agricultural research institute set up to serve northern Brazil, was ignored by the Ministry of Agriculture and Incra when it also warned against short-cycle crops before the TransAmazonica opened. In the event the research of Philip M. Fernacite around Altamira, mentioned in chapter 3, suggests that crop yields have fallen and the fact that Incra is now encouraging farmers to grow long-cycle crops—in spite of the obvious subsistence and economic attraction of those producing annual harvests from the first year—implies that the danger is real enough. (I also observed extremely sickly long-cycle crops—banana groves—between Altamira and Marabá on the TransAmazonica which I was told reflected poor soils.)

However, although it is clear enough that short-cycle crops can be hazardous in Amazonia it is not certain that they must always be ruinous, and of course certain long-cycle crops and possibly grass types can conserve fertility. One factor which can be forgotten is the very local distribution of soils: even a 100-hectare lot with generally poor soil may have fertile patches and in 1974 it was estimated that only 11 per cent of Amazon soils had been surveyed even cursorily. When Mario Andreazza, Medici's transport minister, came back from a visit to the TransAmazonica in August 1972 and said, "Every area that is cleared of forest is excellent for pasture" he was uttering the propaganda of self-delusion. But equally the wholesale dismissal of all agricultural attempts as necessarily inviting disaster is also erroneous. A great deal depends on the way in which the laterite soils are managed. Mulch techniques using waste vegetable compost, or manuring with chicken dung in the manner pioneered by the Japanese colonists, can do much to preserve and add to fertility. Harald Sioli, at a conference in 1969, explained how a combination of animal and pepper growing in the ill-famed Bragantina zone had proved viable and profitable. A Brazilian engineer, Ernesto Rettelbusch, was cultivating 80 hectares intensively with 20,000 pepper plants, 20,000 hens, 500 pigs and 160 head of cattle. He was buying fodder for the animals, whose price was covered by the sale of meat and eggs, and his profit lay in the pepper which was fertilized by his own stock. Soil fertility therefore is still an open question, turning largely on the capacity of Amazonian farmers to learn from their mistakes: although there are grounds for worry the research input since 1970 has been higher than ever before and, even before PIN, the adoption of long-cycle crops like pepper, jute and *malva* (another vegetable fibre) was spreading in the river basin. Even assuming that all of Amazonia was farmed to exhaustion it is unlikely that it would then become a desert; the mixture of dust and coarse grained material in the soil is not generally conducive to such a development.

There is some truth in the comment of Dr Bento de Souza Porto, Secretary of Planning for Mato Grosso, who brushed aside the fears about making deserts by saying, "But we have the technology to make the deserts fertile again!" But what this leaves out is the probability that, in the meantime, vegetable and animal species which exist in the forest will have disappeared for ever. The combination of ignorance among the tree-fellers, the close interdependence of the different plants and creatures, and the intensely local distribution of certain species make it inevitable that a thorough programme of forest clearing will result in irretrievable losses. The tropical forests have already produced so much of medical and commercial interest to man—from quinine to natural rubber—that even the most self-interested could hardly welcome this with equanimity. Selective woodcutting, or even heavy hunting pressures on animal species, may sharply reduce stocks though they can hardly ever eliminate them entirely. But the complete transformation of the heterogeneous forest, whether for agriculture or for an artificial homogeneous forest as in the Jari project, involves an absolute loss.

Nor does the heterogeneous forest return quickly to its original state. Goodland and Irwin estimate that this can take as long as 100 years; the kind of secondary growth that appears in the wake of forest clearing is different from, and contains more soft woods than, the typically undisturbed Amazon jungle. Cutting timber in corridors, which are then given decades in which to recover, might allow foresters to obtain some return from the land without destroying the heterogeneous forest itself: but this first assumes that the principle of the maintenance of the heterogeneous forest has been established, and secondly that it can be policed. There is no doubt in theory that species in Amazonia must be disappearing already, just as recorded Indian tribes have already disappeared. Among creatures that are certainly depleted, especially in particular parts of the region, are jaguars, crocodiles, armadillos, turtles, duck on the River Araguaia, and trees like the rosewood and the massaranduba, whose latex is used for insulators and in the plastics industry.

One of the most tragic cases, which predates PIN and does not involve the forests but the rivers, is the sharp reduction in the turtle population. By 1973 Sioli reported that the giant river turtle and the South American turtle had almost disappeared from the Amazon: this was hardly surprising as, apart from the popularity of turtle meat for food, the annual destruction of turtle eggs for oil in the 1960s varied between 33 million and 72 million. By September 1975 the IBDF was holding "Amazon week for the preservation of the turtle" and an IBDF official in Marabá told me nine months later that there were no problems in protecting turtles on the Araguaia and Tocantins rivers "because they are already extinct here". (It was remarkable that, while the *South American Handbook* stated that "turtle is the main ingredient of many recipes", I never once saw it on a menu during my own travels in Amazonia.)

Most of the environmental worries about what is happening in Amazonia concern the destruction of the tropical forest. It is therefore crucial to discuss the rate of felling. In theory somewhat over 40 per cent of the forest in Brazilian Amazonia could be cut down without infringing the law. The Forest Code (law 4.771 of 15 September 1965) was promulgated just over a year before the law which created SUDAM. The Forest Code provided for controls on the cutting of trees to be supervised by the specialist forestry agency, IBDF. In Amazonia the rule is that no more than 50 per cent of the tree cover on any property may be cleared and all federal agencies are expected to assist the IBDF to enforce this. SUDAM makes this a condition of the allocation of fiscal incentives money. Incra enjoins this on its small colonists with their 100-hectare plots. The existence of Indian parks and reservations and of a few other natural and forest parks brings the proportion that could legally be cut down towards the 40 per cent. However, it is important to appreciate that this 40 per cent plus would not be in one continuous belt, leaving the major part of the forest undisturbed. It would reflect landownership and land management, riddling the whole region with cleared spaces and permitting the survival of substantial forest remnants only where park boundaries were secured or a large proprietor had chosen to leave his forested area in a continuous stand.

But what is actually happening? The best estimate reported in Brazil in 1976 was based on satellite photographs. According to these Amazonia lost 100,000 square kilometres of forest in 1975, or nearly 4 per cent of the total. It was the projection of these figures that leads Kerr, Sioli and others to the conclusion that the forest as a whole may have ceased to exist by 2005. Statistically this would be inevitable if felling was to continue at the present rate. The knowledge that other countries with Amazonian areas are also pressing forward their exploitation of the region makes such a forecast all the more poignant. However, for this prediction to come true the process of law and public education that underpins the 50 per cent rule would have had to break down completely. There is no evidence that this is happening. Although the IBDF supervision procedures leave an enormous amount to be desired there appears to be a developing public opinion in favour of the preservation of the rainforest; my own observations suggest that, although there is considerable clearing beside the new highways, Incra settlers are not disobeying the 50 per cent rule; IBDF has shown the courage necessary to pursue one of Brazil's largest firms, Volkswagen do Brasil, over possible infractions on its land in southern Pará; and, thanks to space satellites, IBDF and the Brazilian authorities now have a useful tool for policing the extensive area concerned.

My own view is that the nearly 4 per cent of destruction reported for 1975 should be visualized as the fast-rising early point on a graph which could as easily describe a parabola as shoot vertically off a page. It would be surprising, for instance, if the recession in Brazil was not to moderate the rate of felling in the course of 1976. Nevertheless—particularly in view of the weakness of IBDF's staffing to be discussed later in this chapter —there is no room for complacency, even about the 50 per cent rule. Two particular factors could put heavy pressure on that rule by the 1980s. The first is the piecemeal encroachment of settlers who may start clearing beyond the permitted proportions if their management of the laterite soils is as disastrous as their predecessors' was at Bragantina. Accident, genuine or deliberate, may also take a hand here: many of the settlers still use a box of matches to clear their land, and a fire can be notoriously difficult to stop at an agreed limit. The second factor is the probable growth in importance of commercial timber extraction both in itself and for Brazil's balance of payments. A SUDAM publication to commemorate the eighth year of the agency's existence put it like this, "The world's major sources of tropical timber, excluding Latin America, are being rapidly extinguished. Hence Amazonia could come to dominate the international trade in tropical wood in the 1980s." *Jornal do Brasil* in an editorial in October 1973 which castigated IBDF for not doing enough to replant woodland, pointed out that the UN's Food and Agriculture Organization estimated that by 1980 the world output of forest products would be worth $110,000 million, of which $22,000 million would come from Brazil.

At present probably nearly all of the cutting in Amazonia is occurring within the terms of the 50 per cent rule, but it would be quite easy to break it. The increase in depredations elsewhere in the world could increase the impetus in Amazonia—and no one should forget that Brazil has been rather unsuccessful in conserving its other forests in the past. Much woodland has been lost within living memory in states like Bahia and Paraná, so that Brazil is now importing timber from Paraguay. In 1971 Glycon de Paiva, an engineer and economist, said that over the previous 450 years the north-east had lost about one million square kilometres of Atlantic forest, and that this destruction explained the region's continuing climatic and agricultural problems. Conservation of the trees in Amazonia, even at the level implied by the 50 per cent rule, would be an historic achievement.

But is the 50 per cent rule anything like good enough— anything like sufficient to avoid the environmental damage that has been suggested? Clearing to the extent implied by the rule would seem likely to have the climatic and water-cycle effects that have been feared even if the type of agriculture used on the cleared areas could be viable. It is a moot point whether more interesting plant and animal species would be lost by this process of selective clearing compared with a system which cleared an equivalent continuous area. Either way, given the local distribution of species, it must be assumed that potentially valuable information will be lost for ever. However, there are two points that may count against the 50 per cent rule in practice. The first is that, if literally followed to the uttermost, Brazil may cease to have anything that can be called a forest in

Amazonia—merely a series of strips of separated woodland. Human disturbance will be everywhere and any natural advantage that can only emerge from large tracts of trees that are not interfered with will be forfeited. The second is that the rule maximizes the risk that weeds and pests will attack the crops and animals which farmers are trying to raise: every plot will have a reservoir of plants and insects nearby, some of them hostile, which would be eliminated if larger areas were cleared or conserved.

The feeling that the 50 per cent rule is just not adequate— both because it will not conserve enough of Amazonia and because the parts it does conserve will be conserved in an unsatisfactory manner—seems to be growing in Brazil, at least among ecologists. In April 1976 for instance Mario Guimarães Ferri, an ecologist at São Paulo University, urged a system of preventative zoning to preserve the country's forest wealth. The 50 per cent rule is, however, supported by Warwick Kerr on the ground that it buys time: at least a substantial chunk of the forest is guaranteed while the risks of clearing and to agriculture are evaluated. A school of thought among those concerned with the development of Amazonia also believes that timber is the best economic use that can be made of most of the river basin: although such a policy leaves open serious questions about the regeneration of the natural forest and replanting techniques, it could provide an economic justification for preserving far more woodland than the 50 per cent rule would allow.

Finally it should be stressed here that around 90 per cent of Amazonia still remains virtually untouched and that, with the possible exception of the river flooding in 1975 and 1976, few adverse environmental effects of the human impacts so far can be confidently adduced. This may be more thanks to good luck rather than good management, and new adverse effects may yet appear. But it is at least possible that some of the environmental alarm sparked off by the TransAmazonica was overstated. Similarly the most prudent use of the Amazonian land space is a question that can still be argued over: in spite of the pessimism of many of those who love its forests their destruction is not yet a foregone conclusion. This is a handicap for the conservationists of course. Because the area is so vast it is hard to imagine that it could lose nearly all its trees within as short a period as 30 years. What the eye sees now can breed complacency. Yet could the Anglo-Saxon invaders of England after the fall of the Roman Empire, or the Pilgrim Fathers in North America, have guessed the destruction that a myriad of their successors could have wrought on the trees they saw? The fate of Amazonia's environment rests in a large number of hands and they have far more powerful tools at their disposal than ever before.

Some of these hands belong to administrators who are supposed to police not only the 50 per cent rule deriving from the Forest Code, but also the protection of Amazonia's wild life in general. How effective are they? Leaving aside FUNAI (though it is often argued that the Indians "are the best ecologists") there are four federal agencies with an interest here: the Special Secretariat of the Environment (SEMA), a dependency of the Ministry of the Interior founded on 30 October 1973; the IBDF; SUDAM and Incra. None of these bodies is in a strong position to take an uncompromising conservationist line. The Environment Secretariat, the newest, had a staff of only 80 in 1976 and is firmly controlled by Interior, the regional development and planning ministry. Although it is now headed by a distinguished zoologist, Paulo Nogueira Neto, it is still having to work hard to sell the idea of conservation. It does have plans for two ecological stations in Amazonia—one on an island in the Amazon near Manaus, another in Roraima—but it is seeking to work on a consensual basis, concentrating on the centre-south, and to avoid polemical topics. Interestingly, however, its Eco-development Division is looking at the impact of large-scale engineering works, including the Rio–Santos highway. Among its high priorities are issues that have already roused public resentment like air pollution in São Paulo and pollution of the beaches. The IBDF has an ambivalence in its make-up. It is supposed to "develop" Brazil's forests, and some commercial forestry practices can counterbalance its conservationist purpose. It can also be played off against SUDAM as happened in the Volkswagen case, where the company claimed that it had approval from SUDAM for its forest clearing while IBDF claimed that its approval was the one that mattered. SUDAM's highest aim, of course, is the development of the river basin; it is not therefore surprising that its natural resources director,

Clara Pandolfo, has often seemed to support proposals that,
like the Jari project, have drawn fire from other ecologists. In
mid 1973 there was a threat to cut off fiscal incentives from all
companies which had done illegal cutting but it does not seem
to have been renewed. Finally Incra's main duty is obviously
to promote the settlement of Amazonia and the disposal of
federal lands there.

The IBDF is the agency in the front line and it is worth
considering its rôle in Amazonia in greater detail. To a depressing extent its offices are documentation centres, giving permits
and collecting taxes, rather than points from which any active
invigilation of their surrounding district can occur. Its sources
of income are a sawmill tax, paid at the rate of sixteen
cruzeiros ($1·5) per cubic metre of wood which is set aside for a
forestry development fund; permit fees of ten cruzeiros ($0·95)
per hectare, paid by anyone for the right to clear trees; and
fines of 1 per cent of the minimum salary for every tree illegally
cut down—and IBDF works on the basis of 800 trees per
hectare in Amazonia. Financially, therefore, IBDF has a
strong interest in the activity of the sawmills: tax paid by the
large sawmill in Humaita varied between 640,000 cruzeiros
($60,950) and 1·6 million cruzeiros (over $152,000) a month in
1976. At the same time the staffing levels are incredibly low
and, because private forestry companies can pay better salaries
for any trained men in government service, there is a high
turnover in the IBDF. The Humaita office, serving a large
municipality, had only two employees in mid 1976: there had
been money for seven as a result of an agreement between
Amazonas state and the IBDF, but when the funds ran out they
were not extended. The whole of Roraima was covered by an
office with only two forestry experts and four forest guards.
Marabá had a staff of nine, but only three of them were
qualified inspectors; the rest were drivers, cleaners, secretaries
and the like.

Such staffing levels belie the bright efficiency of the prestige
wooden buildings which often house the IBDF local offices, and
the apparent thoroughness of the papers which farmers and
proprietors have to sign. One such standard document, for
instance, not only requires owners to preserve 50 per cent of
their land with forest cover, it also lays down that trees should
be kept alongside rivers, lakes, and on the tops of hills or

slopes varying between 25 and 45 degrees—and rules governing the use of fires for burning wooded land. But what happens when such rules are broken? How do the IBDF offices ever find out? With so few employees, and these so tied down with paperwork, the agency has no real means of knowing what is going on in the forest. It relies on complaints of unauthorized clearing which may come in from neighbouring owners whose property has been threatened by fire. The Marabá office was getting an average of five complaints a month in 1976 and each was then investigated.

However, a system of this sort is obviously a hit-and-miss affair. Landowners some distance away from the towns can get away with a great deal and, although IBDF documents may be necessary to enable them to get SUDAM fiscal incentives or Bank of Brazil loans, the agency has no real check on the truth of their statements. Nor, either, is the IBDF quick to inspect properties after receiving a complaint. In the famous Volkswagen case it was several weeks after Roberto Burle Marx, the internationally-respected landscape gardener, had publicized the space photos of a fire before IBDF officials were sent to the scene. The weakness of IBDF's inspection techniques helps to explain why reports of napalm bombing and defoliant spraying periodically surface in the Brazilian press. Burle Marx has denounced these activities too. One of several such cases was reported by the *Folha de São Paulo* from Cuiabá in April 1976: ranchers 450 kilometres north of Cuiabá, in the municipality of Vila Bela, were plane-spraying a defoliant named Tordon-101, used by the United States in the Vietnam war, to clear jungle in the Guaporé valley. They were hiring Commander planes from a firm in Goiás for the purpose. Against this sort of activity the local IBDF offices are often powerless. It is noteworthy that the bigger companies usually clear their tree-cutting requirements through the big regional offices such as Belem, where political leverage can help them in difficulties.

The deficiencies of IBDF, a relatively low status federal body, which had only 300 employees in the whole of Brazil in 1976, are crucial because it is most directly concerned with the forest and wildlife of Amazonia. Without much stronger teams, equipped with larger budgets, helicopters and more instant access to satellite reports, it is not going to be able to enforce any conservation policy effectively. Too much of IBDF's impact is purely rhetorical. On the BR 364 between Rio Branco and Porto Velho, for instance, it has put up posters saying "*Não desmate sem permissão*" ("Don't cut down without permission") and "*Não derruba arvores sem approveita-los*" ("Don't clear trees without making use of them") which have become partly overgrown. As an Acre highway official travelling with me commented, "It's a gesture to salve their conscience." The IBDF's situation is also important because it is concerned with managing an incipient system of natural and forest parks in Amazonia, and with international co-operation with Brazil's neighbours to protect the region's wildlife.

The system of forest and ecological reserves is still at an early stage, but it appears to have received a new stimulus as a result of the increasing interest in Amazonia in the 1970s. Goodland and Irwin listed 16·3 million hectares in nine separate reserves in their 1975 book: nearly all of this land had been set aside as long ago as 1961. However, there have been various developments since their period of study. The federal government set aside one million hectares for a National Park of Amazonia, 73 kilometres along the TransAmazonica from Itaituba in May 1974; the RADAM surveys have recommended the establishment of various new parks (an extra 15,000 square kilometres in its ninth volume, or 10 per cent of the area covered by that survey); and it has become standard practice for Incra, state-development companies and private entrepreneurs to describe parts of their properties as ecological reserves. In the last case this probably means little more than a grandiose description for those parts which ought not to be touched anyway under the 50 per cent rule.

However, the National Park of Amazonia near Itaituba has much higher ambitions. According to the superintendent of the project, Vivaldo Rayol Lobo, by the 1980s this would have an active conservation policy towards jaguars and other endangered species and should be developing as a tourist attraction. At present the IBDF is trying to move illegal settlers out of the area, to replant trees where they have been cut, and to carry out an inventory of the park's animal and vegetable contents. But as in other IBDF operations there is a disparity between the aim and the means available: the park has only two forest guards protecting it from incursions ("though we really need six or ten at least") and subsistence hunting within it is being allowed for humanitarian reasons.

If the IBDF has difficulty in making its parks and forest policy stick, the same is even more true when it comes to preserving wild animals. Here it is up against a powerful semi-legal export trade in furs and skins. A 1967 federal law could not be more definite: "Animals of whatever species, whatever their state of development who live naturally out of captivity constituting the forest fauna, together with their nests, shelter and natural breeding-grounds are state property and their utilization, persecution, destruction, hunting and trapping are prohibited." This is backed up by local rulings from the IBDF. Within Amazonas, Roraima and Rondonia, for instance, the agency has issued regulations which permit hunting for sport only between 1 August and 30 November, and prohibit absolutely the hunting of 86 species. Nevertheless the IBDF is quite incapable of enforcing such provisions without a degree of self-policing in Amazonia of which there is so far no sign.

The line between hunting for sport and hunting for subsistence would be hard to draw even if everyone with a sporting gun were to be challenged by an IBDF official. But this is to ignore the dimensions of the trade in skins and furs: *Realidade* estimated that in 1970 approximately 500,000 crocodiles had died and approximately 400,000 jaguars and other valued members of the cat family. One of the worst features of this holocaust is that one animal is reckoned to be left for dead for every skin which is actually extracted. And perhaps the oddest aspect of this trade is that one of the two biggest tanneries of crocodile skins—the Santo Antonio of Belem—obtained a fiscal incentives grant of 4·8 million cruzeiros (over $1 million) from SUDAM in 1970 although its whole business was theoretically illegal, while in the same year 70 per cent of the value-added tax raised in the state of Acre came from the equally questionable sale of skins. So far the IBDF has had only a slight impact on all of this, although in 1973, by signing a convention on international trade in species of woodland fauna and flora in danger of extinction, Brazil committed itself to stopping the export of certain skins. Eventually the increasing human population of the region may make control easier if it raises levels of enforcement, public education and standards of living: in the meantime there can be no doubt that wildlife has been hit hard by the increased human activity of the last decade.

IBDF is Brazil's instrument in international exchanges and, in spite of the difficulties that all the Amazon nation states have in policing their territory at a period of awakening commercial interest, there has been a growing recognition that conservation involves all of them. If Warwick Kerr, for example, can identify forest clearing in Colombia as a cause of excessive flooding near Manaus, Brazilians with the most nationalistic attitude towards Amazonia can still see the point in negotiating on such matters with their neighbours. The psychological problem is of course greatest for Brazil, because of the historic dialectic between national and international interest which was summarized in chapter 1. For this reason a particularly ambitious scheme for international co-operation, put up in April 1975 by the Colombian Minister for Agriculture at an international conference in Cali attended by representatives of Bolivia, Colombia, Ecuador, Peru, Venezuela and Brazil for a while seemed to fall on stony ground. Sr Rafael Pardo Huelvas suggested that these countries should set up a multinational park for Amazonia to protect animal and vegetable species "across national frontiers".

It was significant of changing attitudes in Brazil that the middle-class quality newspaper of Rio de Janeiro, *Jornal do Brasil*, gave a warm editorial welcome to this proposal. The idea obviously required a great deal more detailed thought. It not only raised the sovereignty issue which had sunk the Unesco institute in the 1940s—and it should be remembered that non-Brazilian countries would be acquiring a voice in the conservation of a large slice of Brazil—but its usefulness would also turn on the amount of Amazonia covered, whether any general guidelines for forest clearing would be included, and its enforcement mechanisms. (A considerable amount of scientific work has now been done on development norms for tropical forest; in February 1974, for instance, a conference was held in Caracas, Venezuela, on "ecological norms for the development of the humid tropics in Latin America" which was organized by the International Union for the Conservation of Nature with financial backing from the UN Environment Fund.)[36] Nevertheless, in future it would not be surprising to see something emerge from the multinational park idea. Brazil in particular has had more experience of international bodies—ranging from the Latin American Free Trade Association to the binational commission with Paraguay which is currently constructing the huge Itaipu hydroelectric dam—and if public opinion supports it such a scheme could be realized.

In the meantime the Itamarati, Brazil's Foreign Ministry, has been actively promoting binational conservation treaties covering Amazonia in the 1970s. The first was with Colombia in 1972. Apart from providing for the exchange of technical information its meat lay in the third article. This provided for the experts of both countries to produce uniform guidelines covering: temporary or total prohibitions on the hunting of endangered fauna; chemical methods of biological control; preservation of forests and other forms of natural vegetation "which, for their ecological characteristics, merit special treatment"; norms for fishing of inland waters; and the introduction of new species into Amazonia. In 1975 an almost identical treaty was agreed with Peru and, according to Itamarati personnel I spoke to, Venezuela is likely to be the next. International treaties of this sort do not of course solve the difficult problems of supervision, but they are significant because they show that the governments concerned recognize that conservation is something important which cannot be handled singly. For Brazil, too, they are a reflection and stimulus for a wider environmental consciousness in élite and public opinion.

This growth of conservation attitudes, as much in the centre-south as in Amazonia itself, is a marked and encouraging feature of contemporary Brazil. Between 1971 and 1976, when I made successive visits, it was as though a new issue had firmly caught the attention of the press and at least certain politicians, military and officials. It was significant that *Veja*, the news weekly, had started a section labelled simply "environment" which not only reported on anything from air pollution to noise in downtown Rio de Janeiro but had the effect of encouraging the enforcement of legislation which had long existed as a dead letter. An example of this last was a *Veja* item labelled "Birds freed" which appeared in this section on 19 May 1976. This referred to the fact that the IBDF had, since the end of 1975, been making new efforts to get the 1967 law observed which should protect wild fauna from capture. In particular it had

been tackling the various "bird markets" which are a traditional feature of some towns. Initially its officials had merely
warned the traders in wild birds that they were breaking the
law. When this had little effect they decided to take more
drastic action—impounding and setting free the birds. Hence
in May, at the Botanic Gardens in São Paulo, the state secretary for agriculture and the commander of the state's military
police were invited to a ceremony at which 1,500 wild birds,
including canaries and other popular varieties, were set free. A
similar strategy had been adopted at caged bird markets in
towns in Ceará.

Reporting of this type, even where it stuck closely to the
concerns of the centre-south—though Amazonia was a source
for domestic parrots and caged birds—has an importance for
the theme of this book. For in so far as the centre-south has a
critical say in the course of development in its dependent region
of Amazonia the importance of a change of heart there can
hardly be overstated. Indeed the quality press of the centre-
south has also reported the arguments surrounding the rainforest in Amazonia with some sophistication. For example the
Estado de São Paulo on 14 March 1976 followed up Burle
Marx's warning that "the desert makers" were moving in on
Amazonia in a particularly thought-provoking report from
Rogerio Medeiros, its correspondent in Vitoria, the capital
of Rio Grande do Norte. He pointed out that ranchers and
cattle men from that state were moving into Amazonia in
considerable numbers chiefly because, in less than 30 years, they
had exhausted the valuable forest of the Rio Doce, the productivity of the pastures they had established there instead had
fallen fast because of a pest nicknamed the "little grasshopper";
where the forests were being replanted it was by a single tree,
the eucalyptus, whose water requirements were large and which
would do nothing to restore the disrupted ecological balance.
The article, of some 2,000 words, was well-documented with
quotations from the IBDF, ecologists and livestock experts in
Rio Grande do Norte. Medeiros estimated that 35,000 cattle
farmers from the state had gone to Rondonia, 50,000 to Mato
Grosso, and 20,000 to Pará.

His figures for the fall in productivity of the state's cattle
pastures were devastating: from five head per hectare they
could now sustain only 0·9 head per hectare and although the

state's total stock had risen from 1·5 million head in 1971 to 2·6 million in 1975 the output had barely increased—a rise of merely 29 million litres of milk (about 20 per cent) and of only five million tons of meat (about 13 per cent). Furthermore the forest clearing had decimated the 2,350 species of birds identified in the north of the state in 1951, had exposed the cattle to cold winds and disease, had increased the number of droughts in the region, and was blamed for a growth of skin allergies in the human population because of increased solar penetration. The comprehensiveness of this account would bring home to readers in São Paulo and the centre-south not only the difficulty of restoring the ecological balance in Rio Grande do Norte, and the short-sightedness of the cattle development there, but the fact that incompetence in recently "developed" regions was both a cause of the impulse into Amazonia and being actively transmitted there by the people concerned. However few the signs of actual devastation in Amazonia so far no one reading this could afford to be complacent about the future: after Amazonia there would be nowhere else within Brazil to go.

Inevitably ecological coverage of this sort has also had an impact among public officials, politicians and the military. An official at the Itamarati, with whom I was discussing the binational Amazon conservation treaties, said that in his view the Stockholm conference had been critical in changing the minds of administrators. The reason this had had such immediate results—in setting up the secretariat in the Ministry of the Interior and the Humboldt project—was because officials were then persuaded that conservation of the environment was not a neo-imperialist gimmick designed to keep Brazil at a lower stage of economic development, but a precautionary approach in the interests of Brazil. The theme that development and defence of the environment are harmonious goals has been steadily pressed by Paulo Nogueira Neto, of the environment secretariat. At an address to a 1975 conference at the Escola Superior de Guerra (Brazil's influential military "Sorbonne") he made telling references to the Japanese problems with pollution. The point was that Brazil's economic growth since 1964 had, however misleadingly, been compared with Japan's, but Nogueira showed that the absence of controls in that country had increased the economic and social costs. "We have in our possession an official publication of the Japanese government, saying that today that country regrets not having taken preventative measures of pollution control. This is for the simple fact that such preventative measures are much cheaper than the corrective measures that they need to take today," he said.[37]

With army officers playing such an influential rôle in the political system it is significant that arguments of this sort should be put before them and discussed by them. The Escola Superior de Guerra runs regular courses on Amazonia and, simply by the processes of rotation and promotion, there is possibly more up-to-date knowledge of Amazonia among the officer class than in any other group of federal employees.

The rôle of politicians, in the system set up after 1964, is influential in a different way. While few of them can be described as exercising power, and the federal Congress has been steadily unrepresentative due to the restrictions of the régime's institutional acts, national politicians have their speeches reported and are significant opinion leaders. Within the Congress in Brasilia there are some politicians, both in the pro-government Arena and the anti-government MDB, who are concerned with ecological issues. In 1976 a group of them were instrumental in setting up a parliamentary inquiry into the conservation of the forests. The spirit of one of these, Senator Nelson Carneiro (MDB senator for Rio de Janeiro) was well expressed in a debate in the foreign affairs commission on the Brazilian–Peruvian treaty for Amazon conservation. "So-called primitive man always lived with Nature, taking his subsistence, combustibles and solid materials from it which he knew how to use without spoiling them or exhausting them. However, from the moment when an allegedly 'civilizing' process occurs in any part of the world it is inevitably marked by the humans annihilating the environment. The exploitation of natural riches then occurs on a big scale and in an intense rhythm and, what is even worse, without any effort to replace it or preserve it in many cases in which it would be possible or even lucrative for man in the long run," he said. The conservationist case could not have been put more persuasively.

No one should assume that the conservationist case has won all the battles since say 1972: other economic and social forces of great power are involved in Brazil. Nevertheless the appearance of an environmental lobby and awareness, so soon after the Medici government launched PIN, has changed the context in which economic development in Amazonia is now being conducted. This awareness—part of the natural inheritance of the Amerindians and *caboclos* in the region—is also finding more modern expression in Amazonia itself. The IBDF's "week of the turtle" has already been mentioned; it is symbolic too of a more respectful urban attitude towards trees that the city of Manaus has lately embarked on a tree-planting campaign for the city's main thoroughfares. A touching example is a new reading primer for Amazonia, prepared by Warwick Kerr of INPA with the help of a psychologist, which was given a trial with 4,500 children in 1976 and is being widely distributed in 1977. It's a reading scheme with a strong local content and ecological slant: the trees, the animals, the birds and fishes are called by their colloquial names, and treated as friends of the Amazon family. As a passionate ecologist this is one of Kerr's most cherished efforts to persuade the next generation to care for the rainforest.

How then is one to sum up the environmental situation? The central question, both for flora and fauna, is whether the tropical rainforest is likely to survive in anything like its present form to the end of this century. In my view, in spite of the 50 per cent rule, this is unlikely on present trends: the real test of the observance and value of that rule will not occur until the latter part of the 1980s. However, it is easy to imagine changes in economics and administration which could drastically reduce the contemporary pressures on the forest—though nearly all of them depend on decisions taken outside Amazonia. Such changes would be of three kinds: those which reduce the value of the crops for which the forest is being substituted, or the market for tropical timber; those which increase the value, as currently measured, of the rainforest in something close to its natural state; and those which sharply raise the efficacy of the protection of the forest from illegal felling. Obviously such changes are inter-related. If for instance the value of the natural forests is enhanced, then the Brazilian authorities may have an incentive to protect them more rigorously. If the alternative uses for the landspace lose their attraction anyway, the forest will conserve itself without needing any help from the IBDF or

similar bodies. Without here going into wider matters of Brazilian government policy, or the socio-economic pressures that are
encouraging poor migrants or rich companies to move into
Amazonia, it is worth speculating on these three sorts of change.

With the first category some changes are already happening.
Most of the large schemes for which the trees are being cut
envisage cattle raising, whose underlying profitability depends
not only on their soil results and fertilizer needs but on the
world market for meat. Protectionism in Europe and the
United States, along with the growth of vegetable protein
alternatives, could help cut the international demand for
Amazon meat (although soya beans are a crop which is displacing cattle ranchers in Rio Grande do Sul); better and more
intensive stock-raising practices closer to the markets of the
centre-south could make it less competitive inside Brazil.
Again one of the main short-cycle crops along the Trans-
Amazonica and elsewhere in the region is rice: this is subject to
similar world-market factors and intense competition from
expanded output elsewhere in Brazil. It is also not generally
realized that if Ludwig's plans for two crops a year of irrigated
rice on the Jari succeed on the scale proposed he could at a
stroke render uncompetitive all the crops being grown on a
smaller scale, for one annual harvest, away from the river banks.
In this respect the Jari enterprise is an enormous advertisement
for the productive potential of the flooded *varzea* lands (also,
perhaps, for water-based freight): if successful it could deflect
agricultural pressure from the higher forested land.

As we have seen the substitution of long-cycle forest crops is
probably the least ecologically damaging replacement for the
natural forests. It is therefore significant that a SUDAM study
has shown that long-cycle crops would be the most profitable
in Amazonia: compared with a profit yield of 18 per cent on
cattle projects and 28 per cent on short-cycle agriculture, the
study estimated that the return with long-cycle products would
be 55·4 per cent. A major determinant for land use in the river
valley is the price that can be obtained for timber. Hence
recycling of paper, the substitution of other materials for timber
products, such as artificial cellulose, or just reafforestation
elsewhere in Brazil or the world, can have a considerable
effect in reducing the pressure to cut trees in Amazonia. (The
impact of artificial leather has already been helpful in the

region: the United States banned the import of alligator skins at the end of the 1960s following the invention of Teflon by Dupont.)

But the rôle of the timber market is hard to analyse. Although its collapse would relieve pressure on Amazonia it is also possible to argue that, if wisely managed and controlled, it could be the strongest force for the preservation of Amazonia as a rainforest region. INPA's successful experiments in making acceptable papers out of the heterogeneous trees of the natural forest suggest that, so long as the natural forest was cut on a self-renewing basis and not stripped entirely, its value as it is is considerable. These experiments, like the harvesting of leaf-protein discussed by Goodland and Irwin, or the rearing of manatees on a commercial scale suggested by another North American ecologist, Betty Jane Meggers,[38] indicate that it is quite possible to put a much higher valuation on the forest region without greatly disturbing it. Many experts believe, for instance, that the output of fish protein from the Amazon rivers could be greatly increased without ecological risk and more economically than meat protein could be produced from Amazon pastures.

Nevertheless, not all woodcutters in Amazonia are as scrupulous or farsighted as the best commercial forestry firms, and even the most enlightened firms would often prefer to replace the natural forest with homogeneous, fast growing commercial varieties of tree. How reprehensible is this latter practice? It obviously restricts the fauna and other flora that will be found in such organized plantations; it is almost as devastating as converting forest into pasture in terms of the ecological information and diversity that is expunged for good. However, it is possible for environmental critics to be too purist about this. Even within the heterogeneous natural forest there are certain homogeneous patches—like the bamboo forest which RADAM located in Acre—and the arrival of new species, which may take a hold on particular districts, is a fact of nature irrespective of any contribution by man. While the best change for the purpose of conservation is one that enhances the value of the natural forest as it has been inherited, controlled commercial forestry—even if it means the "improvement" of parts of the natural jungle—could well be a good second best. Apart from forestry the other main potential prop for the value of natural Amazonia is tourism: though little developed as yet, and with known risks in terms of excessive pressure on popular spots and the erratic financial and employment effects that the industry has caused elsewhere, it too could help to revalue the forest.

The third sort of change lies within the IBDF area of protection and enforcement. It goes without saying that the IBDF would have to be much better staffed in Amazonia, probably relying much more on the support of the air force and army for inspection and policing purposes, if the 50 per cent rule or any other strategy of conservation is to be sustained. But given the size of the area, and the cost of any enforcement system in staffing and transport, only public opinion can really monitor the protection of the forest throughout the region. This is something that would have to happen on the spot and among those in the centre-south (and indeed outside Brazil) whose investments dictate the rate and type of development in Amazonia. It is possible to be moderately sanguine about the problems of protection. One dramatic effect of the Medici government's PIN has been to spotlight both Brazilian and international attention on the risks involved for the rainforest: as a result ecological awareness has increased and is increasing in Brazil in a way that was not true when the rim of Amazonia was being assaulted in a piecemeal fashion in the late 1950s and 1960s.

Finally it is worth pondering one major irony in the effect of the recent drive into Amazonia. It has focused the attention of scientists on to the rainforest with a totally new sense of urgency. Thanks to RADAM, the roads and the concern of ecologists, infinitely more is known about the river valley than was known a decade ago. Leaving the Humboldt experiment aside, all kinds of natural and social scientists have been researching away busily. In 1976 alone a cattle research centre for the humid tropics (Centro de Pesquisas Agropecuarias do Tropico Umido) was opened in Belem, and it looked as though a new flood forecasting agency would be set up too. All this activity is reminiscent of what is known as "rescue archaeology" in Britain—the attempt to examine Roman and other remains which have been revealed as a by-product of new building works. Without the building works the archaeologists would often not know that the remains existed there at all, but they have to work at top speed before the new construction has to start. Although the ecological risks in the present drive into Amazonia should not be under-rated it may be wondered whether the ecological realities and possibilities would have been explored for some time *without* the clear political and commercial incentives which launched Brazil's government and people into the TransAmazonica. There is also one other factor worth remembering when assessing the future of the rainforest and the likely observance of the 50 per cent rule or any strategy that takes its place. That is Brazil's philosophic inheritance of positivism, reflected in the national motto, "Order and progress". Though often authoritarian and neatly attuned to a programme of national development it can equally well foster and defend a considered programme of conservation. It is an element of the national tradition which those who are worried about Amazonia's future should never entirely forget.

8

THE INDIANS

MÃE MARIA, A FUNAI post on the PA 70 between Marabá and Belem, is a showcase Indian village. It belongs to the Gaviões, a tribe who earned 359,000 cruzeiros ($44,320) in 1975—employing 20 Brazilians to help them—from collecting Brazil nuts. They have a school and many of their homes have transistor radios; their "captain" has had an imposing brick house built for him. They have eight cattle and one young man, Raimundo, has been on a cattle and dairy course. When a visitor calls, as I did, they are hospitable and relaxed—speaking Portuguese, offering a fire-grilled piece of armadillo meat, explaining their method of making manioc bread in the village bake-house. On the surface they appear to be a good advertisement for the official policy of "integration".

Yet even the Gaviões have suffered considerably from the new pressures on Amazonia which are symbolized by the road that, running through a cutting, divides their village from their school and the home of the FUNAI official. The road was built in 1968, two years after the Gaviões had been moved there—partly to release other Brazil nut lands which provided the staple crop of Marabá before the TransAmazonica was created. Three kilometres away down the road, but 800 metres from the road itself, is another group of Gavião. Contacted more recently in Maranhão, where their lands were being invaded by *posseiros*, they were then moved at least twice by FUNAI. When the International Red Cross sent a medical mission to observe the condition of Brazil's Indians in 1970 the 48 Gaviões they saw there were described as "in a most deplorable state of health, the worst of all we had seen". This impression was supported by Robin Hanbury-Tenison, when he inspected this second village in 1971, but by 1972 the Aborigines Protection Society team (of Edwin Brooks, René Fuerst, John Hemming and Francis Huxley) found some signs of improvement, although the population was down to 42.[39] Unhappily I was not able to get to this second village, though the FUNAI official informed me that its numbers had increased to 48 again. (It should also be said that the numbers at the vulnerable first village, which is split by the PA 70, have shown a remarkable increase: from 28 in 1970 they had gone up to 40 in 1972 and were 60 by the time of my visit in 1976.)

In spite of their past troubles the Gaviões are lucky, because they have their hands on one of the best extractive cash crops in Amazonia. After a long struggle too they have a reserve of land. The more acculturated group living beside the road is alert to its rights and willing to fight for them. But they still have major cultural and economic problems that hardly existed 25 years ago when the penetration by modern Brazil had barely begun. Game is getting scarce in their neighbourhood and of course having established a reserve of 52,000 hectares—which I was told had been set aside by the state of Pará as long ago as 1943, but whose boundaries and even existence still seemed in doubt when the APS team visited the area in 1972—they are hardly free to move far. The village now beside the road wishes to move away from it, and to rebuild its huts in the traditional circle. The road itself has worsened a generation gap between the adults and the numerous children who are growing up speaking only Portuguese. Even the cash earned from the Brazil nuts is not an unmitigated benefit. According to the APS team, and the official observations on their draft by FUNAI, the Indian workers were at best earning only around 20 per cent of the market price of the nuts; possibly it was below 10 per cent. And the money that came to the tribe had helped to pay for the "captain's" house and was accentuating social divisions within it. Arguably the PA 70 has brought a few gains for the Gaviões—enabling them to transport their nut crop faster, for example—but even in their recovering state it is hard to argue that "civilization" has been of absolute benefit for them. In any social cost-benefit balance on the impact of modern Brazil on Amazonia in the last few decades, Indian suffering must be one of the heaviest weights on the adverse side.

The modern penetration of Amazonia is, however, only the latest chapter in a long, long story which goes back to the arrival of Pedro Cabral in 1500. Since that time almost every Indian group now in existence has moved, often for long distances; many tribes have disappeared entirely and, even allowing for the recent increase in total Indian numbers over the past decade, the population is still only a portion of what it was at the time of Cabral;[40] and the process of moving the Indians off their lands has occurred with all the deceit, unpleasantness and communication of disease that one might expect. Taking the historic record as a whole the Portuguese and Brazilians probably behaved no worse towards their Indians than the English and North Americans in the area which is now the United States. However, the fact that it is still possible to discover uncontacted tribes in Brazil, whereas this has not been possible in the United States this century, is not really a tribute to Brazilian society. It is rather a function of Brazil's lower level of economic development and the great difficulty of exploring and occupying the Amazon rainforest. In the south of Brazil the Indians were vanquished, decimated, and their numbers known by the end of the ninteenth century. As General Ismarth de Araujo Oliveira, the current president of FUNAI, told me in Brasilia, "The problems for the Indians in the south are still a great deal worse than for those in the north because there is greater real pressure on them."[41]

Nevertheless, in the course of this long period of contact and conflict, Brazilians have developed a number of specific attitudes towards their Indians which deserve consideration before we look at the most recent events. In general they believe that their Indians should assimilate into or integrate with modern Brazilian society; they believe on the whole that the land Indians occupy is not quite "their" land in the sense that private property rights apply elsewhere (for if it was, all other Brazilians would be trespassers); and they also, at a practical level, have a healthy respect for the ability of Indians, particularly those who have not been contacted before, to resist intrusion to the death.

The idea of "integration" has proved difficult enough to define and operate for ethnic minorities in countries like Britain and the United States in recent times. Nevertheless Brazil's Statute of the Indian (Law 6.001 of 19 December 1973) establishes this as the highest aim for Indian groups. It describes Indians as integrated "when incorporated into the national community and recognized in the full exercise of their civil rights, even though they still keep the usages, customs and traditions characteristic of their culture". However, behind this modern definition there lie centuries of assimilationist practice, in which cohabitation and intermarriage between individual Portuguese speakers and Indians—whose cultural level was often fairly similar—have helped to make Brazil's present racial mixture. The offspring of these unions, even though sometimes suffering from the snobbery of the dominant whiter groups, have usually been fully recognized as Brazilian citizens. Particularly in Amazonia their influence is visible to all: slanted eyes, high cheekbones, straight black hair and a dark pigmentation which owes nothing to Africa are common hints of Indian ancestry among the ordinary Portuguese-speaking *caboclos*. National historians identify the Indians as one of the three main genetic contributors to modern Brazil—along with Portuguese and Africans—and in the twentieth century the existence of Amerindian physical traits in the general population has probably eased the acceptance of more recent Asian immigrants like the Japanese-Brazilians. In this Brazil is heir to the thorough-going integrationist approach of the old Roman Empire, where the biological needs of early settlers for mates were given official support as part of a policy of pacification and cultural adaptation in newly-acquired territories. It is different from Anglo-Saxon practice in the British Empire where sexual unions between the British and indigenous peoples were frowned on, and British policy emphasized the preservation of existing cultures and political systems, albeit subordinate to the empire as a whole.

Hence the concept of the special preservation of Indian tribes in Brazil, even though it has had administrative backing since the days of Rondon some 70 years ago, is still a difficult one to sell to ordinary Brazilians. It seems to run counter to the whole ethic and practice of their nation-building where the "melting-pot" across ethnic and colour lines is a far greater reality than it has ever become in the United States. How does one persuade a modern Brazilian, who himself may have Indian blood and use Indian inventions like the hammock, and for whom a belief in the merits of civilization blends subtly with contemporary ambitions for economic development, that it can possibly be desirable to separate the remaining tribal Indians from what seems to be progress? The fact that this "progress" has in practice proved so devastating to Indian

H

groups may seem by the way in comparison: the disappearance of tribes has been a regular feature of Brazilian history and was arguably the object even of a peaceful process of assimilation, while the sufferings of Indians were not markedly worse than those of other poor Brazilians.

At the same time, though Brazil today is one of the least racist countries in the world, some close students of attitudes towards Indians believe that some Brazilians, in their views about pure-blooded Indians, come near to holding them in racist disrespect. All the stereotypes that are held by other dominant groups in situations of racial prejudice do recur here: that the Indians are lazy, dirty, with peculiar sexual habits, that they have a bad smell, that they are as irresponsible as children. P. David Price, a US anthropologist who has been working for FUNAI to help the hard-pressed Nambiquara tribe, says that he has come across "cases of racial prejudice of the worst sort" among some Brazilians. Misunderstanding of the culture and language of the surviving Indian groups, and their rapid collapse into prostitution and alcoholism in some cases where culture shock or exploitation has been intense, help to support such stereotypes. So too does the coveting of Indian lands—for how could these incompetent peoples be allowed to keep to themselves territory which other Brazilians, following the historic principle of *uti possidetis*, could put to better use? The fear of reprisals by Indians, too, justifies their restriction, tutelage and stereotyping.

Behind many of the beliefs about Indians held by other Brazilians in the areas of contact lies the fact of competition for land. The appalling scandals revealed in the 1967 report on the discredited SPI—which included selling Indian lands, bombing, poisoning and otherwise removing Indians with the collusion of the service that was supposed to protect them—arose simply from a desire for the ground they were on. Other Brazilians find it difficult to understand the space requirements of apparently small groups who live by hunting and gathering. As Wilson Mendonça, vice president of FAMATO (the agricultural federation in Mato Grosso), put it, "The Indians are like the worst *fazendeiros* [estate owners] for hogging land that they do not use." For those whose minds are conditioned by a more intensive agriculture the needs of hunters seem excessive. Yet increased penetration of Amazonia, with the disturbance and

shooting of game that this involves, may if anything be en-
larging the needs of the Indian hunter-gatherers. A reserve
that would have provided sufficient game if the stocks outside
it were not being depleted becomes too small when they are
disappearing, the tribal numbers are reviving, and the Indians
are no longer free to migrate. The present thrust into Amazonia,
merely continuing past trends, is converting land from a free
commodity into something hedged about with all the restrictions of private ownership. The fact that Indian lands are
in collective or federal government ownership may seem
anomalous to outlooks geared to private ownership: but
most other Brazilians find it impossible to see the real depriva-
tion of liberty and resources for the Indians which occurs with
their restriction to reserves within a sea of private ownership.

Nor do other Brazilians always want to appreciate the
Indians' own relationship to their land. Because Indians have
migrated before, they consider, what does it matter if the
boundaries of their reserves are shifted? A 1976 state map of
Mato Grosso lists thirteen Indian reserves, of which the
boundaries of several no longer correspond with reality. It
rather suits those who want their land to assume that all land
is equally useful for a hunting culture, and that Indians are
always on the move anyway. But in an undisturbed habitat
the villages of most Indian groups are static: it is only when
pressures from incoming farmers or prospectors become
strong, or food resources are hunted out, that they move
spontaneously. In fact even in a purely hunting culture—and
some Indians have been growing manioc and other crops for
some time—the quality of the land is significant. This is why
the boundaries of the more arid Nambiquara reserve, set up to
the eastward of the rich Nambiquara valley in which the tribe
has traditionally lived and where big ranchers have now made
nonsense of their tenure rights, are proving so uninviting to the
Indian communities concerned. A similar point lay behind the
protests of the Villas-Boas brothers when part of their Xingu
Indian Park was cut off to allow for the BR 80 road, even
though the park was extended southward by more than the
area excised to the north. In reality the Indians are often
rather good at locating the better land in Amazonia, using
their own forest skills. As an Incra official in Roraima remarked,
"If Indian villages exist there then it means that there must be

good soil." There seems little doubt that, where soil scientists
have been unavailable, unscrupulous land-grabbers have used
an Indian presence as a guide, then pushed the Indians out,
arguing all the time that one hectare of forest is just like another
for the "uncivilized" persons they have evicted.

The historic relationship between Brazilians and Indians
has been one of constant encroachment by the first and evacua-
tion by the second. In the conflicts that have arisen there have
been no major wars—of the sort that brought southern Chile
under the control of the Chileans or the North American west
under the United States in the nineteenth century. But there
have been many minor engagements. Through the prism of
the advancing culture the deaths of Brazilians at the hands
of the Indians have been regularly recorded; the deaths of
Indians at the hands of other Brazilians often occur in silence.
Over the last 40 years or so perhaps two or three Brazilians
have died most years whereas Indian casualties at the hands of
civilization—whether by shooting, disease or psychological
disruption—could perhaps have run into the hundreds each
year. Partly because modern Brazilians have generally received
only half the story—not knowing the history of pressure or even
abuse and murder that lies behind the incidents in which
Brazilians are killed—the Indians appear more unpredictable
and "dangerous" than they are. Nevertheless half-conscious
attitudes of aggression towards and fear of the Indians have
been an underlying feature of the 20th century. Rondon's great
pacifist injunction to the men of the SPI when he was setting it
up—that they must die if necessary, but never kill—was one
statement of this reality. The fact that the Brazilian air force
has named its locally built fighter the Xavante, after one of the
most celebrated martial tribes of the Xingu, is a recent example.
In the 1940s a famous photograph appeared in *Life* magazine,
Paris-Match and elsewhere around the world: it was taken by a
French photographer with Antonio Basilio, a well-known pilot
in the interior, and showed the shadow of their plane over an
uncontacted Indian village, with tribesmen aiming their bows
and arrows at the plane. Its caption suggested that the Indians
thought this was a "big bird" and at least one of their arrows
stuck to the body of the aircraft. Evocative of the adventure
story view of Indians it symbolized both the aggressive and the
patronizing feelings that have been held about them. For their

willingness to shoot stereotyped them as hostile—yet who else, living in an undisturbed village, would not feel themselves attacked if they were suddenly buzzed by an aircraft out of the blue? Yet the contrast in modern technology between the aircraft and the bows and arrows underscored the weakness of the Indians, and made possible a rather patronizing reference to their perceptions.

With this bundle of commonly-held beliefs it was inevitable that the TransAmazonica programme would put new pressure on Brazil's official policy towards the Indians. On the one hand it was the latest, biggest, most government-organized thrust into the region where uncontacted and "semi-civilized" Indians still lived in considerable numbers. (The numbers of Indians in Brazilian Amazonia are subject to expert dispute, ranging somewhere around 100,000; it is only in the mid 1970s that FUNAI has begun registering all births and deaths.) But on the other hand such a programme was bound to excite concern outside Brazil and create a more effective and sympathetic monitoring of the situation inside the country. It is not surprising therefore that Indian policy has gone through distinct stages since the start of PIN—beginning as a collaborator in the roads programme but becoming more assertive in the Indians' interest as the years have passed. Whether the arrangements for the protection of the Indian communities are yet anything like effective, given the strength and diverse local instruments of the pressure on Amazonia, will be considered later in this chapter.

FUNAI, as a dependency of the Ministry of the Interior which was responsible for regional planning, was never in a good administrative position to object to PIN. In fact, under Colonel Costa Cavalcanti, the minister, and General Bandeira de Mello, the president of FUNAI—President Medici's appointees—FUNAI worked hand in glove with the highway engineers and others involved. The tone was set by Costa Cavalcanti in August 1970 when he said, "We shall take all care of the Indians. But we shall not let them obstruct the advance of progress." General Bandeira de Mello made an unfavourable impression on foreign visitors for his absolute certainty that the roads could do nothing but good for the Indians, and that they could and should be integrated into modern society as fast as possible. Robin Hanbury-Tenison, who met him in 1971, reports that the general shouted at him, "It is no longer necessary to use the old slow process. Now we have new psychological methods for doing it in six months!" When Hanbury-Tenison asked what these methods for rapid integration were he replied, "We have applied psychology to the subject and we resettle them as quickly as possible in new villages and then remove the children and begin to educate them. We give them the benefits of our medicine and our education, and once they are completely acculturated we let them go out into the world as completely integrated citizens like you and me and the minister here." Hanbury-Tenison records that even Costa Cavalcanti, who was present, suggested that in many cases the process of integration must take three generations.[42]

It was inevitable in this climate that all those who advocated a gentler rate of acculturation, and notably the two Villas-Boas brothers whose Xingu Park had been merged into FUNAI on the demise of the old SPI, should fall out of favour. Bandeira de Mello made it clear that he despised the idea of keeping Indians in "human zoos" although Claudio and Orlando Villas-Boas, the two Brazilians best known for their championship of the Indians, were at that time being nominated for a Nobel peace prize. The issue came to a head over the decision to drive the BR 80 (a road linking the Cuiabá–Santarem highway with the east) across the northern part of the Xingu Park: this was carried through, by a presidential decree in July 1971, in spite of the protests of the Villas-Boas and international bodies. Both personal and ideological hostility to the Villas-Boas seems to have underlain this decision, which was not satisfactorily offset by extension of the park to the south. Eliseu Resende, for DNER, said that he would have been quite happy to have routed the BR 80 round the old border of the park, but Bandeira de Mello would not hear of it. He insisted that the alignment through the park was a necessary part of PIN and would bring great benefits to the Indians. At the same time, in April 1971, General Frederico Augusto Rondon, ex-president of the disgraced SPI and with a quite different outlook from his forebear who founded it, denounced the Xingu Park as a "false experiment" which should be wound up.

From about 1970–2, therefore, official Indian policy in Brazil was totally committed to the aims of PIN and the highways programme. The only public objections inside the

country came from the Villas-Boas, the National Council of
Bishops of Brazil (CNBB) and a small handful of others. The
Catholic Church, which through its clergy on the spot was also
expressing concern about labour conditions for road-builders
and the risks of social disintegration in Amazonia, was active
at national level on behalf of the Indians. Its interest was
publicized by its comments on the early drafts of the Statute of
the Indian (first produced by FUNAI in 1970). The CNBB
opposed rapid integration of the Indians, urged that other
Brazilians must be educated to accept them, and emphasized
their unambiguous and inalienable land rights. Foreign
criticism, still coloured by the crimes of the SPI and stimulated
by the TransAmazonica, ran at a high level in the early 1970s.
The three missions of inspection in 1970–2 (by the International
Red Cross, Hanbury-Tenison and the APS) took place against
free accusations in Europe and North America that the Brazilian government was practising ethnicide, a tribal genocide,
against its Amerindian population. Hostility to the Brazilian
military régime on political grounds gave such allegations a
wide audience. International missions which accepted any
facilities from the Brazilian authorities were suspected of betray-
ing their independence, although the officials' willingness to
provide them was a hint that their intentions at least were far
from ethnicidal.

Meanwhile how were the Indians actually being affected by
the road building? As the case of the BR 80 underlines, the
current habitations and hunting grounds of the tribes had no
influence on the routes chosen: the function of FUNAI
personnel, working at top speed, was to go ahead of the road-
builders and attract the Indians to one side. In general, as we
saw in chapter 2, there was remarkably little friction. However,
it is worth looking at five examples of tribes affected by roads
—the Arara and Asurini near Altamira, and the Parakana in
the Marabá region, all of whom were influenced by the
TransAmazonica; the Kreen-Akrore, who were living in the
neighbourhood of the BR 80 and the Cuiabá–Santarem and
were subsequently air-lifted into the Xingu Park; and the
Waimiri-Atroari in the area of the BR 174 between Manaus and
Caracaraí. Taken together these cases suggest that the Trans-
Amazonica programme was considerably more damaging to
the Indian communities in the short run than its planners

supposed or indeed than anyone fully appreciated until the
programme was well under way.

Arara

The Arara were in 1976 the object of one of FUNAI's
"fronts of attraction"—a team that specializes in making friends
with uncontacted tribes by the patient exchange of gifts. In
February of that year a small group of them had murdered
two workers for a minerals firm and probably a third too
whose body was not recovered; this had happened about
60 kilometres south of TransAmazonica and 100 kilometres
west of Altamira. The Araras were scarcely mentioned by
Hanbury-Tenison or the APS mission in their reports, yet,
as I was able to piece it together with the help of FUNAI
officials in Altamira, their story illustrates better than many
how the TransAmazonica intensified existing pressures on the
uncontacted tribes. In the 1960s they lived as close as nine
poisoned sweets kilometres from Altamira but were persecuted by leopard
hunters and on one occasion they were given poisoned sweets.
In 1967, according to Afonso da Cruz, a FUNAI *sertanista*
responsible for making contact with them, they attacked a
party trying to cut the line for a road between Altamira and
Santarem (a road which was abandoned four kilometres from
fired Altamira). In 1969 another group fired on the Arara and, by
the time the TransAmazonica was being built, they were living
100 kilometres from Altamira. The line of the TransAmazonica
passed between two of their villages, one of which was only
three kilometres from the road. They abandoned these and
moved south. Between 1970 and 1974 da Cruz was trying to
attract them but, although he saw them, they made it clear
that they wanted nothing to do with his gifts or civilization. By
February 1976, when they murdered the CPRM employees
who had unwisely persisted into their area in spite of signs of
their presence, they had been on the move and subject to
interference for about a decade. As da Cruz said, "I think
there's a good chance of contact now. They're tired after so
much running away. One man I saw had a bullet in his spine.
As a result he couldn't go as fast as the others."

Parakanas & Asurinis

The Parakanas and the Asurinis were two groups successfully
contacted by FUNAI on the easterly Amazon part of the
TransAmazonica: both suffered initially as a result. The
Parakanas had a village 28 kilometres from the highway and
were contacted in April 1971 after an eight-month period of

attraction. According to the APS team who saw the village the *culture* following year their culture seemed to have been severely affected as a result: some of the Indians had taken to wearing a mixed assortment of clothes, many of the women and children had colds, and the village appeared to have traded most of its artefacts for guns and ammunition. Worst of all there was "strong evidence" that eight cases of venereal disease, one of which caused blindness, had been brought to the village by the FUNAI pacification team. Subsequently these FUNAI employees were said to have been dismissed; by 1976 the tribe, in its reserve of 7,200 hectares set up in July 1971, was receiving a special measure of protection and community aid from FUNAI. Due to psychological disruption and malaria its numbers fell from an estimated 150 in 1970 to only 82 at the lowest point in 1972. They had risen however to 93 by February 1975. A refusal to procreate is a common reaction by Indian tribes to the distress and confusion caused by first contact with other Brazilians. Taken with cruelty and disease this has, historically, been one of the main factors in the disappearance of so many tribes. The Asurini *Asurini* were about 90, according to FUNAI in Altamira, when they were contacted in 1971 as a consequence of the Trans-Amazonica. When the APS team saw them in 1972 they were only 62, partly as a result of a cold-flu epidemic; they also appeared to be deliberately refraining from having children. Between 1974 and 1976 they had three children and FUNAI hoped that they were emerging from their phase of childlessness.

These three tribes were all affected by the TransAmazonica itself. But, as the example of the Arara shows, the road-building merely exacerbated a process of interference that was reaching serious proportions before PIN. The two other examples show opposite consequences of the roads: the Kreen-Akrore had to be airlifted out of the way while the Waimiri-Atroari are a major reason why the BR 174, which was started in advance of the TransAmazonica, took so much longer to finish. The Kreen- *Kreen-* Akrore, living in the area of the BR 80 and BR 163, were *Akrore* successfully attracted by a FUNAI team in February 1973. Their health was studied by Roberto Baruzzi, of the Escola Paulista de Medicina, who had previously worked with the Villas-Boas in the Xingu Park. According to his figures there were 135 in the tribe when he first saw them then. By January

1975 when they were taken into the Xingu Park to improve their chances of survival their numbers were down to 82, and ten more died shortly after they got there. Baruzzi says that the main causes of death were, as so often, colds, pneumonia and influenza. There are rumours in anthropological circles that the numbers of the tribe may already have declined drastically before Baruzzi was able to carry out his first census. It was suggested to me that there might have been as many as 500 of them; I have no sure evidence here but it is a fact, which FUNAI tries to guard against, that the process of attraction and pacification can itself be the means by which Indians are infected with diseases to which they have little resistance. Significantly the Kreen-Akrore were moved to the Xingu Park after President Geisel had succeeded President Medici, and the new FUNAI leadership under General Ismarth held the park itself and the work of the Villas-Boas in greater respect. Nevertheless even then the Kreen-Akrore weren't entirely well off. Due to a mishap they were placed alongside other tribes in the park with whom they did not get on, and they had to be moved again within the park.

Waimiri-
Atroari

The case of the Waimiri-Atroari is the most remarkable because, although engineering difficulties are quoted by DNER, the hostility of this tribe appears to be the principal reason why the opening of the BR 174 was consistently delayed. Originally the Manaus–Caracaraí road was planned to run to the west of the lands occupied by this tribe (which has already had to move as a result of outside pressures over the past half century). But the ground was too flooded and, before plans were laid for the Perimetral Norte, it was decided to put the road directly through the Waimiri-Atroari areas. The authorities, and FUNAI which was responsible for the pacification of the tribe, already had a healthy respect for them: in 1942 they had killed two Brazilian brothers and in 1946 they killed nine members of the SPI. Since the pressure to pacify them in advance of the BR 174 there has been a whole string of incidents: in 1968 Padre Giovanni Calleri and eight others were killed at an "attraction post"; in 1973 three FUNAI staff were killed; in 1974 ten more were killed in two incidents; since then two road-builders under contract to the army have been killed by them. Although the Waimiri-Atroari have probably suffered from incursions in the same way that other tribes have done

there is no obvious explanation for their particular resistance to
FUNAI's techniques of attraction. FUNAI's bulletin (number
15/16) which analysed the killings in 1976 suggested that
language difficulties, a shortage of presents for the tribe, or
some little understood warrior ritual could all be responsible.
In the meantime the BR 174 stands out as the one case where
the Indians have lived up to a stereotype held of them, and
have put a spanner in the roads programme. Even before the
BR 174 was formally opened, in April 1977, FUNAI had
already made clear that the Waimiri–Atroari stretch would be
exceptionally well invigilated, with four FUNAI posts, and no
drivers would be permitted to stop in their territory.

Not all the effects of the road-building have been bad for the
Indians, and some of the bad ones have been shortlived.
Access to isolated FUNAI and Indian mission posts has
improved, making it possible to get medical help to Indians
more quickly. At Catrimani, in the Yanomama tribal area
affected by the Perimetral Norte, it used to take three weeks to
reach a mission station by river. Now it is possible to drive. In
the same region, on the Ajarani river, all the Indians in one
village were so overwhelmed by the arrival of the road-builders
that they abandoned their slash-and-burn system, and failed
to sow their crops at the right time. But, by the time the
construction teams had moved on, they had recovered and
were able to feed themselves again.

Still the road-building and the international missions put a
harsh spotlight on official policy for the Indians which even the
Bandeira de Mello administration turned to some benefit for
them. There were three main areas in which something was
achieved: the legal support of the Statute of the Indian; the
delimitation of parks and reserves; and a more energetic
vaccination drive. None of these was wholly satisfactory, but
they were an earnest of good intentions which later FUNAI
administrations might turn to better advantage.

The Statute of the Indian divided Indians into the three
categories—"isolated," "on the way to integration" and
"integrated". The first two groups would be under the tutelage
of FUNAI and would only be enabled to enjoy the full civil
rights of the third after they had proved to a judge that they
could understand the Portuguese language and the customs of
modern Brazil. This definition left a certain ambiguity about

the status of "integration" but should protect the most vulnerable groups. The statute required all Indian lands to be surveyed and marked out (a task for which FUNAI subsequently hired the RADAM aerial survey team and which, by the end of 1978, was due to be complete). All Indian land was to be regarded as territory belonging to the federal government, which could not be sold, and of which the Indians would benefit from any economic exploitation. (The president of the republic could decree an intervention in Indian areas for the exploitation of underground resources of interest "for security and national development".)

Indian lands would be of three types: lands which they had traditionally occupied (defined as "effective occupation of land which the Indian . . . holds and where he lives and exercises activity which is indispensable for his subsistence"—a definition which could be elastic on a map); areas set aside as reserves, parks, agricultural colonies and "federal Indian territories" (the last, suitable for places like Roraima where Indians are relatively numerous, covered districts where Indians were more than a third of the population); and a holding for an Indian, whether or not he was "integrated", of up to 50 hectares for his personal use where he had occupied it for ten years running (the similar article in the Brazilian constitution which is designed to protect *posseiros* allows them up to 100 hectares). The statute authorized FUNAI to call in the armed forces and police to remove interlopers from Indian lands and also laid down special penalties for crimes which were particularly noxious for the Indians: prison for up to six months for exploiting them for tourism; prison for up to two years for selling alcohol to those who were "not integrated"; and sentences lengthened by a third where a FUNAI employee was the culprit. The "Indian income" (*renda indigena*) which the APS team had found confusing in theory and practice was defined as the income from Indian property which should be reinvested in profitable activities of benefit to the Indian community concerned.

This statute, of course, was worth only what the integrity and efficiency of FUNAI could make it worth. Here the record prior to the 1973 statute had been weak. Apart from the case of the BR 80 and the Xingu Park there had been numerous recent examples of FUNAI itself failing to maintain the boundaries of Indian lands against incursions: the Aripuanã

Park had moved westwards from Mato Grosso into Rondonia because a São Paulo property company had penetrated its eastern flank; the boundary of the Waimiri-Atroari reservation north of Manaus left out a number of tribal villages on its northern side. In all cases where a developer laid claim to lands which might contain Indians he had to obtain a certificate from FUNAI saying that there was none there. This was a procedure vulnerable not only to corruption but to the genuine ignorance of FUNAI offices. Even the RADAM survey could not entirely guarantee that all tribes would be sighted, even if they were still not contacted, for those which are totally nomadic may leave few traces which are visible from the air. FUNAI's problems of supervision are comparable to those of IBDF and, although the Statute of the Indian was a useful achievement on paper, its practical value would depend on policing and public education.

A report published at the end of Bandeira de Mello's presidency of FUNAI (FUNAI bulletin 9/10) quoted eleven new reserves and three Indian parks with their size readjusted as among his successes. Parks, reserves and so on with 3·8 million hectares had been marked out, while 6·4 million hectares of traditional Indian areas had been surveyed by air. All of this activity might be inadequate, and fragile in the real security that it provided for the Indians, but it was possible to argue that the outcome of Medici's government had been to put some controls on a process of interference in Indian areas which had been much more perilous in the piecemeal era of the 1950s and 1960s. The immunization campaign, in particular, was one explanation of the rising Indian population which the APS team reported for many areas in 1972 and which seems to have continued since. In the four Bandeira de Mello years, over 103,000 general vaccinations were carried out, as well as nearly 29,000 BCG vaccinations against TB. Nevertheless the medical progress achieved should not be exaggerated. *Veja* in May 1976 reported that a tiny mission hospital belonging to the Salesians on the upper Rio Negro, near the Colombian border was providing the only health service for 15,000 Indians. The two health workers in charge had to deal with an outbreak of 80 cases of TB and were desperately anxious that FUNAI would keep its promise to send 7,000 shots of BCG vaccine.

In what ways has Indian policy and the actual administration

of FUNAI changed under General Geisel and the new head of
FUNAI, General Ismarth de Araujo Oliveira? There seems
little doubt that, within the resources at his disposal, General
Ismarth has been acting as resolutely for the Indians as is
possible. He has never been so rash as to suggest like his
predecessor that they could be integrated in six months, or
anything like it. And in two particular areas, Aripuanã and
Gorotire, FUNAI under his management has successfully
resisted powerful economic interests. The example of Aripuanã,
the municipality in northern Mato Grosso which is one of the
Polamazonia growth poles, is of particular interest because the
integrity of the Indian park there has already been compromised in the past and a 1976 map of the state suggests that
two new roads will run through it and that the new town of
Fontanillas lies within its boundaries. In fact, as far as I was
able to discover, the eastern boundary has been moved westward from the River Juruena to the River Aripuanã in order to
accommodate one of the CODEMAT colonization schemes
(see chapter 3). The effect of this new boundary has been to
leave Fontanillas outside any designated Indian area, but across
the River Juruena from a new reserve for the Canoeiros tribe.

The significance of this is that the main road from the BR
364 and Cuiabá to Fontanillas, and thereafter to the town of
Aripuanã, is marked on the municipal map as crossing that
reserve. All but the twelve kilometres across the reserve were
actually built when FUNAI dug its heels in. As a result a
300-kilometre alternative, the BR 174 from Vilhena to Aripuanã
and Fontanillas, has had to be built instead. This stand by
FUNAI inside the Ministry of the Interior, which has naturally
infuriated the state of Mato Grosso and the highway authorities,
may be seen as a piece of belated and possibly futile justice on
behalf of the Indians in that area. It is belated because the
Medici government, by moving back the boundaries of the
Aripuanã Park, made possible the Aripuanã growth pole. It
is probably futile because the CODEMAT settlement plans
are bound to cause a major influx and disturbance on the edge
of the Indian park while, if Fontanillas grows in the 1980s to
the extent one may expect, the future of the four Canoeiro
villages opposite cannot be too peaceful even if the road and
bridge are never built.

The case of the Gorotire in southern Pará is interesting in a different way. The tribe here is growing rapidly. According to FUNAI officials in Belem its numbers were 258 in 1958, 415 in 1973 and 529 in mid 1976. Furthermore their reserve is situated on a major coal discovery. But FUNAI appears to be cautious in permitting the coal to be prospected or exploited, somewhat to the irritation of the National Department of Mines (DPNM). This promises to be a test of those parts of the Statute of the Indian which insist that the Indians should benefit from any subsoil resources that are developed, but that the Brazilian government has the right to insist that the development takes place. The attraction of the Gorotire deposits are that they are within reasonable distance of the Carajas iron reserves, and of the other interesting minerals in that neighbourhood. Although any major development is bound to affect the life-style of the tribe radically, it does at least appear so far that FUNAI is seeking to defend the Indians' rights.

The one major criticism that can be made of the Ismarth administration so far is that it has ordered thirteen non-Brazilian anthropologists out of the border zone, thereby crippling two community-aid projects—P. David Price's for the Nambiquara and Peter Silverwood-Cope's for the Maku—and preventing Kenneth Taylor's project for the Yanomama from getting started at all. For each of these rather exposed tribes this has involved some loss: the Maku and Yanomama are tribes which have only been recently contacted which lie in the area of influence of the Perimetral Norte. The Nambiquara have been suffering since the mid 1960s from the agricultural activity induced by the BR 364. When I was able to speak to some of those concerned it was still not clear how far the decision had been taken on national-security grounds, rather than because of personality disagreements, and it was possible that some of the work of these teams would continue. (FUNAI's regular staff are not always informed by an anthropological perspective, although most young recruits have now completed a special university course. I was told that FUNAI often prefers to recruit agricultural technicians rather than those who have studied anthropology.)

Bearing in mind the changes, both in Amazonia and in its own organization over the past few years, how effective a body is FUNAI? It still appears to be reactive, lacking the strength on the ground to define and defend Indian lands before the pressures have become so intense that they have eroded traditional Indian areas. Its attraction work is very obviously road-related (indeed FUNAI obtained extra funds for this purpose at the time of the TransAmazonica) although it might benefit from a slower pace. General Ismarth told me that, for the number of uncontacted Indians, the western stretch of the Perimetral Norte from Benjamin Constant to São Gabriel was probably the most difficult area for FUNAI in Amazonia. Yet, because of the delays to the roads programme, the prospect of making that stretch was still three years away at least in 1976. Far from taking advantage of the extra time to do a more gradual pacification FUNAI was leaving the tribes alone and was planning not to start attraction until six months before road-building commences. "There's no point in going in sooner as it just upsets the Indians unnecessarily," he said. There may have been other reasons for the organization's reluctance— shortage of funds for itself, or scepticism about the timetable for the Perimetral Norte—but on the surface it seemed to be opting to do a difficult job in a rush in a case where that was not necessary.

FUNAI, as the APS team noticed, is feebly represented north of the Amazon where the Indians are relatively numerous. In practice the Roman Catholic and Protestant missions, and the Brazilian air force, are much more closely involved in their welfare. (In the 1970s, for instance, United States Protestant missionaries have transferred several hundred members of the Wai Wai tribe from Guyana into Brazil.) Roraima has an estimated 22,000 Indians, or over a third of the population of the territory, yet many of their lands are not demarcated as such. With the probable increase in immigration to the territory over the next decade land friction is bound to rise also, partly because the savannah lands of northern Roraima are poor and extensive areas are needed for successful cattle raising. In this respect it was worrying to find that a problem of incursion by cattle ranchers into a Macuxi area at São Marcos, which had disturbed the APS team in 1972, still did not appear to have been resolved by 1976. I was told that some 20,000 to 40,000 head of cattle were being raised within the 630,000 hectares set aside for the Macuxis there. In such cases in the past FUNAI and its predecessor have always tended to give ground to the outside interests, rather than insisting on their removal, and my impression in Boa Vista was that the ranchers were not going to be required to move out.

The Macuxi, who are bilingual in Portuguese and their own language and highly acculturated to Brazilian society, are the main tribe in Roraima. At one of their villages I visited (the Maloca de Contão, where the people are Baptists), the school with 68 pupils was a hive of activity. Some of the Macuxi are active cattle farmers themselves, while others have become *garimpeiros*, or miners. In a sense, therefore, their future is not a bad test of the prospects for the more "integrated" Indians. They have some skills and education and are being left to sink or swim. Many of them must depend more on the normal services available to them as citizens of Roraima (which ran the school at Maloca de Contão, for example) than on any special protection they might have as Indians. Nevertheless, for at least some of the Macuxi, this could be a depressing and unjust future for it is doubtful whether they could retain their lands and sustain their cultural adjustment against a much more powerful impetus of development. Like the territory as a whole their progress has been underwritten in the past by the obstinacy of the Waimiri-Atroari and the delays to the BR 174.

FUNAI's capability in the field is limited by the difficulty of holding on to good staff. In the middle of 1976, for instance, the chief of a post would get 7,000 cruzeiros ($666) a month. Without many expenses this was not a bad salary. But the isolation of the job, particularly for young city-bred people and their wives, often undermines their intitial idealism. Many of the young products of the special "*indigenismo*" course have fallen by the wayside for this reason. And, although I was impressed by the calibre of many FUNAI personnel I met, I was told that three out of the six Indian posts run from Altamira lacked heads and each of the remainder lacked other staff. When a landowner such as Dorival Kniphoff finds Indians on his property he cannot confidently rely on help from FUNAI.

At a philosophic level the rôle of FUNAI is also compromised by the fact that it is the agent of a government with an active commitment to economic development, and by the ambiguities of the "integration" to which it aspires. Although General Ismarth may be putting more effort into the defence of Indian lands from encroachment, and the Statute of the Indian may

guarantee these on paper, in the last resort the needs of the
national community are seen as paramount. (Indeed there is a
connection between the objective of "integration"—which
would give the Indians a share in the material improvement of
Brazilians as a whole—and a justification for removing them
from land in the meantime.) The Aripuanã growth pole could
not have been declared without excising territory from the
Aripuanã Park and, in the outcome, there are now Cintas
Largas (a tribe which suffered from a massacre in 1963) outside
its boundaries and, indeed, living on land belonging to the
INPA experimental station. Yet if it is true that Aripuanã
possesses one of the few belts of really fertile land in Amazonia
then the "national" case for making it a centre for agricultural
development was strong. In many parts of Amazonia the
ground had literally been sold from under the Indians' feet
in the 1960s and early 1970s so that by the time FUNAI under
General Ismarth was willing to take a more robust attitude in
defence of the Indians it was impossible to resurrect the
status quo ante for them, while there was a danger of injustice to
the incoming Brazilian farmers who had often paid good money
for their land and who had not themselves been party to any
negligence of Indian rights. As one anthropologist remarked,
"Where landowners are occupying traditional Indian lands
the only way in which the constitutional rights of the Indians
can be preserved is by taking the landowners to court. But the
legal process may take years, its result is uncertain, and by the
time you win the Indians are all dead."

    When the RADAM survey of Indian lands is finished
(perhaps in the course of 1978) it may be realistic to expect a
better protection for them. In the past bad cartography as
well as unscrupulous land dealing have contributed to an
erosion of their territories. What would perhaps be unrealistic,
given the whole slant of government policy and indeed the
whole history of land settlement in Brazil, is to imagine that
FUNAI can now start on a great legal campaign to wrest back
Indian lands which were wrongfully occupied in the 1960s.
(Some day better-educated Indians themselves, following the
precedents of their cousins in North America, may try.) One
reason why FUNAI has been active in creating parks and
reservations by decree law—which may be in non-traditional
Indian areas, and require the decanting of tribes into them—is

because it finds it easier to protect newly-established areas rather than the traditional lands allegedly guaranteed by the constitution. (In a decree of January 1976 President Geisel gave FUNAI sole responsibility for demarcating Indian lands. Previously it was traditional for FUNAI's boundaries to be narrowed as a result of lobbying, first by the Ministry of the Interior, and subsequently by the Presidency.) In practice this means that the effective protection of lands traditionally occupied by the Indians, in the few cases where it has occurred, has rarely been due to FUNAI, the law or the armed services, but usually thanks to the Indians themselves. Their own belligerence, whether in the "primitive" style of the Waimiri-Atroari, or the more sophisticated manner of the Xavante, has been their best defence.

Meanwhile, although FUNAI and others may take satisfaction from Indian numbers which are increasing by as much as 8 per cent a year in Pará and Amapá, and from the programme of reserves, the long-term future of the tribes depends largely on how the concept of "integration" works out. The moment of contact with Brazilian society, even when conducted skilfully by FUNAI's *sertanistas*, is of course revolutionary for the tribe concerned. Their whole world is changed overnight. Where the initial contact is brutal, traumatizing and involves the transmission of disease the tribe itself may die out. *O Globo*, the Rio paper, published a report in September 1976 by a research worker, Paulo Lucena, on the Mayuruna tribe near the Peruvian border. Here the contact was taking place in the worst fashion, the tribe was being evicted from its traditional lands, and their numbers had dropped in three years from 2,000 to 400. Lucena said that the tribe was killing both male and female children in what can only be seen as a desperate act of suicide. As P. David Price, working with the much encroached-upon Nambiquara put it, "Their attitude is 'better dead than Brazilian'."

However, the tribes that survive this phase of contact are in different stages of acculturation. On the whole, the more adapted to Brazilian society they become the less interesting do they seem to many anthropologists and those who feel the plight of the stone-age cultures most keenly. Yet this is unfortunate for the really hard questions, about the cultural and economic rôle for "integrated" Indians, arise more sharply with

Culture

their adaptation to the dominant society. And it must not be forgotten that their "integration" is being played out against radical changes to the traditional environment of Amazonia: tribes that were used to obtaining their living from the jungles of Pará, for instance, must expect that the same areas will be agricultural and industrial complexes in the 1980s. The first phase of contact often establishes habits which are not conducive to economic and cultural survival thereafter. The attraction process of FUNAI, with its free gifts for a tribe, can make for dependence and the idea that Indians can get something for nothing from the authorities. The unpoliced contacts with rubber tappers and the like can lead to alcohol addiction and prostitution. Where missionaries are involved—either those like the Salesians who run boarding schools for Indian children or the Protestants who stress the need for pagans to be "born again"—the process of conversion itself involves a sharp break with their Indian culture.

The trouble is that the ultimate object of the "integration" policy is still rather obscure. In the absence of anything better it could easily mean assimilation and intermarriage, at the lowest social level, into ordinary Brazilian society: this is what has happened regularly throughout history and still happens where Indians feel the attraction of the dominant culture is great and they have sufficient Portuguese to be able to survive as individuals within it. This spells death to the Indian communities and cultures, and to the lifestyle and knowledge that that they have developed over thousands of years. But is it really more reprehensible, particularly at an individual level, than a decision by a Japanese-Brazilian or German-Brazilian to abandon his immigrant community and become a fully-fledged Brazilian? In parts of Amazonia, after all, the genetic and cultural gap between a *caboclo* and a full-blooded Indian may be quite small.

FUNAI and the Geisel government undoubtedly define "integration" as a stage in which FUNAI tutelage is no longer necessary. They do not want to run the political and psychological risks of trying to keep Indian groups indefinitely in a legal state comparable to minors. Rangel Reis, the Minister of the Interior, said in June 1976, "If we do not reach the emancipation of at least some Indian communities, already in President Geisel's government, we will have failed in that objective, at least in the south of the country." He cited the case of the Carajas on the island of Bananal (in the Araguaia Indian Park) as a community in an advanced state of acculturation which was ready to be emancipated in this way. However, both the APS team and Hanbury-Tenison had expressed concern about this tribe, partly because of the steady swarm of settlers coming on to the island (around 6,000 in 1972), the agricultural developments centred on the neighbouring town of São Felix de Araguaia, and the fact that the Indians were becoming a tourist attraction. Although emancipation for the Carajas might be a good thing if it gave them full control of the income from settlers who graze their lands, and stimulated and made possible their own agricultural and fishing projects, it would be perilous if this meant that FUNAI was backing down from its responsibility to defend the integrity of the Araguaia Park. There is a risk that "integration" and "emancipation" could involve further blows to the Indians' ill-secured property rights.

For the real question about "integration" on a basis which maintains the continuity of the Indian communities is economic. This is a question that existed before the Trans-Amazonica programme, but which has become far more insistent now that nearly all tribes have been contacted and the level of Brazilian activity in Amazonia has increased so sharply. The Indians need to be able to feed themselves, and to have some surplus which they can trade for items they require, if they are to maintain their self-respect and control the pace and direction of their adaptation to general Brazilian society. They have three likely options: to carry on as hunters and gatherers (though this may involve considerable sophistication where a cash crop like the Gaviões' Brazil nuts can be traded); to become agriculturalists or to raise cattle (which for some tribes requires adaptation which does not come easily); or to become day labourers, hired by Brazilian employers when required like the other *boias-frias* of the countryside.

Each of these options has its difficulties. The first assumes that the Indian lands can be defended and will be sufficient to feed a growing tribe, now armed with shotguns as well as bows, which may have increasing desires to purchase manufactures. It is possible, however, that this way of life could serve other contemporary purposes acceptable to the dominant society—

if the Indians were to be regarded as ecological guardians and
park-keepers, for example, or came to play a part in commercial
forestry. The second option, of agriculture, raises problems
akin to those faced by the TransAmazonica settlers—the
Indians will need to retain a share of the good soil, they must
use appropriate techniques, and they will need a fair return on
the surplus to their immediate subsistence. Obviously if the
Nambiquara, for instance, abandon the good soil of their
traditional lands in the Guaporé valley for the park set aside
for them on cerrado land to the east they will handicap their
chances of developing a successful agriculture. For other
tribes, which have been ejected from good lands entirely,
agricultural self-sufficiency may be hard to achieve and
maintain. Nevertheless the first two options seem to hold out
the best prospects for the time being: a study by a Brazilian
anthropologist, Paulo Amorim, has shown that Indians in the
north-east who have adequate land are totally independent of
government financial support. The third option, which has
been bitterly criticized by Orlando Villas-Boas, frankly offers
the Indians only a marginal, proletarian existence. This is what
has already happened where they have lost their land and
morale. They become day labourers with the low wages and
insecurity of employment that is in the nature of the *boia-fria*
system. This is no worse than the experience of millions of
rural Brazilians, although as Indians arousing prejudice and
more limited than others in their social and linguistic confidence
there is a danger that they may become an under-class in an
under-class. In any event such a subservient and partially-
employed way of life makes a mockery of the offer of full
citizenship which "integration" implies. If this was to be the
main outcome of the present impetus into Amazonia for its
Amerindians it could be a far more enduring blow than their
immediate loss of life during the contact phase.

To conclude this chapter, however, it is worth giving snap-
shot accounts of three different tribes—the Yanomama, the
Nambiquara and the Xavante—to underline the diverse
problems and responses of groups at various stages of acculturation. The Yanomama, who number perhaps 6,000 inside
Brazil but who straddle the Venezuelan border, speak related
languages and prize a warrior culture which leads to recurring
warfare among themselves. Although the Perimetral Norte

passes through part of their territory and some 500 tin miners are panning up by the border, most of the Yanomama have not yet been contacted by other Brazilians. According to Kenneth Taylor, responsible for the abortive Plano Yanomama for FUNAI which was designed to give the tribe medical and other assistance, and to give road-builders some insight into how to deal with them, only twelve out of 150 villages actually had mission or FUNAI posts in 1976. One small group of Yano-mama, who numbered 82 in 1973—they had been decimated by measles six years before—were living about 100 kilometres west of Caracaraí when the Perimetral Norte builders started to come through in that year. Two years later their numbers were down to 66: of the sixteen deaths nearly all were due to flu, although a couple of road-workers took measles back into the district in June 1974, which caused deaths further afield. At this period neither the construction companies nor the regular health agencies were inoculating the Indians and road-workers thoroughly. Nor was FUNAI's special plan for assistance able to help much: while FUNAI had allowed funds for eight medical helpers in the area it was never possible to recruit them because of the low salary scales and, perhaps, the isolation and difficulty of the work. With the postponements of the Perimetral Norte the Yanomama may have bought a temporary respite from outside pressure. They represent one of the largest pacification tasks left for Brazil and an opportunity to provide a coherent strategy of protection and acculturation, perhaps in concert with the Venezuelan authorities, while the outside pressures are temporarily relaxed. If the chance is not taken—and the ban on foreign anthropologists means that FUNAI now has total responsibility—there will be another saga of disease, culture shock and pauperization, mitigated only slightly by rescue anthropology, of the kind that has occurred elsewhere.

The Nambiquara, by contrast, now amount to only 530 people in 24 villages scattered over an area of 57,000 square kilometres. They have been in some sort of contact with other Brazilians since at least the start of the 20th century, when General Rondon was laying telegraph lines through their territory. At that stage the tribal group, which speaks four related languages, is estimated to have numbered around 6,000 to 7,000: that is to say their numbers have been steadily falling, at about 1 per cent a year, throughout this century. Since the construction of the BR 364 from Cuiabá to Porto Velho in the early 1960s, which skirts their traditional territories and allowed access roads to be built westwards into the Guaporé valley, they have been under increasing pressure from agricultural developers. Contrary to article 198 of the Brazilian constitution—which, even before the Statute of the Indian, supposedly guaranteed Indians in their lands—the developers began purchasing these lands and cutting the forest. In 1968, in what in retrospect seems close to collusion with these interests, FUNAI established the new reserve for the Nambiquara east of the BR 364. Thereafter, according to a series of articles in *Jornal do Brasil* in September 1972 by Mario Chimanovitch, FUNAI was issuing certificates for the absence of Indians to the developers while simultaneously trying to remove them into the new reserve. In a report dated 5 February 1971 four local FUNAI employees expressed their opposition to this policy: apart from the abandonment of the Nambiquaras' constitutional rights that it involved, many of the tribal sub-groups did not get on well, and the game resources of the new reserve were likely to prove insufficient. Chimanovitch reported that some of the groups in their traditional areas were close to starving, because of the deforestation, while the APS team who also looked at the new reserve which was being nibbled away at by *caboclos* "left the Nambiquara with a deep feeling of unease". One small group, whose condition had been described by the Red Cross and Hanbury-Tenison as amounting to semi-slavery, was still working half the year for a trader and land-owner named Faustinho, being paid only in goods and medicines. All told, the events in the Nambiquara region, a delayed response to the construction of the BR 364, could hardly have been a greater warning of the risks that the Indians run from road-building in Amazonia. One group of about 25, living by the road, has become a demoralized source of prostitutes for lorry drivers.

According to P. David Price, an anthropologist who has studied the Nambiquara since 1967, and who was put in charge of a FUNAI project to assist them in 1975, the tribe has not yet recovered from the power, impersonality and environmental changes wrought by the big firms in their region. Although they had a rich oral literature these Indians had only a simple technology. As Price told me, "Most of them can't speak Portuguese. They have no idea what has hit them, and they don't know what their future is." In two villages for which he had figures the population had dropped from 59 to 34, and from 56 to 26 in the seven years to 1975: in 1975 every death in the Nambiquara region was an infant death. The principal causes of death were colds and bronchitis which tended to become pneumonia, dysentery and measles (though by 1976 three-quarters of the tribe were inoculated against measles). Their land situation remains precarious. Some are still living in enclaves of their traditional Guaporé valley, while others have gone to the reserve. However, the FUNAI project, set up under Price, suggests a genuine willingness to help within the limitations of resources and the bureaucratic inertia of the agency itself. Although the ban on foreign anthropologists has cast some doubt on its future it was able to provide medical help, to seek a herd for an acculturated village which wanted one, and to press for schools. Between 1975 and 1976 its budget rose from 198,000 to 600,000 cruzeiros, more than doubling it in real terms. Nevertheless, without a project of this sort, and continuing attention from FUNAI, the outlook for this tribe must be poor. With small villages, encroached on by the salami development process of the entrepreneurs, it would be quite possible for the Nambiquara as such to have disappeared within a couple of decades.

The Xavante, by contrast, look well set to be around for a long time yet. The APS team in 1972 noted the high birth rate—an annual population increase of over seven per cent—at two of the three Xavante reserves they visited. When I was in Cuiabá in May 1976 *O Estado de Mato Grosso*, a morning paper, had a front page story about 500 Xavantes causing terror among settlers at a place called Nove Paraiso. The account was fascinating because this was a group which had formerly lived in this fertile area and had then been transferred, in the early 1950s, to the less fertile region of the River Couto Magalhães. The APS team, who saw some of them there—though many villagers were away working for diamonds and in plantations—felt that they were less well off than other Xavante groups. The team was frankly sceptical of their hopes of returning to the Culuene. However, they proceeded to do so and friction with the incoming *posseiros* increased when they discovered, in the middle of 1975, that the *posseiros* had violated an old warrior cemetery. Ever since they have been campaigning to get the invaders out—destroying a bridge to the settlement, surrounding it and threatening it, and forcing FUNAI to come and remove the *posseiros*. The whole issue has galvanized the Xavante who have never been shy of lobbying FUNAI and the state government of Mato Grosso for their rights. Although they still have land and other problems they now have five reserves and their acculturation has been an example for other tribes. They were first contacted in 1946 by the famous *sertanista* Francisco Meirelles—who named his son after Chief Apoena—and thereafter, with the aid of the Salesian mission at São Marcos in particular, they have learnt Portuguese with success. Yet at the same time they have preserved much of their culture and martial traditions. No one pushes them around without a struggle and, at the River Culuene, they seem to have achieved the unheard-of—a return to good traditional lands and the expulsion of those who have encroached on them. If more groups could understand and imitate the survival of the Xavante, there would be less reason to worry about the Amerindians' fate in Amazonia. In the meantime their determination stands out like a beacon.

9

CHANGES OF DIRECTION

SCATTERED THROUGHOUT AMAZONIA are the relics of
policies that have failed within living memory. They are quite
as poignant as the pieces of pre-Colombian pottery found near
Santarem or on the island of Marajó, or as the bones of Colonel
Fawcett's expedition would be if they were ever satisfactorily
identified. For they testify not only to the errors that have been
made in the attempt to "conquer" Amazonia, errors which
have been more recently repeated. In some cases they represent
approaches to development which may well be valid in future,
which have already become fashionable once more for the
policy-makers, and which were only abandoned in the last
decade or so.

For myself this sense of wasted history, and of the volatility
of human objectives in the river basin, was felt most strongly
when I journeyed beside two abandoned railway lines: along
the BR 364, which parallels and borrows bridges from the
Madeira–Mamoré railway; and from Belem to Bragança,
close to a line which took 25 years to build (from 1883 to 1908)
and which then had only 58 years of useful life, being shut down
as uneconomic in 1966 by the military government. The
Madeira–Mamoré has left several mementoes (indeed in
Britain one cannot help feeling it would still be run by volunteer
enthusiasts). There are rails still visible, though covered in
places by tarmac. There are stations still in existence in towns
like Abunã, and rows of housing for maintenance workers on the
line are visible at intervals in the forest. In Porto Velho itself
one of the small engines is a decoration for the local army
barracks; other trains and rolling stock are kept by the station,
which is preserved as a museum by the port on the River
Madeira; and the iron water towers, erected by the railway
company on a bluff over the river, are a sufficiently symbolic
landmark to decorate the Rondonia telephone guide. This is
the quaint Toytown railway which was the product of an

international treaty and cost over 6,000 lives to build. Its closure
in 1972, with Bolivian approval and after 60 years of operation,
seemed totally justifiable on economic grounds. Until, that is,
the jump in petrol prices and the new emphasis on rail investment after 1974 would plant a seed of doubt in the minds of the
impartial. Had a transport system which was really part of the
waterways (because the line by-passed nineteen rapids) been
written off just when price changes and a new potential in
Brazilian–Bolivian trade could have made it economic again?

The Bragança line has left fewer memorials—apart from the
fact that this district is still one of the most densely-populated
parts of Pará. But the sense of history which appreciated the
pioneer rôle of the Madeira–Mamoré railway in Rondonia has
been more negligent in the Bragantina. What is left of the station
in Bragança was merely a foundation of rubble in front of the
municipal bus station when I visited the town in June 1976.
The object of the Bragança line was not just one of transport,
like the Madeira–Mamoré. Its rôle was to stimulate a ribbon of
agricultural colonization, as described in chapter 3. Inadequate
motivation and ecological incompetence have made the
Bragantina a byword for how not to go about such colonization
schemes in Amazonia. When I travelled through the district
there were few visible signs of prosperity, with the exception of
some well-kept black pepper fields. There were patches of
scrub, some apparently abandoned fields, and poor crops of
manioc. Nevertheless, the view from a bus alone would not have
been sufficient to persuade one that this was the scene of a
major agricultural and social disaster. For that the condition of
Bragança itself was far more telling. It is a typical "abandoned"
riverside town, as people of Amazonia categorize it. Economic
activity seemed limited. There was only one bank, and no
restaurant open on Saturday apart from a cafeteria at the bus
station. If the Bragantina had been a resounding agricultural
success, Bragança would have been a thriving market town and
there might even have been a bit more argument about closing
the railway line in the anti-rail era of the 1960s. Ought not the
Medici government to have first demonstrated its capacity to
reclaim the Bragantina before embarking on another linear
colonization scheme, the TransAmazonica?

Whether looking at the causes or effects of the contemporary
push into Amazonia it is impossible to ignore the rapid

changes of official policy that have already taken place. Before drawing wider conclusions in the final chapter it is desirable to look more closely at these policy changes, some of which are specifically aimed at Amazonia and some of which will impinge on the region although they have been adopted for the whole of Brazil. National policy changes since PIN was launched have occurred in three main areas: economics, transport and social policy. Regional policy changes have occurred in development strategy (with the adoption of Polamazonia by the Geisel government), in Incra's agricultural and settlement approach, in ecological awareness, and in policy towards the Indians.

General economic policy for Brazil altered course sharply with the arrival of the Geisel government in 1974, and the new guide-lines were expressed in the second national development plan (PND) for 1975–9. Although this shift coincided with the coming of a new government, which made a fresh start easier, something of the sort would probably have happened anyway under the pressure of international events. The Geisel government was faced by a bad dent in its balance of payments caused by the rise in the price of oil, about 80 per cent of which was imported. The price of oil imports jumped from $726 million in 1973 to getting on for $3,000 million in 1974 and approaching $4,000 million in 1976. Secondly, President Geisel was confronted with a world-wide recession: this was hurtful to Brazil, whose extraordinary growth rate under Medici had depended heavily on foreign investment to assist the restricted capacity for domestic saving and on an uninterrupted expansion of Brazilian exports. Brazil's gross national product growth rate, which was 11·4 per cent in 1973, had dropped to a mere 4 per cent in 1975; although by 1976 it looked as though it would be around 7 per cent, close to the historic average over the previous 40-odd years. Thirdly, Geisel's ministers had to deal with a resurgence of inflation, in part imported, which took annual price rises from 15·7 per cent in 1973 to 34·5 per cent in 1974 and had them heading towards 50 per cent in 1976 until the public spending cuts of November that year.[43] The general strategy with which Geisel's economic ministers— Mario Henrique Simonsen and Joaõ Paulo dos Reis Velloso— responded to these circumstances involved the following: an attempt to reduce the dependence on imported energy, which meant more emphasis on hydroelectric projects and a nuclear power deal with West Germany which annoyed the United States, plus enlisting multinationals in the search for oil reserves, so ending the Petrobras state monopoly on exploration; a new drive to develop exports and substitute for imports —whether in the further encouragement of agricultural exports like soya or meat, or import substitution and export of "intermediate products" like paper and cellulose, or by a stimulus for fertilizer output and the capital goods industries; a new effort to obtain international financing, pursued in government-to-government fashion on President Geisel's visits to France, Britain and Japan in 1976, and by a sharper pressure on the multinationals who were suspected of exporting less than they were importing; and, in 1976, by a reining in of public expenditure, particularly on telecommunications and road transport.

Although these policies were changed for the benefit of Brazil, it goes without saying that they would all have consequences for Amazonia if persisted in with some determination. While Brazil's internal recession, which was most sharply felt in 1975, might reduce business investment in Amazonia those policies which stressed the export of meat, minerals and timber products must over time give economic activity there a new fillip. The demand for hydroelectricity was articulated just when the electricity authorities were getting a clearer idea of the enormous reserves which existed there. Amazonia too could help in more experimental types of oil substitution— whether by solar power, or by a process for making anhydrous alcohol out of manioc which in 1976 had a São Paulo group interested in investing 100 million cruzeiros ($9·5 million) in a plantation and factory, and which could also put money into the hands of 100-hectare settlers. On the other hand the stimulus for meat and agriculture might have more immediate effects on the cerrado or savannah lands of Goiás, Mato Grosso and the forest rim rather than on the rainforest area proper. Although there are technical and ecological problems about the management of the cerrado lands the general consensus in Brazil in the mid 1970s was that it was quicker and more straightforward to incorporate these than the forest land. Dr Bento de Souza Porto, the secretary for planning in Mato Grosso, put it unequivocally when he was commenting on cattle and rice output, "Cerrado is the best short-term hope for the state." This view was also held in the federal government and therefore could mean a diversion of possible pressures on Amazonia. It chimed in too with the continuing difficulties of cattle ranchers in the river basin. *Veja* (3 November 1976) reported that only 10 per cent of SUDAM's 337 cattle projects were considered to be satisfactorily established and that Hugo de Almeida, its superintendent, was hostile to new cattle schemes in the forest itself.

The second national policy switch was in transport. This was beginning before the end of the Medici government as Minister Andreazza began to plan new railway construction; but the new emphasis, which was designed to reduce dependence on oil and to give priority to "export corridors" for natural products and manufactures, came to fruition under Geisel. On the one hand this meant a reining in of the rate of growth for road-building. This had been conducted at a high level for roughly two decades, resulting in a quadrupling of the total extent of first-class paved roads to 40,000 miles between 1957 and 1972. The slowdown became even more marked after the the public-spending cuts in November 1976. At the same time other transport systems were strengthened. The federal railways (RFFSA) received 85,000 million cruzeiros ($12,500 million) to invest in the five years 1974-9: this would pay for extensive modernization and 2,500 kilometres of new track, of which the "steel line" linking Belo Horizonte, São Paulo and Volta Redonda was the most prestigious.[44] The railway programme was largely geared to electric power and regular movements of freight in bulk. Other attempts were made to serve the heavy passenger movements of the growing conurbations. Both Rio de Janeiro and São Paulo were building underground railways while in April 1976 a law was passed to set up the Empresa Brasileira de Transportes Urbanos, a body designed to find mass transit solutions for nine cities ranging from Belem to Porto Alegre. These solutions were dubbed "pre-metro": studies in the Ministry of Transport suggested that systems which borrowed the features of tramcars and trolleybuses could be established for a tenth of the cost of underground railways, and carry 5,000 travellers an hour compared with 8,000 by metro. Simultaneously the government tried to stimulate the growth of Brazil's merchant shipping, the improvement of ports, and the use of water-borne transport.

This change of policy inevitably had repercussions in Amazonia, as had been hinted earlier. The rail enthusiasm was echoed in the hopes for a line from the Serra dos Carajas. The use of the natural waterway of the Amazon itself was crucial to the extraction of bauxite from the Trombetas. However, the clampdown on road-building in Amazonia was relatively slow to take effect, principally because the case for it had been couched in terms of settlement and national development rather than transport alone. Although the Geisel government had its own Polamazonia strategy it did not repudiate such arguments entirely. Hence the brakes were not applied sharply until 1976, which allowed for the completion of the Cuiabá–Santarem (the BR 163) in October of that year, but postponed the completion of the Perimetral Norte and the asphalting of the BR 364.

The third national change was in social policy. The preceding governments since 1964 had all encountered criticism, at home and abroad, for apparently sacrificing the interests of the poor and the working class in pursuit of their model of economic modernization and capital accumulation. This model frankly required tight political controls by the army-backed régimes, no genuine freedom for wage bargaining by labour, and a warm welcome for foreign investment. It was justified by the aim of achieving an advanced Western capitalist standard of living and, ideologically, by a horror of "communism" widely defined. The governments before Geisel's had not been totally negligent on the social front—they had, for example, overseen a great expansion in education and the Medici government itself had introduced the Funrural scheme for pensions for rural workers—but whenever they had tried a mild political liberalization, as under President Castello Branco in 1965 or President Costa e Silva in 1967, they had been caught between the hammer of the right-wing military and the anvil of electoral hostility. President Geisel, therefore, whose government's political ancestry lay with the more liberal Castello Branco position, in reaction to the harder, more nationalist Medici line, came to power with a programme of political decompression and social reform. The two things went together because he wanted to demonstrate that the government was popular enough to win elections, and some social benefits for the mass of the public would help him to do so.

President Geisel's second PND was specific in its intentions.

Its chapter on social development strategy began, "The government has rejected the position of waiting until economic growth by itself solves the problem of income distribution, or the theory of 'waiting for the cake to grow bigger'. It is necessary, while maintaining an accelerated rate of growth, to undertake redistributive policies 'while the cake is growing'." The plan therefore attempted to tackle the problem of an inequitable income distribution by doubling gross national product per head from $546 in 1970 to $1,121 in 1980, by aiming to expand employment by 3·5 per cent a year from 1975–9—0·6 per cent a year faster than the predicted growth of the labour supply—in order to mop up under-employment, to spend 267,000 million cruzeiros ($32,900 million) on education and health in an effort to improve the quality of "human resources" and to invest 384,000 million cruzeiros ($47,400 million) in welfare benefits which were intended to reach the poorest groups and ensure that the workers kept pace with the growth in national output and productivity. In all, what was defined as the social budget comprised 43 per cent of the funds allocated under the plan and a presidential advisory body, the Council for Social Development, was empowered to co-ordinate the work of the ministries involved.

Now the forecasts of planners are notoriously fallible, ever vulnerable to economic changes and the politically unexpected. Few in 1976 would have anticipated that early the following year Brazil would have abrogated its treaty of military co-operation with the United States, in protest at President Carter's campaign for human rights. The world recession and Brazil's balance of payments difficulties since make it less likely that the country will have achieved the GNP per head which the PND forecast for 1980. Nevertheless, partly through astute control of the army commanders and partly because he was able to claim a victory in the municipal elections of November 1976, President Geisel so far has tried to stick to his political objective of decompression. (There was a hiccup in October, 1977, when Geisel fired his right wing Minister of Defence.) And this socio-political stance is likely to have real consequences for the assault on Amazonia, even though official government policy is to persevere with the incorporation of new lands there. Better wages and more jobs in the cities are likely to continue the drain from the countryside—the second

I

PND assumes that the rural population of Brazil will be almost static at around 45 million between 1970 and 1980, while the urban population grows by 25 million—and in Amazonia that is bound to weaken the pressure of migrants, whether they are *posseiros* or officially-organized colonists. If the overall social policy for Brazil is successful it is likely to intensify a type of settlement in Amazonia that stresses the towns and the cities and relies on a high wage, big capital approach to the forest and rural areas. Instead of being conceived of as a sponge for an excess population of poor people, Amazonia would have its share of a materially-advancing urban standard of living, and its riches would be exploited in a more capitally-intensive fashion to sustain it. In terms of the rate of transformation of hitherto untouched rainforest of course it may not make much difference whether the principal agent is a large company and a handful of well-paid men using the latest machinery, or a large number of poor men using machetes and spades. The companies, perhaps, have more options as to where to put their money than do poor men who must exert their labour.

All three changes in national policy, described above, have been reflected to some extent in Polamazonia, the Geisel government's regional strategy for the river basin. The fifteen poles (or sixteen if the Bragantina one is included) would if successful have important benefits for Brazil's exports and balance of payments; would add to the country's hydro power reserves and be less road-related than the PIN programme; and involve an urban and capital concentration which was a step away from the undiscriminating strategy of occupation of the Medici government. Polamazonia treated the region as an archipelago, not a continent that must everywhere be settled at once: significantly, only three of the original fifteen poles were north of the main river.

What does Polamazonia consist of? Basically it consists of canalizing federal funds available in funds like PIN and Proterra to provide an infrastructure of development in the following districts: Xingu–Araguaia, for ranching; Carajas, for its minerals; Araguaia–Tocantins (including Marabá), for its hydro power, cattle and agriculture; Trombetas, for the bauxite and agriculture; Altamira, for agriculture; the Maranhão "pre-Amazon" region, for land settlement and private-sector agriculture which may expand naturally with the building of the Carajas–Itaqui railway; Rondonia, for tin, minerals and agriculture; Acre, for rubber and forestry; Juruá–Solimões, for forestry; Roraima, for agriculture, especially cattle and pigs; Tapajos (including Itaituba and Santarem) for agriculture and hydro power; Amapá (the central and northern parts of the territory, not including the Jari project), for agriculture; Juruena (around the Teles Pires, Juruena and Arinos rivers in northern Mato Grosso), for agriculture, hydro power and cattle; Aripuanã, for cattle, agriculture and energy; and Marajó, for agriculture, cattle and forestry.

Within Brazil's development budget as a whole Polamazonia is cheap. The sum set aside for the fifteen poles was only 4,000 million cruzeiros ($493 million) (compared, for instance, with 100,000 million cruzeiros, $12,345 million, for the north-east over the same five years). This budget was also only a quarter of the size of the resources set aside for the first phase of the mining and metallurgical complex which included Trombetas and Belem, Carajas, Tucuruí, Marabá and Itaqui. Looked at in terms of its own investments this huge mineral and industrial operation, with its export potential and supporting agriculture, is by far the biggest initiative of the Geisel government in Amazonia. And this owes almost nothing to its predecessor's roads. Although Itaituba, Altamira and Marabá get some reinforcement in this regional strategy another striking feature is its recognition of the power of natural, rather than artificial, avenues into Amazonia. Seven of the poles stretch in an arc from Acre to Maranhão, beneficiaries of the south-to-north or south-to-west axes of migration and settlement. The Carajas-related developments in southern Pará may well have attractions for migrants from the north-east, helping to raise traffic levels on the north-eastern section of the TransAmazonica. But in the light of the original Medici aims for the Trans-Amazonica it is perhaps more significant that Carajas will be relying on its own railway to extract the ore, while the over-whelming investment to better conditions in the north-east is being put into the north-east itself.

The changes of policy in other areas—for Incra, ecology and the Indians—may be summarized more briefly. Incra's switch of interest westwards from the TransAmazonica in the early 1970s reflected the bad publicity the agency had received and an

awareness of the greater power of the spontaneous land pressures
coming up from the centre-west. Its switch to sales of larger
land areas to any one proprietor, when its rôle as land salesman
overtook its rôle as patron of small colonists, reflected a certain
loss of confidence as a colonization agency. But it was inevitable
from its duty to sell the federal lands in Amazonia. Nevertheless
this change of emphasis, which preceded the replacement of
President Medici by President Geisel, also converged with the
notion that only big organizations could successfully cope with
the difficulties of Amazonia, and with an approach which
looked favourably on projects with an export bias. The
"privatization" of Amazonia which is entailed by the process
of land sales and the discrimination of doubtful land titles is
almost certainly more important for the region's ecology and
Amerindian inhabitants than the specific measures adopted to
help them. Nevertheless, in the ways suggested in chapters 7
and 8, official policy has moved in a more sensitive and
conservationist direction.

In evaluating the prospects for Amazonia in future it is
worth trying to synthesize the reasons why official policy has
changed so considerably within the last decade, and then trying
to understand the relationship between these policies and the
underlying social, economic and political realities. Among the
reasons why the policies have changed have been economic,
political and international pressures; internal investigations by
non-governmental institutions like the press and the church;
and a certain pragmatic learning from trial and error in the
river basin itself.

In all the fields in which policies have changed the rôle of
economics has obviously been important. The acquisition of
new resources by businessmen, allied to poverty in the rural
areas, helped to account for the steadily growing pressure on
Amazonia even prior to the TransAmazonica. Yet it is important to stress that Medici's PIN programme might well not have
occurred in that precise form at that point in time for economic
reasons alone. The roads, after all, involved a diversion of
fiscal incentives money and the economic value of the Trans-
Amazonica in particular was far from clear. On the other
hand economic expansion in the river valley would have
required a more extensive road network at some time. The
TransAmazonica was a political decision which was much less

important in calculable economic terms than the RADAM minerals survey. It was economics, however, which caused the reappraisal of transport priorities after the Yom Kippur war and a certain slackening of pressure in 1975–6 in Amazonia itself. Between 1974 and September 1976, for instance, SUDAM approved only sixteen new cattle and agricultural enterprises for fiscal incentives, and a mere five industrial projects. The history of the Carajas and Trombetas ventures, enjoying the most vigorous government support, underlines the power of adverse economic conditions to delay even the most profitable schemes.

This power could become more important as Amazonia was increasingly seen as a region that was too expensive for Brazil alone to develop, as somewhere whose development had to be largely justified by the export revenues it could earn. This approach contains some irony, bearing in mind the traditional nationalist sensitivity about foreign incursions in the region. Instead of being just a colonial appendage of the centre-south, the river basin's fortunes would be more tightly tied to the markets and investing capacity of the United States, Western Europe and Japan. Yet in this history was repeating itself. It had been the force of North American and British and European capital which had powered the rubber boom at the start of the 20th century. Unless Brazil was going to opt for a controlled and isolated economic and political system, it was almost inevitable that the huge costs of undertaking meaningful development in Amazonia would have to be raised abroad. Compared with Japan, at its formative period of economic growth after the Second World War, Brazilians were poor savers who already desired to participate in a modern consumer society. They were not able to exploit Amazonia on their own. Their choice was between almost no development and development with a foreign input.

This message became clearer as they sought to grapple with the problems of developing the region. SUDAM, the main state agency involved, had approved 536 projects of all types by September 1976, worth only 70,518 jobs when they were all fully operational, at a price of over 20,000 cruzeiros (probably well over $2,000) per job. In an area of the size for which SUDAM was responsible this was a relatively small product after a nearly a decade. Nevertheless, even in the

foreign-owned enterprises, it was normally Brazilians themselves who were carrying out the undertakings in Amazonia,
and supposedly within laws and rules set out by their own
federal and state governments. The types of project which
caused the most extensive forest cutting were also cheaper and
much more likely to be owned by Brazilians themselves—
namely the cattle and agricultural schemes. Although they too
might be launched with an eye on overseas markets their initial
capital outlay was lower, and it was feasible to extend the
cleared areas gradually as funds were available.

Worldwide, as well as Brazilian, economics therefore were
responsible for the ebbs and flows of the pressure on Amazonia
over the last decade or so. Rising standards of living and
population numbers outside Brazil were the unseen forces
which, behind the more visible Brazilian factors, propelled the
incorporation of the resources of the river valley. This was at
its most obvious in timber extraction, the activity which,
destructively conducted, could be most ruinous to the region:
sensitively conducted it could be one of the strongest forces for
conservation. But the chain-saws of Amazonia were and are
playing to a score which is at least partly dictated from
thousands of miles away. Daniel Ludwig launched his venture
in the Jari, for instance, after calculating in the mid 1960s that
there would be a world shortage of timber products in the
1980s. By the same token, however, the successful development
of recycled paper and paper substitutes—and in Britain alone
in the 1970s there have been dramatic technical advances in
de-inking and in substituting plastics for newsprint—could
throw such calculations and chain-saw music awry. The old
story of natural rubber, with the appearance of cheaper
competitors elsewhere which undermine economic purposes in
Amazonia, could still recur for many of the potential products
of contemporary Amazonia. It is, however, unlikely to recur for
all of them at once.

The economic determinant in Amazonia was not always
overt and licit. There are numerous private airstrips in the
region and there is still plenty of smuggling. Gold from the
Tapajos region near Itaituba, for example, finds its way to
Bolivia and other countries without ever having declared its
existence to Brazilian authorities. Official awareness of this, and
a fear that it would spread unless prevented, also helps to

explain certain changes in official policy. The concept of the customs-free zone at Manaus was designed to offset the attractions of smuggling and turn the free movement of goods to better public advantage. Again the Medici government's objective of "occupation", supported by the despatch of more military units to the river basin, was in part designed to counter the filching of the area's riches.

Finally, having stressed the world factor in the economics that affect policies in Amazonia—and having noted that the world recession of the mid 1970s eased the pressure on the region—it is worth considering one historic parallel. World recessions can prove extremely stimulating for Brazil, so long as the country's internal purchasing power is maintained. Economists are generally agreed that the impetus for industrialization in the 1930s came from the collapse in world trade, which was then followed by a Second World War which made it virtually impossible for Brazil to import manufactured goods. If the world economy is now moving into a phase of slower growth following the 1973 oil-price increase it does not follow that the economic pressures on Amazonia will necessarily slacken for long. It could be that a strengthening Brazilian economy, operating with greater autonomy, is more able of its own volition to "conquer" Amazonia. If so, however, the nature of this process would be more controllable by and responsible to Brazilians.

But although economic trends in general may be the most powerful agent in Amazonia, it is also clear that there is a substantial political element in the various policy changes for the region. It was Castello Branco who launched fiscal incentives, SUDAM, and remodelled the Manaus free port; it was Medici who backed roads, linear occupation and a jamboree of national propaganda; it was Geisel who downgraded roads and went for selective development and the big mineral projects. Different consequences for the ecology, Amerindians and human settlement of the region flowed from each new emphasis. What may be surprising, however, to those who imagine that the military-backed régimes since 1964 represent one homogeneous whole, is the extent to which a change of federal government has also marked an alteration in approach. Hence the regular alternation of military presidents, even though none has been elected by universal suffrage, has provided some of that renewal of administration that "democratic" countries achieve through elections every four or five years. Each incoming government in Brazil brings a new set of personalities, a new range of contacts and personal experience, and a new consensus on policy objectives with it.

All the régimes since 1964 have been working to create a more modern system of capitalism in Brazil under state direction and leadership: this would aim to combine high growth rates with improving incomes, better social provision and the trappings of an advanced consumer society; some, particularly in the Castello Branco and Geisel governments, look forward to a gradual dismantling of political controls, allowing a greater freedom to the electorate to choose their government, as living and educational standards rise. Actual achievement, of course, has been somewhat erratic when set against such goals. But it is possible to distinguish between what might be described as Castellista and Medici tendencies in the military governments so far: they do stand at different points in the internationalist versus nationalist debate which has been—not only in Amazonia as discussed in chapter 1—a recurring theme in Brazilian history.

For the Castellistas it is desirable to welcome international firms with open arms on the grounds that their expertise provides the quickest short cut to developing the country; they believe Brazil is so big that no foreign firm can become too powerful. With this goes some respect for the liberal political and judicial values professed by the states of North America and Western Europe: they are part of the advanced capitalist model which Brazil is buying. The Medici line, however, stresses nationalist goals even though it has been equally dependent on foreign investment to achieve them. President Medici used to emphasize that the TransAmazonica was a nationalist programme and, in the priority it gave to planting small farmers in the region and ensuring a stronger military presence and communications system, there was some truth in this. At the same time the Medici line is much more open about the need for repressive controls, whether these are justified by anti-communism or the requirements of a developing state. Brazilian political commentators describe the Castellista position largely followed by Geisel as "liberal" while Medici's approximates to the "hard line" (*linha dura*). In certain perspectives, for example the Amerindian, there may be less to choose between them than first appears. An Indian group on land belonging to a large-scale owner such as Daniel Ludwig may or may not be more roughly treated, more pressed into acculturation, than a group that found itself in the way of one of President Medici's roads.

Politics of this kind, however, is not the only variety which is important in the region. There are also state and inter-state politics to remember, and a sort of administrative politics both federally and locally which have helped to determine policy changes. There was always a reservoir of hostility at state level to Medici's roads strategy: in Amazonas (especially), Pará and Acre, where electors choose their governors, there were always more citizens who were not benefiting from the roads than those who did. Even if road programmes of some sort seemed important these were often state and access roads rather than the federal roads which were devouring local budgets. In 1976 for instance, Mario Frota, a federal deputy from the tolerated opposition party, MDB, put forward a scheme by which municipalities in Amazonia might switch up to 50 per cent of their quota from the National Road Fund (Fundo Rodoviario Nacional) to improve water navigation. Hence there was local pressure, waiting to be harnessed by the Geisel government, to change the regional-development strategy.

Inter-state friction is another factor which alters the formation or application of policy. The quarrel between Pará and Maranhão over the extraction of iron ore from Carajas was one cause in the delay of that project. However, the rivalry between Belem and Pará on one side, and Manaus and Amazonas on the other, helps to explain the enthusiasm for big export-orientated agricultural and industrial schemes in Pará. An interesting policy statement for 1975–9 published by the incoming Aloyisio Chaves state government in Pará pointed out that the success of the Manaus free-trade zone was destroying Belem's traditional rôle as an entrepôt for the whole river basin, and at the same time undercut any hope of building up the economy by import substitution. The region was in any case too thinly populated to provide a good home market. The logic of this analysis led towards an export solution for Pará, with all its implications for large-scale industry and extensive ranching. But a major reason for this option is the Manaus customs-free zone whose defence and prosperity is, for politicians in Amazonas, a major plank for survival and re-election.[45] There is also an administrative politics at work in the background. The first father of the TransAmazonica was not a politician but a civil servant—Eliseu Resende of DNER —and subsequent policy shifts within the Ministry of Transport are at least as likely to have occurred because of officials rather than due to ministers. This less publicized dimension includes the interplay between ministers, civil servants and military which has continued throughout the governments since 1964. No officer of the Brazilian navy has had a major say in national-transport policy in recent years—although obviously the priorities for Amazonia might have been different otherwise. Army officers, who have been influential, have nearly all had their thinking conditioned by the construction and use of roads. When President Geisel appointed a soldier with experience of rail construction to be Minister of Transport (Dirceu Nogueira) it was an important break with a long tradition.

External pressure, aside from general economic forces or the interests of particular overseas firms, has also helped to change the policies in Amazonia. Just when the World Bank was helping to finance the TransAmazonica roads other international bodies—the International Red Cross, Survival International and the APS—were hastening to investigate the state of the Indians who were affected. Their representations were to some extent influential in persuading the Medici government to promulgate the Statute of the Indian and create more parks and reserves, and in stimulating FUNAI to become a more robust and sensitive body after General Ismarth became its head. Similarly the Stockholm conference had a definite impact on official policies towards conservation. However, it is important to keep the rôle of such humanitarian and conservationist pressures from outside Brazil in perspective. They did not prevent completion of any Amazon roads by themselves, nor did they deflect international financing for them. Some of the Brazilian government responses—like the Humboldt initiative—belonged to the politics of gesture. The overseas concern was not easily transmitted to the *caboclos* who were actually in conflict with ecology and Indians, and even where companies based outside Brazil were responsible for transforming Amazonia they have rarely had to face the kind of challenge that Walt Hardenburg posed for Julie Arana at shareholders' meetings nearly 70 years ago. If a different attitude to the conservation of the rainforest really becomes effective in Amazonia it may be much more the product of simple economics—like the SUDAM study which showed that cattle ranching in the region could only yield an 18 per cent profit and agriculture 28 per cent, whereas forestry made 55·4 per cent profit.

Certain international institutions have also been important in the policy changes that have already occurred. The press and Roman Catholic Church stand out for their independent critiques of successive emphases in the region. The press has helped to change policies merely by faithfully describing the effects of existing ones, and in spite of censorship which was particularly restrictive during the Medici period. Whereas local papers in Amazonia were often uncritically "developmentalist" in tone, some were quite willing to publish impartial accounts of land and Indian disputes. The quality press of Brazil—papers like *Estado de São Paulo, Jornal do Brasil* and weeklies like *Veja* and periodicals like *Opinião*—gave their middle-class readers an early intimation of the failures of Incra settlement along the TransAmazonica, of Indian suffering, and of the ecological risks of deforestation. Some of this work was carried out at risk to the reporters concerned. Mario Chimanovitch who wrote three outspoken articles in *Jornal do Brasil* in September 1972 under the title "The sad history of Indian integration" was sent abroad for his own safety. Others who left the beaten track to investigate labour conditions or the state of *posseiros* were threatened by gunmen.

Of particular significance under President Medici was the line taken by the *Estado de São Paulo*, the conservative paper renowned for its financial coverage which had been a warm supporter of the 1964 revolution. It became a vigorous critic of the TransAmazonica programme, partly because it did not help the north-east and partly because it diverted resources wastefully. Its forthright attitude, which was backed by a thorough coverage of Amazonian affairs, rallied other critics and blunted the charges of unpatriotism. It was still maintaining the same line six years later when the Cuiabá–Santarem road was eventually opened by the Geisel government. A thoughtful editorial criticized Brazil's dependence on road transport and quoted some comparative statistics: whereas Brazil carried 65 per cent of its tonnage by road and only 17 per cent by water and 18 per cent by rail the figures for West Germany were respectively 18 per cent, 29 per cent and 53 per cent; for the United States 25 per cent, 25 per cent and 50 per cent; for France 28 per cent, 17 per cent and 55 per cent; for Japan 20 per cent, 42 per cent and 38 per cent; and for Russia 4 per cent, 13 per cent and 83 per cent. "One of the greater crimes committed against the national interest is represented by this numerical comparison," the paper commented. Nor did it pull any punches in suggesting how this state of affairs had come about: the roads and their bridges were highly "inaugurable" and attractive to publicity-conscious politicians who wanted to cultivate the electorate; and a roads programme always offered opportunities of graft, both for officials and contractors. Although the international figures may have been inaccurate, the general thrust of the argument was cogent enough in Brazil.

The position of the Catholic Church was significant because, even at the most politically restrictive times after the 1964 military takeover, it remained independent of the government of the day and its views were reported to the public. It was not homogeneous in its social and political attitudes—a conservative establishment was under consistent attack from a leftist, progressive minority—but as an institution it still has considerable respect. Its ability to act as a national conscience after 1964 was enhanced by the fact that the preservation of Brazil's Catholic heritage from marxist atheism was one of the justifications claimed for the successful rebellion against President Goulart: in 1973 the National Council of Brazilian bishops made an important declaration in favour of human rights and social justice. In Amazonia its complaints or denunciations could have the more force because it was well represented in the region long before the TransAmazonica programme was conceived: small towns with well under 5,000 inhabitants were the seats of bishoprics, while many Indian tribes were looked after by Catholic missions. The length of its commitment, and the extensive knowledge which many priests have of an earlier Amazonia, equipped them to judge the new economic impetus from the angle of the indigenous *caboclos* and Indians. While welcoming anything that raised living standards and morale in the river basin the clergy in general were hostile to the more vicious and acquisitive aspects of contemporary development. They would speak up for the Indians, the road-workers, the poor *posseiros*. They pointed out morally corrosive features of the sudden wealth that the TransAmazonica had brought to the towns it passed through. (Unlike the decentralized Baptist congregations, the Catholics were slow to build churches outside established towns along the new roads: a lot of settlers are out of range of a mass.)

One bishop who has a reputation for castigating the rich and defending the rights of workers and Indians is the charismatic Bishop of São Felix do Araguaia, Pedro Casaldaliga. His see in north-eastern Mato Grosso has been transformed by the activities of the big ranchers and he is regarded as saint by the poor people who bring him their grievances. But other bishops have been ready to make their displeasure known as the occasion requires. Dom Henrique Froehlich, Bishop of Diamantino in Mato Grosso, wrote to the United States ambassador when he discovered that a man who had been using gunmen to evict 200 *posseiros* and their families was getting a US salary as Peace Corps co-ordinator in the region. Although it is not easy to identify the Catholic Church as responsible for any one policy change in Amazonia—with the possible exception of the move to protect Indian rights in the course of the Medici government—its presence has, in concert with the press and media, been a humane influence which has reminded the authorities of the social costs of their actions.

The other major factor in the changes of policy can only be described as pragmatism, learning capacity, or a kind of natural selection as those involved discover which approaches will or will not work in the rainforest region. SUDAM's talk of concentrating new ranching on the cerrado lands at the edge of the forest, and Incra's encouragement for the long-cycle tree crops along the TransAmazonica, are two cases of this. The point is that both ranching and short-cycle crops have been tried on the non-flooded rainforest land and, in too many cases, they have been found to be unsuccessful on average Amazonian soils. The lesson is the more clear because the experiment has been tried so widely in the last few years under government supervision and before considerable national attention. This possibility was sometimes ignored by the more vehement ecological critics of the TransAmazonica programme (who also failed to appreciate that this was a government attempt to win control over a piecemeal invasion of Amazonia which was already under way) although if indeed farming was going to be such an ecological disaster it would have been impossible to have persisted in it for long. But the same type of natural selection that is at work in deciding the most viable forestry or agricultural uses for the land has its counterpart in other changes of policy. The reason why a halt was called to Incra's original programme for 100,000 settlers beside the Trans-Amazonica was largely that too many difficulties had emerged in trying to establish the first colonies. This "difficulty" factor should not be underestimated either in the slowdown of SUDAM investment in Amazonia under the Geisel government, and the much tougher line on priorities: if there were fortunes just lying around to be picked up in the region the investments would still have roared ahead when Brazil was suffering from balance-of-payments and other economic problems. The whole boom psychology about Amazonia which had been propagated by the Medici administration had been deflated by Amazonian realities as much as anything. Problems of technique, transport, markets, the size of finance required for almost any enterprise, ecology and so on could not be wished away by sweatshirt slogans about the TransAmazonica making Brazil a giant. Nevertheless, although this natural selection effect may seem comforting to those who worry about the survival of the rainforest, the very acquisition of knowledge which at present may seem to be restraining the impetus into the region may in future lead to solutions of the various problems. Nor does it remove one possibility—that predatory logging of a kind that has wiped out Brazil's other former forests may continue to march across Amazonia, whatever happens afterwards to the land that has been cleared.

Having looked at some of the changes of policy that have taken place recently, and at reasons why they have changed, it is worth asking how far the official policies relate to some of the underlying realities. It is no good SUDAM and Incra insisting that 50 per cent of any property should remain covered by trees if soil depletion and absence of supervision make an owner cut them down. It is little help to Indian communities for FUNAI to say that their lands are inviolate if *posseiros* and cattlemen, squeezed from their own homes by forces with which they cannot contend, start biting into the reserves. It is folly to expect a complex road network to be postponed indefinitely if this is regarded as essential by military strategists, and the military are going to continue to have a decisive say in Brazil's affairs. It would be unwise to expect a reduction of migration into Amazonia, even if Brazil's birth rate turned down more sharply, if at the level of individual psychology one of the mainsprings is a man's desire to abandon his wife and family and go adventuring. (For some Freudian psychologists[46] to be lost in a forest symbolizes a person's desire to find his own identity.) It would be a mistake to suppose that Amazonia will be immune in future from sudden political interventions of the TransAmazonica type if another president scents national glory in the region. Nor, of course, will it easily be protected if the international economy finds it the source of some much-desired product—like rubber in the past, or possibly beef in future—whose extraction can revolutionize conditions in the region. In what is bound to be a somewhat arbitrary analysis it is necessary to emphasize from the outset that the social, economic and political realities which have a structural importance for Amazonia, which is more profound than the policies of governments, mostly originate outside the region.

The first underlying reality is that Amazonia represents available space which is free or nearly so. The fact that it already contains flora, fauna and Indians is by the way. Far more important for other Brazilians is that, by the titles of private ownership and the claims of visible utilization, there are enormous quantities of land which are still available. And, although the creation of Incra as a sales agent has somewhat bureaucratized the process of purchase and occupation, it is the duty of Incra to settle title and transfer all but the parks and reserves to private ownership. What this means is that, until all the Amazon lands are in effective private ownership, they will continue to be a magnet for companies and *posseiros* who desire them: only much higher prices for these lands, or effective prior possession, or a complete cessation of the pressures causing rural migration from the north-east, Paraná, Rio Grande do Sul and elsewhere could halt this.

But there is more to it still. The low valuation for the rainforest as it is, in strictly monetary terms, means that what is
there now is despised and value is only created as forest land is
transformed for other purposes. This has consequences for the
style of contemporary settlement: the cheapness of the land
encourages extensive ranching operations which are often
wasteful and highly inequitable in the income distribution that
they create. The kind of intensive agriculture practised by the
Japanese community at Tomé Açu—where from black pepper
they are now planning to move into other high-value tropical
crops like cloves, cinnamon, vanilla and nutmeg (where
INPA researchers have discovered 35 varieties growing wild,
some with hallucinogenic properties)—is not automatically
stimulated by land availability. Related to this is something
else. It would be unrealistic to expect, in a system where land
is up for sale, the property distribution within Amazonia to be
markedly different from the distribution in Brazil as a whole.
According to Incra figures quoted in a Ministry of Agriculture
report of January 1975 the situation in 1970 was that little
over 25 per cent of the land in Amazonia was in private ownership (roughly 123 million out of 487 million hectares). But the
distribution of this land was as inequitable as elsewhere in
Brazil; over half the properties occupied less than 50 hectares
each, and a mere 1·5 per cent of the total land, while just over
2 per cent of the properties, occupying over 5,000 hectares
each, accounted for nearly 52 per cent of the land in private
ownership.[47] The operations of Incra itself, particularly after
it began selling land in larger tracts from 1973, seem merely to
have reinforced this type of disparity.

The conclusion must be that availability of space alone does
not ensure a greater equality of distribution. This was an
implicit hope behind Medici's policy of diverting population
from the north-east into Amazonia. In the outcome the
settlement of the river basin is including *latifundia* (large
estates) of a type familiar to north-easterners, whose existence
in the north-east has been a cause of agrarian friction and
poverty. Although Incra is still trying to prevent mergers of
100-hectare plots along the TransAmazonica the workings of a
cash economy there too are tending to make the land
distribution more unequal.

The second underlying reality is that Brazil is, has been at least since the mid 1950s, and is likely to go on being highly committed to the idea of economic development. *Desenvolvimento*, the Portuguese word for it, became a catchword under the presidency of Juscelino Kubitschek, who built Brasilia: its ancestry as a national motivation can be traced further to the governments of Getulio Vargas in the 1930s. The objective of this future-oriented philosophy is not always clearly stated by its supporters. But their general remarks imply that it includes a high (North American or West European) standard of living; educational, cultural and social services levels to match; and an international status for Brazil which would recognize the wealth and skills of well over 100 million Brazilians, living in such a "developed" manner. This philosophy is extremely attractive to a country where gross national product per head is still less than half the West European average, and where income distribution is extremely inequitable. It offers a relief in future for the frustrations of the present. It has also become widely diffused in the army, where it chimes in with a positivist tradition and a self-assessed doctrine of political intervention in the national interest: since 1964 economic advance, enforced by military discipline, has been a major justification for the army's continued involvement in government.

But if development is part of the socio-political reality in Brazil, neither officials nor public opinion could allow Amazonia to remain in the sort of limbo of stagnation in which it was stuck for much of the 1940s and 1950s. This is for two reasons. The first is the absolute and relative poverty of the region's inhabitants during that period. The second is because to realize the possible resources of the region is seen as both a requirement for and symbol of Brazil's development. The work of RADAM and the actual confrontation with Amazonian natural conditions sponsored by SUDAM and the Trans-Amazonica programme have shown that there are indeed valuable resources in the region. But the geographical connection between occupation of the interior and national development had already been established by President Kubitschek with Brasilia and the roads he planned from there to Belem and to Acre. Other things connect with the idea that Amazonia is part of and ripe for development: the spreading of private ownership and a cash economy there; a certain disregard and ruthlessness towards anything that is there already; its increasing attractiveness for migrants who want to better themselves; the welcome for big and overseas firms who offer apparent short-cuts to development, and who come knowing that the federal government has defined this as a region of expanding activity while local state governments and institutions are poor and vulnerable.

The third underlying reality is the sheer size of Amazonia. The regional population would have to multiply many times, and become much more dispersed, before this space could in any real sense be described as occupied. What this means now is that officials and others still have only a dim, second-hand and outdated idea of what is happening in different parts of the region. Officials in Rondonia, Acre and the other states simply do not know precisely the size of their own populations —a basic tool for social and economic planning. The policing and monitoring problems to which the vastness of Amazonia gives rise are most evident in conservation and Indian matters, but they also help to explain the belated and intermittent official action where there are land conflicts with *posseiros*, or labour grievances on the big estates. In spite of ham radios, which are actively used by companies and official agencies in the region, local officials can feel very isolated and reluctant to upset local power groups. This is the more so because the availability of land allows everyone to think that conflicts can still be painlessly resolved by migration, while the "privatization" of land ownership marks an officially sanctioned award of authority to the new proprietors. Chiefly because of the size of Amazonia the federal government has subcontracted much of its law enforcement along with its development policy to the private companies: the power of officials can easily be reduced to the rhetorical.

Most importantly the size of the region makes it extremely hard for those living there, and those planning its destinies in São Paulo and elsewhere, to realize that it is not virtually limitless. Flying over the forest for hours at a time, with only occasional clearings for crops or huts, it is hard to believe that the rainforest or soils can ever be depleted. This seeming immensity has not only encouraged Brazil to plant roads and distribute ownership with abandon, it has also introduced a shriller note into the debate with ecologists and anthropologists who see more clearly that the rainforest is highly vulnerable to a sustained rate of "development", but whose warnings based on trend projections and personal knowledge are easily dismissed as exaggeration. Sometimes they have exaggerated, because so few involved can see that a forest disappears with its trees.

The fourth underlying reality is that the kind of cost benefit estimates which the government and companies apply to projects in Amazonia give a relatively low rating to the benefits that may accrue to inhabitants already there. The benefits that count are national or international. In so far as the local inhabitants are seriously considered it is just assumed that material and cultural improvements will trickle down to them. But President Medici's TransAmazonica was justified for north-easterners, newer colonization projects have been for people from Rio Grande do Sul and elsewhere, and even the Polamazonia strategy is primarily designed to assist Brazil's balance of payments and requires outsiders to the region to play a leading rôle. This disparagement, or at least underimportance, allowed for Brazilians already living in the region stems from the idea of development and from the practical recognition that they were too unskilled, undercapitalized and thin on the ground to do much for themselves. Yet the *caboclos* and Indians often knew plenty about vegetation and soil conditions, and their river-based transport and settlement patterns, which seemed "reactionary" when viewed from Brasilia, appear more progressive after the oil crisis. Their cultivation of the flooded varzea lands looks the more sensible in the light of the fertility problems on higher ground, and the shortage of cheap available fertilizer.

The national objectives, to be reached by outsiders with the aid of modern technology, brought the new lifestyles and skills of middle-class engineers and agricultural experts and federal officials along the TransAmazonica. Elsewhere private-enterprise people were more in evidence—cattle ranchers, geologists, bank managers. Numerically such arrivals were outweighed by the labourers and small farmers and *posseiros* who were coming at the same time. But it was the coming of a new middle class into the small towns of Amazonia which created new services and demands. Financially and in status this group is doing well—however much it complains about the backwardness of the society around it. But for the poorer migrants who came with them, and even more for the poorer existing inhabitants, the benefits of this process are much less clear. To generalize, it appears that the poorer immigrants have gained where they have found land, work, or access to medical and other services which they did not have before. But they have often had to work hard for these benefits, and providing them has often been subordinated to other needs of companies and federal agencies. Few such people have dramatically or quickly raised their standard of living, and some of them are already being squeezed out as a second wave of more moneyed immigrants is arriving, buying up the farms which have so arduously been cleared and made workable.

The obverse of the fact that non-local people are spearheading the development process is that the local people are often distanced and left on one side by it. *Veja* (3 November 1976) reported that Altamira had that month completed 65 years of existence. But, of the 3,000 inhabitants which the town had had at the beginning of 1971, before the TransAmazonica boom, "only few remain". It would be unrealistic to imagine that all these were beneficiaries rather than victims of the transformation of their town. There is little doubt that the more economically backward inhabitants of Amazonia can suffer directly from the process that has been unleashed—whether they are other shopkeepers in Humaita who cannot compete with the lorry-supplied supermarket which is a branch of another in Porto Velho, or growers who must accept what prices they are paid by transporters and are always liable to be undercut by bigger producers, or smallholders and fishermen who watch as a cash economy is created around them, suffering a loss of game and the supports of their simpler life-styles. The traditional inhabitants have gained something from the surge of development—especially in inoculations, health services and education. But even a bank manager in Belem told me that in his view their immediate losses outweighed the gains. Only a second generation, better educated and more capable of dealing with the new economy and society that is emerging in Amazonia, can hope to be full participants and beneficiaries. The reality of costs and benefits stems from the economic and political weakness of the region. Now, and for some time to come, the intention of its developers is that a disproportionate amount of the pecuniary benefits should accrue outside the region. The costs of a process which, as with the Trans-Amazonica roads, does not necessarily serve the priorities of local inhabitants, bear much more hardly upon them in real terms.

While much therefore has changed in Amazonia over the past decade or so, particularly government policies and the real rate of private investment from outside, certain constants have remained. In the final chapter it is possible to reach more general conclusions.

10

CONCLUSIONS

"Nature and the climate are nowhere so favourable to the labourer, and I fearlessly assert, that here, the 'primeval' forest, can be converted into rich pasture and meadow land, into cultivated fields, gardens, and orchards containing every variety of produce, with half the labour, and what is of more importance, in less than half the time than would be required at home, even though there we had clear, instead of forest ground to commence upon." Alfred Russel Wallace (*Voyages on the Amazon and Rio Negro*, 1853), an ecologist who made a mistake.[48]

"Would Brazil have been discovered if the Portuguese government had made economic viability studies before permitting the voyage of Cabral? Do the United States and USSR justify the realization of journeys into space economically? Do they see some immediate benefit in them for their peoples? No. Their decision, in relation to the conquest of space, is political. The TransAmazonica is, also, a political decision of the Brazilian government." Eliseu Resende, speaking to the graduates' association of the Escola Superior de Guerra, an engineer who put his finger on a truth.

ELISEU RESENDE WAS right when he said that Brazil had never conducted serious cost-benefit studies before embarking on the TransAmazonica adventure—nothing of the sort that helped persuade a British government to set aside its plan for a third London airport at Stansted. A political decision was carried out, at first regardless of the consequences. But that does not mean that it is necessarily impossible to draw up some assessment of the costs and benefits of the recent move into Amazonia. The fact that this is a difficult task, involving value judgements and an awareness of the trajectory of time, should not divert one from making the attempt. (The importance of time, of course, is that it can change uses and valuations of the same space dramatically: in an appendix to his book on *Latin American Development*, 1974,

Alan Gilbert pointed out that cost-benefit analysis was particularly difficult to apply to development roads in areas whose economy might only expand many years after they were built.) Above all one must be careful not to make a false antithesis based just on fears or intentions. We do not, for example, have to weigh the total destruction of the rainforest against the material betterment of several million north-easterners: whatever may happen in future, the rainforest is far from destroyed as yet, while it is already obvious that economic activity in Amazonia is only making a modest contribution to the well-being of a few poor north-easterners. In the last analysis, however, the case of Amazonia could yet raise some fundamental ethical issues in the debate on conservation and economic development. If the cutting down of the forest *was* essential to the relief of world starvation, or to a higher standard of living for poor Brazilians, would it be justified or not?

So what do the costs currently look like? In terms of Brazil's gross national product the financial investment in Amazonia over the past decade has been small; some of this money, as in the case of Ludwig's Jari project, has come from outside Brazil. Even at the height of the TransAmazonica road-building spree it was easier to argue that the region was at last getting its share of the federal transport budget than that it was getting far more than its due. Since the arrival of the Geisel government and tougher conditions for the Brazilian economy much of the waste in public and private investment in the region has been eliminated. In principle each of the fifteen original Polamazonia poles should be capable of a fair return on investment, even though that may be over as long as 20 years. However, the relative smallness of the financial input into the region should not blind one to the possibility that it might have been better spent elsewhere, or that it was being spent in a socially regressive way. Certainly if the Medici government had wished to be more effective in its impact on the problems of the north-east it is now clear that it would have done better to spend the funds for its strategic roads and colonization programme in the north-east itself: in extenuation for that government it should be said that the north-east seemed like a bottomless pit for public money, where nothing except the radical land reform which it was not prepared to consider could have a real effect on poverty. Firms investing in Amazonia would often have expected a better or more immediate return elsewhere, and only went into the region because of the fiscal incentives. Finally there was a social cost implied in the mode of financial investment. The SUDAM-supported projects tended to be capital intensive, just as those of SUDENE had been in the north-east, while the land-purchase and colonization patterns sponsored by Incra foreshadowed the same kind of inequity and distortion that existed elsewhere in the Brazilian countryside.

The human and social costs of the move into Amazonia have been high, and borne chiefly by the indigenous Amerindian and *caboclo* inhabitants, as well as by the poorest migrants into the region. Thousands of Amerindians have died, more by disease and cultural trauma than by direct cruelty; their situation in the new social environment that is being created is insecure and questionable. The *caboclos* have suffered through being elbowed aside, like the Acre rubber-collectors who have been squeezed over the border into Bolivia by developers from the centre-south. Like the Amerindians they have seen their interests neglected and themselves undervalued. Road transport for them was often only helpful if they were prepared to move beside the new highways, a change in their river-oriented way of life. For them development could be upsetting, although they were supposed to be its beneficiaries—making some prices cheaper, but creating more competition; preferring main roads when they wanted access roads; turning landownership upside down; making a higher, cash-based standard of living possible for their children, but despising their own values and knowledge. The poor immigrants into Amazonia, although they too carried some of the social costs and suffered individual hardship, were usually no worse off than they had been in their place of origin. Any exploitation they found on arrival in Amazonia was of a type they were probably used to. Where they found land or better public services, as along the Trans-Amazonica, they could find their gains outbalanced their privations; they often had advantages of skill or dynamism over the indigenous inhabitants they met on arrival. Although they too are bearing the social costs of the development process a number of them are obtaining rewards with time.

Thirdly, the ecological costs have also been considerable. Their real significance depends, however, on the medium-term future of the rainforest. For reasons discussed in chapter 7

I conclude that the 50 per cent rule designed for its protection, whose logic would only preserve separated stands of timber of greatly varying sizes, will on present trends be suffering breaches in the 1980s. Obviously the pressures are much greater south of the river Amazon, where the road network is more extensive. The specific costs already include the disappearance of locally-distributed flora and fauna; the blighting of land in those places, which will become more clearly identified by the 1980s, where inappropriate agricultural techniques are being used on former forest soils; and flooding and climatic changes which are the result of tree-felling on a large scale.

What, on the other hand, have been the benefits? Economically, as was stressed in chapter 5, the profits from Amazon enterprises have been slow in coming. This does not mean that they will never come—indeed the timber and ranching businesses ought to be increasingly successful as they get organized, while the minerals projects depend only on obtaining the large initial capital investment. The exact profitability of the big schemes will relate to the state of world markets at the time they come to fruition. In the early 1970s money was being sunk into Amazonia which has not yet borne interest: when it does so it will be instructive to see how much is reinvested in the region. The problem is that by going for export-orientated businesses, often involving multinational firms like Bruynzeel or Liquigas, Brazil must expect that much of the profit on the transport and marketing sides will never come back to the country. At the same time too many of the export activities— of which ranching is a classic example—combine few jobs with wide disparities of income. (By definition, of course, Amazon beef which is sold on world markets will not feed the starving: it will feed those who have the money to buy it.) So far, with the exception of the Japanese colonies which preceded the recent impetus into Amazonia, neither government nor inhabitants have been successful at finding the products, transport and marketing that would yield high agricultural incomes from small plots. The TransAmazonica rice surplus illustrated the difficulties that have not yet been overcome. Great imbalances still exist in the regional economy, so that Manaus cannot feed itself cheaply from its own surroundings, while the city's industrial zone is not yet geared to local raw materials. Nevertheless there is no reason why some of these distortions should not be removed in time, just as commercial fisheries or even the harvesting of leaf protein could develop with a larger economic infrastructure. In spite of the social and ecological costs now it would be short-sighted not to recognize that the bigger economic commitment is itself an economic gain which could have other uses: Amazon products could increasingly benefit Brazil rather than the world (industries now being created could be nationalized in different political circumstances) while fiscal and employment policies could ensure that the poorest in the region benefit more.

The benefits of President Medici's road-transport commitment have become more doubtful with the enormous rise in petrol prices. Roads which duplicate each other, as do the BR 319 and the BR 163, are now hard to defend. So too are roads which are built between towns which have little prospect of generating mutual traffic, when settlement does not take place beside them. However, traffic levels on the more easterly sections of the TransAmazonica do support Eliseu Resende's original contention that where roads and colonization are planned together they can both be viable. They would be viable more quickly if the budgeting and the structure of federal and state responsibilities allowed for proper upkeep of the access roads. A more unexpected but equally pertinent effect of the roads programme, coinciding with the Yom Kippur war, has been to stimulate a general reassessment of transport needs in Amazonia. More investment in water transport, in conjunction with hydroelectric dams on some rivers which can smooth out rapids,[49] is bound to take place. It might not have done so but for PIN.

The social and human benefits of the movement into Amazonia have so far been concentrated on groups from outside the region—the middle-class technocrats, the more recent purchasers of Incra land, the lorry drivers. But it would be churlish to ignore some benefits, particularly in health and educational services, for existing inhabitants of the region. TransAmazonica publicity helped to focus attention on mundane but pressing needs for piped water and sewage in the smaller towns; the arrival of army troops put such claims in channels that could influence governments, while the soldiers themselves could provide some of the services which the civilians had long lacked. Health and educational levels in the region are now climbing from the abysmal state of the late 1960s. But the rate of improvement appears faster along the Trans-Amazonica, where the federal government has taken so much responsibility, and in Roraima, which has been protected from much of the pressure, than in Rondonia, Acre or parts of Amazonas.

There have also been *ecological benefits* from the recent increase of interest in Amazonia, although ecologists may be reluctant to admit them. A great deal more is now known about the region, thanks to RADAM and the many other scientific surveys which have been recently launched, than would otherwise have been discovered. It is perfectly true that the hazards of attempting to transform rainforest land for agriculture were known to scientists in the 1940s and 1950s. But thanks to the reaction and research stimulated by the Trans-Amazonica this is now a part of public understanding, and the quotation from Alfred Russel Wallace, at the head of this chapter, is widely realized to be misleading. It could well be argued that the piecemeal penetration of Amazonia in the 1960s was more dangerous to the chances of the rainforest than the government-supervised TransAmazonica of the 1970s. Incra's encouragement of long-cycle crops, Hugo de Almeida's indication that SUDAM is trying to keep ranching out of the rainforest proper, even the Geisel government's Polamazonia programme—all reflect the fact that the Medici government chose to confront the realities of Amazonia under a blaze of publicity. Had it not done so in this way the conservation issues would not have been thrown up so sharply, the vulnerability of the rainforest would not have been so well advertised, and the bulldozers and chain-saws could have cleaned out most of the forest without the authorities or public taking stock of what was happening. None of this is to forget the losses and dangers which weigh so heavily on the cost side of the ecological account. But it should be admitted that if, against the odds, the Amazon forests survive in recognizable form into the 21st century it will be partly because the Trans-Amazonica programme set off the alarm before the damage was overwhelming.

But the case of Amazonia is not just a vast essay in comparing costs and benefits. It is also an instructive study in the real meaning of development as it is practised by many different

new
colonialism

countries today. This involves justifying today's pioneering
hardships and social inequalities in terms of tomorrow's
prosperity for all, while at the same time expanding present
class relationships and property patterns into areas that had
been free of them—indeed, inequality in the more populated
and "advanced" parts of Brazil has been one of the motors for
the occupation of Amazonia. It also means treating the area
to be developed—in this Amazonia is just an example—as an
internal colony; its priorities will be set elsewhere, the bulk of
the profits to be made from the development process will go
elsewhere, and the values and preferences of its people may be
subordinated to those of outsiders. Development is the new
colonialism. The fact that some in Amazonia wholeheartedly
welcome the process that is under way, just as some colonial
subjects identified the British empire with progress of all types,
should not deflect attention from the relationship of dependence
and subjugation that exists beneath the surface. It is easy to
forget, in all the talk of the "conquest" of Amazonia, that it is
people who are being conquered as well as space, and that
these people are not only Amerindians. However, and here is
the catch in any simplistic critique of development, it must also
be remembered that before the 1960s the people of Amazonia
themselves were in a poor condition to raise their own standards
of living and culture. They needed an injection of finance and
expertise from elsewhere. But anyone else, Brazilian or non-
Brazilian, would be looking at the region from his own perspective and with a view to what he could get out of it. From the
national standpoint it would be almost criminal not to realize
some of the resources—like bauxite and iron ore—which
the region contains. Brazil's difficulty here, given the shortage
of investment funds for projects in the rest of the country, was
that even assured reserves like these required foreign funds
and foreign markets, so that Brazil's benefit would be limited
to taxes, wages and any multiplier effects.[50]

military
govt.

How far is the type of development that is occurring in
Amazonia the peculiar product of Brazil's military governments? There is no doubt that there has been a military
interest in the region which was different from that of civilians—
a strategic and geopolitical concern with a large part of Brazil's
landspace adjoining most of its neighbours. The Trans-
Amazonica and its related roads have a strategic as well as

a developmental purpose. The publicity surrounding PIN reflected the needs and possibilities of a régime which lacked democratic legitimacy and needed to blazon its nationalist integrity. Only a strong government could divert the resources to make a splash in Amazonia, but only a military régime which had ruled out fundamental change in the north-east would have grasped at an unopposed invasion of Amazonia as a diversion. At the same time the nature of the development programmes in the region—whether SUDAM's fiscal incentives, the TransAmazonica colonization, or Polamazonia —reflected different aspects of the capitalist, free-enterprise model which the governments since 1964 have been promoting for Brazil as a whole.

Yet it would be easy to exaggerate what is peculiarly military, or even peculiarly capitalist, about aspects of the occupation of Amazonia. Several other Latin American states, with somewhat different social and political systems, have been pressing roads and settlement into their parts of Amazonia. It was Peru, under the elected President Belaunde Terry, whose trans-Andean jungle road was a precursor of the TransAmazonica. Ecuador, like Peru, has sought to use available Amazon lands as a solvent and diversion from land frictions in already settled areas. The self-proclaimed marxist government of Guyana, under Forbes Burnham, has been quite as ruthless as Brazilians in removing Amerindians from their fertile traditional lands in order to build the Upper Mazaruni hydroelectric plant. As in Brazilian Amazonia the national interest was seen as paramount over the interests of local inhabitants.

Outside Latin America there are other examples where thinly-populated regions have been held to require development, giving rise to similar dilemmas. A case from North America in the 1970s involved the provincial government of Quebec which is now flooding traditional hunting grounds of the Cree Indians of James Bay in order to build a hydroelectric scheme. At issue were not only the rights of the tribe, stemming from Indian treaties with the British Crown, but the survival of moose, caribou and a wetland habitat of streams and lakes. As in Amazonia there was an appearance of ecological abundance in this colder area which qualified scientists said was spurious. The legal and political situation in Canada being so different from the position in Brazil, it was possible for the

Cree and the Eskimo to sue to prevent the hydro works from starting. Legal action proceeded for over two years, 1972–4, and in November 1973 the plaintiffs obtained an interlocutory injunction ordering the hydro development corporation to cease work and cease trespassing on tribal territory. However, this was rapidly set aside and ultimately overthrown at law, while the Quebec government finally agreed with the Grand Council of the Cree that the Cree should surrender all rights in the land to be flooded in return for $150 million in cash and royalties and special rights in other lands. Although this settlement appeared generous—also giving the hunters possession of the animals and controls over new environmental intrusion—it amounted to only just over 10 per cent of the estimated cost of the project in 1974. There was no doubt either that the needs of Quebec—and the needs of New York to whom much of the power would be sold at preferential rates—had triumphed over those of the local inhabitants. In this case, too, the agency was not even a fully-fledged national government.[51]

Nor is it clear that the Soviet Union has shown much more sensitivity for the environment and the rights of local inhabitants in its contemporary development of Siberia. This, like northern Canada, is an area of great ecological interest. Like Amazonia it contains one of the world's greatest forests. The strategically motivated trans-Siberian railway was one of the many conceptual precursors of the TransAmazonica. But, in spite of the indistinct reporting of this remote and extensive region, it appears that national Soviet interests have been regarded as overriding the claims of the environment and local and native peoples; in spite of the Soviet Union's tradition of greater economic autonomy it too has drawn in Japanese and other outside capital in order to realize its far-flung assets more quickly.

One conclusion that should be clear even from this brief look at other examples is that the imposition of national priorities implicit in the idea of development is far more the product of territorial control and national material ambitions than of any one political or social system. The case of Quebec, apparently different in being a province rather than a nation state, in fact demonstrates the great determination of a French Canadian identity endowed with territorial boundaries which has felt subordinate to the economic and cultural needs of the rest of Canada. In the case of Brazilian Amazonia it is probable that a non-military government would also at some time have launched an attempt at occupation. The logic of President Kubitschek's attitude to the interior did not stop at Brasilia. The bigger the territory to be "developed" and the fewer the people it currently contains, the more overwhelming the rights of the national developers are in their own eyes. Yet both their practices and attitudes would be labelled as colonial if the territory to be developed was separated from their own, and in many colonial empires the subjects have had more redress than have the more remote and culturally-impoverished citizens of some nation states. Where the nation state is at one with powerful and sophisticated multinational companies there may be less chance of objections being aired on the spot than at shareholders' meetings in the firm's own country. In Amazonia, of course, the Brazilian government claims to be supervising the bigger firms and there is no doubt that some of them are working to high standards in their environmental and employ-ment practices. Nevertheless it is questionable whether it is the government or the firm that has the upper hand in this mutual relationship. The government has offloaded much of the practice of its development policy to the companies and, even where they are not as secretive as the Jari schemes, it has to take what they are doing on trust.

Another rôle for development, which emerges sharply from the preceding chapters, is as a sidestepping of social change. Amazonia is carrying the costs of poverty and rural back-wardness in other parts of Brazil in a way that does not threaten prevailing patterns of ownership. This was the government's intention behind the original TransAmazonica programme. Instead of tackling poverty, agricultural backwardness and ecological mismanagement in the north-east itself, many thousands of people were to be displaced into the Amazon forest. The fact that this particular exercise in planned coloniza-tion missed its targets should not blind one to the realization that a similar process is at work, often spontaneously, involving migrants from other parts of Brazil as well as the north-east. Development has become a vast diversionary movement because the problems of raising living standards where the poor currently live seem so intractable: the political strength and economic ineptitude of the richer classes is hard to overcome in a non-revolutionary way, while the real health and skill levels of the poor may be so low that, as the Incra recruiters discovered, it seemed a bad risk to take them as official colonists along the TransAmazonica. Nevertheless the poor can still move of their own volition, hoping for land and a second chance in a more fluid frontier society. And their hopes can indeed be realized. This is why the option of migration is so attractive while the possibility of fresh lands still exists, and why Amazonia can expect to be under pressure for decades to come.

However, any conflicts that arise in the frontier zones of Amazonia should be set against the much bigger ones that are avoided because this safety valve exists. Migration of this kind is a relatively cheap investment in social peace in other parts of Brazil. The development option is cheap because in private ownership terms the land is virtually free and, as the discussion of Rondonia's budgetary difficulties in chapter 4 indicated, the allocations of public money to the receiving states and territories are not large. At the same time, for participants in the development process, it offers a clear futurist goal: every new bank branch or kilometre of asphalted road gives them the feeling that they are achieving it by measurable instalments. But what neither the individuals themselves, nor the framers of development policy will admit, is that their fashioning of the future is so often a retreat from an intransigent past. This is a retreat that takes them into new landspace but, like an army of veterans, they are taking only the baggage of skills and unfulfilled ambitions which they had before. Ironically the developed society which they hope to build may end up remarkably similar to the one from which they are escaping.

But what will happen when Brazil recognizes that Amazonia can no longer serve as an escape valve, either because all the land is occupied, or because more effective conservation measures have put restraints on its development? Maturity for nations, as for individuals, represents a knowing acceptance of limits, a deliberate refusal to exercise power in destructive or anti-social ways. Brazil, which Henry Kissinger described as an "emerging power", has been going through the type of changes which, by the end of the 20th century, might cause its society to be described as "developed": gross national product has been growing sharply even if income distribution has remained unequal; educational and other social services have been expanded rapidly so that culture and skill levels in the working population are bound to be much higher; falling birth and death rates mean that the population structure is gradually taking on a more mature quality. Assuming that the process of growth itself has not completely destroyed the rainforest, ecology, Amerindians and life-styles of Amazonia—a big "if"— these could all be generally prized as among the glories of a more prosperous and developed Brazil by the end of the century.

But such an outcome depends on more than just conservation attitudes and policies, backed up by more efficient enforcement. It will also require the kind of income egalitarianism and rural reforms in the settled parts of Brazil which have proved so difficult to achieve in the past, but whose absence has promoted land speculation and occupation in the developing areas of Amazonia. There is little doubt, comparing the Geisel government's much larger allocations to SUDENE rather than to SUDAM, that the present government appreciates the need here. The task is, however, to maintain this kind of priority for several administrations and to obtain results. At the same time Amazonia itself needs to be spared from political gimmickry by the federal government; its own inhabitants, through their state governments, need to obtain more control over the development process so that they genuinely obtain benefits from it; and, while ensuring that economic growth is not of a destructive type, those responsible for the region must go on obtaining new investment so that the inhabitants do not revert to the status of Brazil's poor relations.

A combination of conservation with judicious economic exploitation ought also, ideally, to involve Brazil in co-operation with its Amazon neighbours. The sovereignty issue has been delicate for all the nation states in the river basin, as has been described in chapter 1. Nevertheless, in geographical terms, the river basin has a unity. Either destruction or achievements in one nation's territory may well have effects in another's. In terms of regional planning or conservation, for instance, Amazonia lies midway between the north Canadian or Siberian situation, where a large and distinctive land mass is the responsibility of one state alone, and Antarctica or the oceans where usage and responsibility are truly international. If

K

Amazonia's rainforest is to be conserved while some of its mineral and other riches are realized, Brazil must take the lead in multinational measures of economic liaison and conversation. As geography suggests that Brazil will be the biggest beneficiary and financial contributor this is something to which it must be wholeheartedly committed. Multinational co-operation of this type could cover scientific research, ecological guidelines and practical policing, Amerindian affairs and economic co-operation. The multinational park proposed by the Colombian Minister of Agriculture in 1975 might be just one practical outcome of a system of collaboration covering various fields. And in this co-operation it would be just as important that SUDAM and the development agencies of neighbouring countries should play their part; for a strategy of conservation that ignores the legitimate claims of economic development will be worthless or subverted. The alternative to collaboration by the nations of Amazonia is clear enough: this would involve a duplication and waste of economic resources; the individual rediscovery of forest, agricultural and climatic knowledge; and the piecemeal destruction of the rainforest.

But Amazonia requires more than just a mature willingness to recognize the interdependence of national interests. It also needs a more sophisticated and responsible attitude to the private ownership of land for the destruction that a private owner can cause is, proportionately, quite as large as that of a national state. As an expression of its own political and economic philosophy Brazil has been stepping up the proportion of Amazon land which is held in recognized private tenure. As we have seen this "privatization" of a resource which was previously "free" is part of a process of agricultural transformation and growing land values. Although certain areas are set aside for parks and a system of zoning for forest uses only could be introduced with advantage, the position now is that the Brazilian authorities have no control over what happens to the land in private ownership apart from exhorting obedience to the 50 per cent rule for maintaining the tree cover. Private ownership is not an unmitigated evil for the conservation of Amazonia, for an owner who damages the soil may have to bear the losses, while the lack of defined ownership has contributed to the past depredations of those who could plunder and move on. Nevertheless, if the rainforest is to survive in a worthwhile form a huge programme of public education and inspection will be required. The new owners must learn that the forest has a value which does not just consist in cutting it down, and they must in real cash terms be able to participate in this value—whether by selective forestry, improved methods of natural rubber collection, or by the regulated hunting and export of game. Ecological guide-lines must be credible and capable of being observed by illiterate *caboclos*. At the same time the standards of conservation in public forest parks must be exemplary for the private owners. It is not impossible to imagine that private owners could be an important buttress for the unique character of Amazonia. In Scotland, after all, estate owners whose main concern is with deer and game shooting have maintained the moors in an ecologically good condition, which also makes them a tourist attraction, for generations; such owners have had little difficulty in observing the rules laid down by national park authorities. In Amazonia, so far, something of a contrast has been assumed between park areas and private ownership; foreigners were concerned that the limited parks programme undertaken before and during the Medici government in fact permitted the transformation of the whole of the rest of the region. But if conservation is to be meaningful it will be attained as much by integrating the support of the private owners as by greatly extending those publicly-owned areas which are supposed to have total protection, but which in reality are difficult to police. Another way of changing the valuation of land in Amazonia is by recognizing how precious are those areas whose transformation for agriculture is permitted. Here the attitude of the Medici government, aiming for small but highly-productive plot areas, seems to have been more farsighted than the sale of large expanses. If Japanese levels of productivity could be achieved on the Incra 100-hectare plots there would be less justifiable pressure on other parts of Amazonia.

Is there anything that concerned people outside Brazil can do to help—whether in minimizing the costs to fauna, flora and local and Amerindian inhabitants, or in ensuring that a fair proportion of the benefits of development do reach local Brazilians? As this book has underlined, the main responsibility for what is happening in Amazonia lies with Brazil and Brazilians; given the fundamental importance of territorial possession for Brazil, ill-considered international interventions risk creating further examples of the unpredictable dialectic referred to in chapter 1. Nevertheless, in schemes in Amazonia which require foreign money to be established at all, there is no reason why shareholders and citizens of countries outside Brazil should not insist that the environmental impacts and social benefits be assessed in advance. Such precautions are now being taken in other countries. At the Caura dam, on a tributary of the Orinoco in Venezuela, the Venezuelan authorities have insisted that not a single tree be cut down unnecessarily, and a lot of money has been spent on surveying the biological matrix of the area. Questions about the situation, rights and employment prospects of Indian groups who may have traditionally lived on land earmarked for a development scheme should be satisfactorily answered before their environment is overwhelmed.

Secondly, where international agencies and funds are assisting in major projects—as the World Bank did with the TransAmazonica programme—it is incumbent on them to assess the environmental and social impacts before they award the loans. In the sort of political situation which existed in Brazil in mid 1970, where the government wanted to make a dramatic gesture quickly, theirs is the only pressure which can ensure that these other factors are properly discussed in time. When the International Monetary Fund was asked to give a major loan to the British government in November 1976 its officials spent some weeks in London, cross-questioning civil servants, checking their arithmetic and making sure that all possible options were considered by the British treasury. Similarly the World Bank might, before underwriting some of the cost of the TransAmazonica, have questioned whether the same money might not have been better spent in the northeast, whether the plans for agricultural colonization were soundly based, and what the environmental and Amerindian consequences would be. Obviously international agencies could not have a veto power on schemes like this, but they can insist on reflection. In the case of the TransAmazonica there was instead a somewhat ridiculous sequence—an international outcry after an international agency had already underwritten the scheme. Ideally the United Nations, both in its concern for development and the environment, ought to monitor the more far-reaching schemes in the third world which rely on international aid; in reality, as a club of sovereign states, the UN is not well placed to intervene in policies that they regard as matters of sovereignty. However, environmental groups have already found some means of forcing the international agencies to pay more regard to ecological issues; a consortium of them have brought a test case over the section of the PanAmerican highway which was planned to cross the Darien Gap between central and south America; their argument was that United States government funds should not be used to implement a scheme which would not meet United States environmental standards.

Thirdly, the rest of the world, which should perhaps include the citizens of Brazil's more developed centre-south, can minimize destructive incursions in Amazonia by changing some of their own habits. Effective recycling of wood products in the developed world, higher agricultural productivity elsewhere, or even dietary changes which reduced the potential demand for Amazon beef—world market changes of this kind must inevitably alter the valuation that is put on Amazonia. Economically the region is a dependent variable. Although this makes it vulnerable to sudden desires from outside, it can also be drastically affected, as at the decline of the rubber boom, when a demand collapses. While no one would wish to repeat the plight of the rubber collectors between the First and Second World Wars conservationists could act on the world market connection at the points where the demand originates. If timber deficits and food deficits in the rest of the world could be reduced by a better use of already occupied landscape—and this obviously includes effective reafforestation in the centre and south of Brazil—there would be much less cause to incorporate new space in Amazonia and elsewhere. It might even be possible for Incra to call a halt to its land-sales programme in Amazonia, holding the undistributed areas in trust for the nation and the world.

Fourthly, there is a great deal that the international community can do to further the scientific understanding of Amazonia and to assist its ecology and Amerindians without incurring the errors of neo-colonialism. Much of this ought to involve continuing co-operation with Brazilian institutions, and should avoid what Warwick Kerr describes as "environmental tourism"—the quick study-trip followed by the immediate report. But it is clear that, whether we are considering complex ecological questions about the forest mass and climate, detailed points about soil properties, or even the taxonomy of animal and vegetable species, there is still a great deal to be learnt. A much heavier scientific investment will not guarantee a wiser use of the river basin, but at least the scientific issues in its development will be better understood. There is scope for help at a more practical level also: the IBDF could make more of a reality of its forest parks programme with technical assistance from outside, while its inspection systems could be greatly enhanced with the aid of helicopters; the Indians, in spite of FUNAI's conflict with foreign anthropologists, still need some support during the difficult course of acculturation. Even quite modest assistance from non-Brazilians, offered in a spirit of partnership and without the supercilious pretence that they know all the answers in Amazonia, can have a real benefit in an area where resources are thinly spread. It also helps to meet the criticism that the rest .of the world is quick to point to human and ecological disasters in Amazonia when it is often at least a sleeping partner with the forces that create them.

In spite of the special characteristics of Amazonia and of the Brazilian military governments the TransAmazonica venture was perhaps representative of the style of modern nation states in general. A national interest was asserted. National benefits were averred in a spirit of faith. A programme was launched to which other factors, whether economic or environmental, simply had to accommodate as best they could. As Eliseu Resende pointed out, this affirmation of political will was not so different from the way in which the United States embarked on its space programme; he could equally have compared it with the joint Anglo-French commitment to the high technology, supersonic aeroplane, the Concorde. The political needs for a visible and immediate action—whether in assisting Brazil's north-easterners, matching Russia's triumph with Sputnik, or preserving employment and an advanced aeronautical industry in Britain and France—override the time requirements for cost-benefit analysis. Governments are not expected to evade a crisis: they must do something. In any case it is often difficult to predict the real costs and benefits of a project until it is under way. But when national governments act in an atmosphere of heightened excitement, calling on the national interest in justification, they become coercive. The balance between decisiveness, and humane and rational decision-making, is a source of tension even in countries which are better equipped for public debate than the Brazil of President Medici. And of course it must be recognized that many national achievements, which are widely accepted as such later, would never have begun but for an act of faith and a diversion of resources which may have borne heavily on others who could have used them.

I have tried to be dispassionate in chronicling the different aspects of the contemporary assault on Amazonia: to explain why it is happening, who is involved, and how its style and direction has changed. In drawing attention to greed and violent conflict one should not forget that the whole movement also contains many examples of patient labour, selflessness and idealism. Indeed many of those who have a "colonial" attitude to the development of Amazonia combine it with a strong idealistic desire to see the cultural and material betterment of its inhabitants, and the products of a more developed Amazonia relieving hunger and need throughout the world. My own perspective is not one of "hands off Amazonia at all costs". Although I give a high priority for the real preservation of the bulk of the rainforest I do not think that economic advance could or should be excluded from the region. What I do feel strongly is that poor Brazilians, among whom I include the Indian groups, should benefit from the economic development that takes place, and that the modes of development should harmonize with preservation of the forest wherever possible. But the picture is moving all the time. Amazonia was under assault before the TransAmazonica programme. Now its future lies in more hands. High intelligence and widespread public support will be necessary if it is not to become a memorial to the despoliation of the planet. If Amazonia ever did have anything in common with the Garden of Eden it is just that many have now tasted of its tree of knowledge. It is important for humanity, as well as for Brazil, that good should outweigh evil.

NOTES

GLOSSARY

BIBLIOGRAPHY

INDEX

NOTES

Chapter 1

1 Calentura was a fever occurring on board ship in hot climates. Raleigh's claim is quoted by Betty J. Meggers in *Amazonia: Man and Culture in a Counterfeit Paradise*, Chicago, 1971.

2 Vera Pacheco Jordão, an art critic for *O Globo*, made this off-the-cuff comment to the author. It is representative of the historical view of many educated Brazilians.

3 This total was quoted by Arthur Cesar Ferreira Reis in an address entitled "Ocupação da Amazonia e Cobiça Estrangeira" (literally, "Foreign greed and the occupation of Amazonia") reprinted in *A Amazonia Brasileira em Foco*, number 8. He stated that the Franciscans of St Anthony, who established a convent near Belem in the early seventeenth century, were the first order in the river basin; they were soon followed by the Jesuits, the Carmelites, a Spanish order coming via Quito, and two other bodies of Franciscans.

4 Variations in the definition of Amazonia itself account for some divergences in past estimates of population. This set, which is higher than some others, is taken from Meggers, *op. cit.*

5 Interview, 7 June 1976. On the same day INPA also had 94 scientists based at the Goeldi Museum, Belem, and two at the Aripuanã field station.

6 These figures are published by the quasi-official Fundação Instituto Brasileira de Geografia e Estatística in *Sinopse Estatística do Brasil 1975*.

Chapter 2

7 Literally, "Hello wood, hello timber / pretty wood. / Mother mine / Most holy Mary / Help / to get down this wood."

8 Resende's article was reprinted in Alberto Tamer, *Trans-Amazonica, solução para 2001*, Rio de Janeiro, 1970.

9 The first section of the TransAmazonica was put out to tender on 26 June, ten days after the announcement of PIN.

10 It is not easy to establish the real average costs of the Trans-Amazonica per kilometre which is why the range of $51,000–$60,000 is so wide. The lower average is obtained by accepting

the estimate of 810 million cruzeiros in 1974 and dividing it by the 2,322 kilometres involved. The top one is based on a sum of 410,000 cruzeiros per kilometre which was quoted by *O Estado de São Paulo* on 20 October 1976 in an article discussing the inauguration of the much cheaper (330,000 cruzeiros per kilometre) Cuiabá–Santarem road.

11 Interview, 9 June 1976.

12 Use of the pools could give rise to friction and jealousy. At Altamira, for instance, DNER workers' children looked on longingly, having to be chased out at intervals, when the engineer's guests were using the pool. He permitted them to swim, however, when his guests had gone home.

13 Interview, 27 April 1976.

Chapter 3

14 Where privies exist they are not always built at a safe distance from a house and its water supply. A SESP doctor at Altamira, who pointed this out, also observed that the standard height off the ground of Incra houses was insufficient to keep the occupants clear of mosquitoes. They are normally on stilts one metre high. In his view they should have been three metres off the ground to have been safe. Specifications for the Incra utility houses were probably settled by officials far from the TransAmazonica. Initially the houses were imported in prefabricated form from the centre-south.

15 In "Confronto de Adaptação em Projetos de Colonização", reprinted with other seminar documents by the Nucleo de Altos Estudos Amazonicos, Federal University of Pará, 1974.

16 Interview, 7 May 1976.

17 This means, nevertheless, that nearly all the schemes currently possessing SUDAM grants are using land obtained from the states or private proprietors prior to Incra's sales.

18 Quoted in *O Estado de São Paulo*, 6 November, 1975.

19 Interview, 1 July 1976.

Chapter 4

20 *O Estado de São Paulo*, 25 April 1976.

21 Susan George in *How the Other Half Dies*, Pelican, 1976, blames soya-bean farming for export, promoted by United States agribusiness firms, for displacing black beans (*feijões*) which were a staple for poor Brazilians. However, she wrongly states (p. 93) that "Brazil, like Argentina, was one of the few developing countries where meat was cheap enough to be a staple food for much of the population". Outside areas like Rio Grande do Sul this has only been true for the better-off. Senator Benedito

Ferreira told Congress on 12 October 1971 that annual average Brazilian consumption of meat was only fifteen kilos per person, compared with 51 kilos in Argentina and 70 in the United States. Brazil has long needed to raise the output and productivity of its cattle sector. This is why, whether the meat was destined for the home or export markets, SUDAM was able to assume general support for the ranching programme in Amazonia.

22 These figures for Aripuanã, Barra do Garças and northern Mato Grosso come from the *Anuario Estatístico, 1974,* Governo do Estado de Mato Grosso, Departamento de Geografia e Estatística.

23 Interview, 31 May 1976.

24 The same feeling in western Amazonia has led to periodic attempts to have the headquarters of SUDAM transferred from Belem to Manaus.

25 This argument is developed in particular by Janice Perlman, *Myths of Marginality: Migration and Integration in a Brazilian City,* University of California Press, 1975. See also Francine F. Rabinovitz and Felicity M. Trueblood (ed.) *Latin American Urban Research,* SAGE Publications, Beverly Hills, 1976.

26 *Opinião* 2 July 1976.

Chapter 5

27 *Wall Street Journal,* 8 October 1976. This newspaper report also spelled out the details of the trade deficit and foreign debt which was causing the Brazilian government to cut public expenditure and squeeze the multinationals. The adverse trade balance was then forecast as $2,500 million, while the net foreign debt for 1976 was forecast at about $23,000 million. Three years before Brazil's net foreign debt had been only $6,200 million.

28 Interview, 3 May 1976.

29 Roberto Campos, who played a part in introducing Ludwig to Brazil, states that he is the outright owner of these Jari lands. The idea of the lease probably originates in the autonomy of the Jari enterprises. Ludwig, who is a strong opponent of all forms of government interference anywhere, has made it clear to successive Brazilian presidents that he wishes them to be left alone and, to a large extent, they have been. Persons like Arthur Ferreira Reis found it hard to believe that Brazilian governments had made such an absolute cession of so much territory, and therefore assumed that there must be a lease agreement.

30 Interview, 9 June 1976.

Chapter 6

31 Interview, 1 June 1976.

32 Traffic figures given here were kindly supplied by local DNER offices. The months of April and May are among the drier months along the TransAmazonica (especially May) and traffic is likely to be much heavier than it would be in November or December.

33 Brazil is turning to railways for regular bulk freight. It is significant that Daniel Ludwig, for instance, is building a 220-kilometre railway to transport timber on his Jari property to the pulp mill.

34 Interview, 2 July 1976.

Chapter 7

35 Interview, 7 June 1976.

36 A précis in Spanish of this conference, prepared by Duncan Poore, IUCN's principal ecologist was published in 1975 as *Normas Ecologicas para el Desarrollo del Tropico Humedo Americano*, IUCN Occasional Paper 11. A similar conference run by the IUCN later in 1974 in Indonesia resulted in *Ecological Guidelines for Development in Tropical Forest Areas of South East Asia*, IUCN Occasional Paper 10. The latter concluded, "The conversion of humid forests to open grasslands for the grazing of ruminant livestock should be approached with caution. These pastures have sometimes proved productive, particularly where they have been developed on fertile soils, but more often they have failed, resulting in degradation of the areas and low productivity of the livestock." It recommended the rehabilitation of degraded soils, restriction of cattle to savannah regions (though there are problems of year-round forage there), and the integration of livestock with tree crops.

37 His address was on 29 September 1975, reprinted as *A Poluição no Brasil* by his environment secretariat.

38 R. J. A. Goodland and H. S. Irwin, *Amazon Jungle: Green Hell to Red Desert?*, Elsevier, Amsterdam, 1975; Meggers, *op. cit.*

Chapter 8

39 See "Tribes of the Amazon Basin in Brazil 1972", a report for the Aborigines Protection Society, Charles Knight, London.

40 Adrian Cowell, author of *The Tribe that Hides from Man*, Bodley Head, London 1973 (about the Villas-Boas contact with the Kreen-Akrore), states that only four out of fifteen known tribes of the Timbira group survived into the twentieth century; the rest had been exterminated by cattlemen advancing into the

interior of Maranhão and southern Pará, some in the early
nineteenth century. Appendix four to his book lists nine extinct
tribes of the Xingu, five of which were wiped out by tribal
warfare and three by disease.

41 Interview, 10 May 1976.

42 See Robin Hanbury-Tenison, *A Question of Survival*, Angus and
Robertson, London, 1973.

Chapter 9

43 At the beginning of January 1977, Mario Henrique Simonsen
told *Jornal do Brasil* that the inflation rate in 1976 had been
46 per cent. This was a jump of nearly 17 per cent on the
previous year, and the highest annual rate since 1966.

44 An advertisement in the *Financial Times*, London, on 6 January
1977 listed a consortium of 38 international banks which had
subscribed to a loan of $200 million for the purchase of British
goods and services for the "steel line". This railway loan
provides a useful perspective on the foreign loans raised for the
Amazon roads programme. As with railways in the nineteenth
century, Brazil still regularly looks abroad for finance for major
transport projects, and international bankers are happy to
support loans which are guaranteed by the Brazilian government. However, the Amazon roads loans—whether raised from
the World Bank or on the Eurodollar market—appear not to
have required the purchase of goods from outside Brazil, or
from any particular country. The "steel line" loan was specifically geared to purchase from British exporters.

45 This was notably true of Governor Henoch Reis, the pro-
government Arena governor.

46 Among them Bruno Bettelheim, as he makes clear in his psycho-
analytic interpretation of fairy stories, *The Uses of Enchantment*,
1976.

47 These figures were quoted in an unpublished report from the
Ministry of Agriculture of January, 1975, *Atuação do Ministerio
da Agricultura no desenvolvimento agricola da Amazonia Legal.*

Chapter 10

48 Wallace was writing here about the region round São Gabriel
de Cachoeira, on the upper Rio Negro. He spoke of it with a
promoter's enthusiasm akin to Sir Walter Raleigh's, and
suggested that he would like to get together some British friends
to develop the area. More recently, during the TransAmazonica
boom, his statement was quoted in Brazil as applying to the
whole rainforest. Elsewhere in the same book, however, he

noted the slash-and-burn and poor crop yields in other parts of Amazonia and his enthusiasm at São Gabriel is not entirely characteristic. The contemporary lesson is that, in such a large and diverse region, even respected ecologists can be misled and misinterpreted.

49 The flooding associated with hydro schemes also raises ecological and land-use issues. Amazonia may offer much simpler and less ecologically harmful sources of energy. It has an obvious potential for solar power. In addition Engineer Astor Modesto de Souza, of the State University of Campinas, has suggested that a power station could be established at the junction of the Negro and Amazon near Manaus using ammonia gas. The gas would be activated by the difference in temperature between the two rivers and a power station could produce 20 MW at a cost up to 40 per cent less than conventional stations.

50 Roberto Campos and certain other economists argue, however, that the multiplier effects are a great deal more important than the original projects that make them possible.

51 The whole story is told, from the viewpoint of the Cree Indians, in *Strangers Devour the Land* by Boyce Richardson, Alfred Knopf, New York and John Murray, London, 1976.

GLOSSARY OF PORTUGUESE TERMS

Agropolis	centre, with a secondary school, planned to serve 20 agricultural villages
Agrovila	planned agricultural village containing 50 families
Balsa	ferry
Boias-frias	rural labourers, not continuously employed
Caboclo	man of the interior
Cachaça	cheap rough rum
Castanha	literally a nut, used to describe a starvation diet in Amazonia
Clareira	clearing
Desenvolvimento	development
Farinha	manioc flour
Favela/favelado	slum/slum dweller
Fazendeiro	farm estate owner
Fim do mundo	at the end of the earth
Garimpeiro	miner
Gatos	literally cats, used to describe labour recruiters
Gaucho	literally cowboy, used of inhabitants of Rio Grande do Sul
Gleba	large area to be divided up for colonization
Indigenismo	study of Amerindians
Latifundia	property system of large estates
Linha dura	hard line rightist in politico-military spectrum
Malva	a natural fibre akin to jute
Minifundio	property system of non-viable tiny holdings
Movimento	bustle
Patrão	boss
Peon	poor manual labourer
Pistoleiro	gunman
Posseiro	rural squatter
Prefeito	mayor of municipality
Renda indigena	Indian fund
Ruropolis	planned town intended at every 140 km along TransAmazonica
Seringueiros	rubber tappers

Sertanista	explorer grade within Incra, responsible for contacting Indians
Sertão	interior of north-east
Sorva	variety of rubber
Vaqueiro	cowhand
Varzea	land beside river banks flooded in rainy season

SELECT BIBLIOGRAPHY

Ministerio da Agricultura, *Atuação do Ministerio da Agricultura no desenvolvimento agricola da Amazonia Legal*, Brasilia, 1975

Allen, Robert, "The year of the rain forest" (article in *New Scientist*, London, 24 April 1975)

Estado do Amazonas, *Plano do Desenvolvimento do Amazonas, Programa 1972*, Manaus, 1972

Banco da Amazonia, *Amazonia: Instrumentos para o desenvolvimento*, Departamento de Estudos Económicos, Belem, 1969

Araujo, Galileo Antenor de et al., *Transamazonica—uma experiência rodoviária nos trópicos*, DNER, Rio de Janeiro (undated)

Arruda, Marcos et al., *Multinationals and Brazil*, Brazilian Studies, Toronto, 1975

Bates, Henry Walter, *The Naturalist on the River Amazon*, Dent, London, 1969

Benchimol, S., *Estrutura Geo-Social e Económica da Amazonia*, Governo do Estado de Amazonas, Manaus, 1966

Bodard, Lucien, *Massacre on the Amazon*, Tom Stacey, London, 1971

Bourne, Richard, *Getulio Vargas of Brazil*, Charles Knight, London, 1974

—— *Political Leaders of Latin America* (chapter on Juscelino Kubitschek), Pelican, London, 1969

Brazilian Government, *II National Development Plan (1972–1979)*, editions in English and Portuguese, Brasilia, 1974; also matching plans for individual states and territories in Portuguese

Brazilian Embassy, London (pamphlet series)
Amazonia (1976)
Amazonia—Humboldt Project (1975)
Brazil's Indians (1975)
The Jari River Project Grows the Biggest Forest in the World (1976, translation of an article in *O Estado de São Paulo* by Robert Appy)
Polamazonia—the new development strategy of the Amazon (1975)

Brooks, Edwin and Fuerst, Rene, Hemming, John and Huxley, Francis, *Tribes of the Amazon Basin in Brazil 1972*, Charles Knight, London, 1973

Casement, Sir Roger, *Correspondence respecting the Treatment of British Colonial Subjects and Native Indians employed in the Putumayo District*, HMSO, London, 1912

Collier, Richard, *The River that God Forgot*, Collins, London, 1968

Commissão Nacional de Defesa e pelo Desenvolvimento da Amazonia, *A Amazonia Brasileira em Foco* (irregular journal), CNDDA, Rio de Janeiro, 1970s

Corrêa, Antonio Camarão *et al.*, *A expansão da fronteira económica como estrategia de Desenvolvimento*, Nucleo de Altos Estudos Amazonicos, Universidade Federal do Para, Belem, 1974

Cowell, Adrian, *The Tribe that Hides from Man*, Bodley Head, London, 1973

Departamento Nacional de Produção Mineral, *Anuário Mineral Brasileiro 1975*, Brasilia, 1975

Departamento Nacional de Produção Mineral, *Projeto RADAM* (continuing series of volumes)

Empresa Brasileira de Planejamento—GEIPOT, *Plano Integrado de transportes da Amazonia* (7 vols), Ministerio de Transportes, Brasilia, 1971

Ferreira, Manoel Roderigues, *Nas Selvas Amazonicas*, Grafica Biblos, São Paulo, 1961

Fleming, Peter, *Brazilian Adventure*, Jonathan Cape, London, 1933

FUNAI (Fundação Nacional do Índio), *Informativo FUNAI* (quarterly journal), Brasilia, 1970s

FUNAI, *Legislação*, Brasilia, 1975

Furneaux, R., *The Amazon*, Hamish Hamilton, London, 1969

George, Susan, *How the Other Half Dies*, Pelican, London, 1976

Gilbert, Alan, *Latin American Development*, Pelican, London, 1974

Goodland, R. J. A. and Irwin, H. S., *Amazon jungle: Green Hell to Red Desert?*, Elsevier, Amsterdam, 1975

Hanbury-Tenison, Robin, *A Question of Survival*, Angus and Robertson, London, 1973

Haskins, G. P., *The Amazon: The Life History of a Mighty River*, Doubleday, New York, 1943

Hopper, J. H. (ed.), *Indians of Brazil in the Twentieth Century*, Institute for Cross-Cultural Research, Washington, 1967

IBDF (Instituto Brasileiro de Desenvolvimento Florestal), *Proteção a Fauna*, Delegacia do Amazonas, IBDF, Manaus, 1972

IBGE (Instituto Brasileiro de Geografia e Estatística), *Sinopse Estatística do Brasil 1975*, IBGE, Rio de Janeiro, 1975

Incra (Instituto Nacional de Colonização e Reforma Agraria), *Metodologia para Programação Operacional dos Projetos de Assentamento de Agricultores*, Brasilia, 1971

Incra, *PIN—Colonização da Amazonia* (two pamphlets), Brasilia, 1972

Incra, *Urbanismo Rural*, Brasilia, 1973
IUCN (Internal Union for Conservation of Nature and Natural Resources), *Ecological Guidelines for Development in Tropical Forest Areas of South East Asia*, Occasional Paper 10, IUCN Morges, Switzerland, 1974
IUCN, *Normas Ecologicas para el Desarrollo del Tropico Humedo Americano*, Documento Ocasional 11, IUCN Morges Switzerland, 1975
Kleinpenning, J. M. G. *The Integration and Colonization of the Brazilian Portion of the Amazon Basin*, Nijmegen, 1975
Linke, Lilo, *People of the Amazon*, Robert Hale, London, 1963
Estado de Mato Grosso, *Anuário Estatístico 1974*, Cuiabá, 1974
Meggers, B. J., *Amazonia: Man and Culture in a Counterfeit Paradise*, Aldine-Atherton, Chicago, 1971
Mendes, Armando, *Viabilidade Economica da Amazonia*, Universidade Federal do Pará, 1971
Morais, F., Gontijo, R. and Campos, Roberto, *Transamazônica*, Brasiliense, São Paulo, 1970
Nucleo de Altos Estudos Amazonicos, *Documentos* (on colonization, by Nigel Smith, Emilio and Eve de Moran and Robin Anderson), Universidade Federal do Pará, Belem, 1974
Estado do Pará, *Diretrizes de ação de governo 1975–9*, Belem, 1974
Peregrino Junior, João, *Panorama cultural da Amazonia*, Rio de Janeiro, 1960
Pereira, Osny D., *A Transamazônica: Pros e Contras*, Civilização Brasileira, Rio de Janeiro, 1971
Perlman, Janice, *Myths of Marginality*, University of California, 1975
Pinheiro, Francisco P. *et al.*, "Public Health Hazards among Workers along the TransAmazon Highway", paper presented at the 18th International Congress on Occupational Health, Brighton, England, 1975
Prata, Aluizio and Marsden, Philip D., "Infectious Disease in Brazil Today", paper for the Tropical Medicine Unit, University of Brasilia, 1976
Rabinovitz, Francine and Trueblood, Felicity (eds.), *Latin American Urban Research*, SAGE, Beverley Hills, 1976
Rangel, Alberto, *Inferno Verde*, Rio de Janeiro, 1917
Realidade, "Amazonia" (special issue), Abril, São Paulo, October, 1971
Reis, Arthur C. F., *A Amazonia e a Cobiça Internacional*, Grafica Record, Rio de Janeiro, 1968
— (ed.), *Problematica da Amazonia*, Casa do Estudante, Rio de Janeiro, 1969
Resende, Eliseu, *As Rodovias e o Desenvolvimento do Brasil*, Ministerio dos Transportes, Rio de Janeiro 1973 (edition in English

prepared for International Road Federation meeting, Munich, October, 1973)

Ribeiro, Darcy, *Os Índios e a Civilização*, Civilização Brasileira, Rio de Janeiro, 1970

Secretaria Especial do Meio Ambiente, *Legislação Basica*, Brasilia, 1976

St Clair, David, *The Mighty, Mighty Amazon*, Funk and Wagnalls, New York, 1968

Smith, Anthony, *Matto Grosso, Last Virgin Land*, Michael Joseph, London, 1971

Souza, Filho, Rui, Guilherme and Souza, Dulce Leoncy, *Incentivos Fiscais Estaduais: a experiência do Pará*, Instituto do Desenvolvimento Económico-Social do Pará, Belem, 1975

Staniford, Philip, *Pioneers in the Tropics (The political organization of Japanese in an Immigrant Community in Brazil)*, Athlone, London, 1973

SUDAM (Superintendencia do Desenvolvimento da Amazonia), *Amazonia; Desenvolvimento e Ocupação*, Belem, 1969

SUDAM, *Plano de desenvolvimento da Amazonia 1975–1974*, Belem, 1971

SUDAM, *Amazonia Novo Universo/New Universe* (Portuguese and English), Belem, 1974

SUDAM, *II Plano Nacional de Desenvolvimento, Programa de ação do governo para a Amazonia (1975–1979)*, Belem, 1975

SUFRAMA (Superintendencia da Zona Franca de Manaus), *Anuário Estatístico 1974*, Manaus, 1974

Tamer, Alberto, *Transamazônica. Solução para 2001*, Apec, Rio de Janeiro, 1971

—— *Nordeste os Mesmos Caminhos*, Apec, São Paulo, 1972

Vergara Filho, Otto (coord.), *II Seminario de Contribuição ao Desenvolvimento da Pesquisa sobre as Consequencias socio-económicas decorrentes da implantação da Rodovia Belem-Brasilia*, Instituto de Pesquisas Rodoviarias, Rio de Janeiro, 1975

Villares Moscoso, Jorge W., *Geografia Politica y Economica de la Hileia Amazonica*, Hispano-America, Guayaquil, 1965

Wagley, Charles, *Amazon Town*, Macmillan, New York, 1953

Wallace, Alfred R., *A narrative of travels on the Amazon and Rio Negro*, London, 1853

Zweig, Stefan, *Brazil, Land of the Future* (translated by Andrew St James), Cassell, London, 1942

INDEX

by

Michael Gordon

Where subjects and organizations appear *passim*, reference is given only to the initial or definitive entry and other selected passages. TA = Trans-Amazonica highway; pop. = population

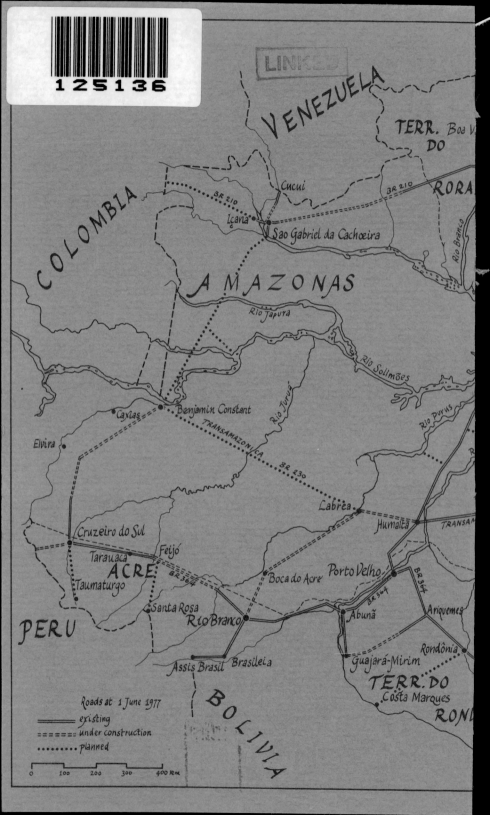